Child and Youth Care

Child
and Youth Care

Critical Perspectives on Pedagogy,
Practice, and Policy

EDITED BY
ALAN PENCE AND JENNIFER WHITE

UBCPress · Vancouver · Toronto

20 19 18 17 16 15 14 13 12 11   5 4 3 2 1

Printed in Canada on FSC-certified ancient-forest-free paper (100% post-consumer recycled) that is processed chlorine- and acid-free.

Library and Archives Canada Cataloguing in Publication

Child and youth care : critical perspectives on pedagogy, practice, and policy / edited by Alan Pence and Jennifer White.

Includes bibliographical references and index.
ISBN 978-0-7748-2130-8

    1. Social work with children. 2. Social work with youth. I. Pence, Alan R. II. White, Jennifer

HV713.C386 2011   362.7   C2011-903958-3

Canadä

UBC Press gratefully acknowledges the financial support for our publishing program of the Government of Canada (through the Canada Book Fund), the Canada Council for the Arts, and the British Columbia Arts Council.

This book has been published with the help of a grant from the Canadian Federation for the Humanities and Social Sciences, through the Aid to Scholarly Publications Program, using funds provided by the Social Sciences and Humanities Research Council of Canada.

Printed and bound in Canada by Friesens
Set in Sabon and Myriad by Artegraphica Design Co. Ltd.
Copy editor: Dallas Harrison
Proofreader: Lana Okerlund
Indexer: Noeline Bridge

UBC Press
The University of British Columbia
2029 West Mall
Vancouver, BC V6T 1Z2
www.ubcpress.ca

Contents

Preface: A Personal and Professional Journey / ix
ALAN PENCE

Introduction / xv
ALAN PENCE AND JENNIFER WHITE

Acronyms / xxiii

Part 1: Teaching and Theorizing Child and Youth Care

1 Articulating a Child and Youth Care Philosophy: Beyond Binary Constructs / 3
J.N. LITTLE

2 Rethinking Developmental Theories in Child and Youth Care / 19
VERONICA PACINI-KETCHABAW

3 Re-Stor(y)ing Professional Ethics in Child and Youth Care: Toward More Contextualized, Reflexive, and Generative Practices / 33
JENNIFER WHITE

Part 2: Critically Interrogating Gender in Child and Youth Care

4 Doing "Sissy" and "Tomboy": Exploring Childhood Participation in and Resistance to Discourses of Gender and Sexuality / 55
JONATHAN MORRIS

5 Bottom of the Food Chain: The Minoritization of Girls in Child and Youth Care / 70
SANDRINA DE FINNEY, ELICIA LOISELLE, AND MACKENZIE DEAN

6 Father Involvement Initiatives: Social Inclusion or the (Re)Construction of Hegemonic Masculinity? / 95
B. DENISE HODGINS

Part 3: Expanding Perspectives in Child and Youth Care Practice

7 Northern Canadian Practice as a Site for Exploration of Child and Youth Care Identities: Inside and Outside Professionalization / 121
BROOKE ALSBURY

8 Considering Street Outreach to Youth: Politics, Policies, and Practice / 139
MARK L. KELLY

9 Contextualizing Care: Generating Alternatives to the Individualization of Struggles and Support by Considering Loss / 158
JANET NEWBURY

Part 4: Policy Discourses in Child and Youth Care

10 Constructing and Regulating the Young Offender: Trends in Punishment from Colonial to Contemporary Canada / 179
LORINDA STONEMAN

11 Once upon a Time There Was a Ready Child: Challenging Readiness as a Single Story / 199
KATHLEEN KUMMEN

Afterword / 219
JENNIFER WHITE AND ALAN PENCE

Contributors / 221

Index / 226

Preface
A Personal and Professional Journey

ALAN PENCE

I seek the kind indulgence of the reader in allowing me a brief reflection on a journey – a journey that reminds me of T.S. Eliot's words in "Little Gidding" ([1942], 1965, 114):

> We shall not cease from exploration
> And the end of all our exploring
> Will be to arrive where we started
> And know the place for the first time.

Eliot captures precisely my sense of this volume not only as part of a personal exploration, which it certainly has been, but also as providing possibilities for further explorations of a profession – that of child and youth care (CYC).

This is a very different volume than the ones that Carey Denholm, Roy Ferguson, Jim Anglin, and I developed in the 1980s (Anglin, Denholm, Ferguson, and Pence 1990; Denholm, Ferguson, and Pence 1987, 1993; Denholm, Pence, and Ferguson 1983). In looking back, those books seem to me like the place "we started" – very important work that helped to establish the broadly based profession of CYC not only in Canada but also beyond. I value those volumes as part of a professional "coming of age" in which we, both as an educational institution and as a profession, could access our own literature in addition to the literatures of allied professions and disciplines.

I believe those volumes continue to have much to offer – they are not simply historical markers along the way. They were framed within certain paradigms, and they sought to accomplish certain things. Those paradigms and objectives remain relevant and important today.

But, in addition, we now have other paradigms and other objectives available. This volume speaks to them, and it speaks in critical and "post-" frames of reference (see the introduction for the use of terms in this volume). This book was not planned – it basically spoke itself into existence as part of a course that sought to ground and operationalize critical perspectives into the broadly based practices and policies of the CYC field. As the course instructor, I was very pleased as the course moved from initial encounters to fuller engagements with diverse ideas, experiences, and contexts. There was much I wanted to share and much I wished to learn.

Part of what I wanted to share was my own experience in moving from a more positivist and modernist position as an academic and professional to a more critical and post- (post-structural, postmodern, postcolonial, etc.) position and how that had opened up possibilities in my work that lay outside what other paradigms might allow, with each paradigm providing different possibilities and potentials. What I was interested to learn is captured well by the chapters in this volume.

I began to explore critical perspectives and postmodern ideas at the same time that I began to focus primarily on work across cultures. The critical perspectives I had begun to explore not only complemented but also extended in ways not possible through some other paradigms my work with diverse communities in Canada and internationally.

Insofar as personal journeys are not reflected in this volume, it seems appropriate to offer an example of one such journey in which one might arrive where he or she "started / And know the place for the first time." As suggested earlier, my starting place in the 1970s and 1980s to a great extent referenced "objectivity" as a value and was in alignment with a positivist orientation. Although I was greatly influenced by Urie Bronfenbrenner and his ecological framework (Pence 1988), my ability to move into or understand various perspectives within an ecological web was limited by the strictures of both "science" and "professionalism." Both began to be disrupted in 1989-90 when I received an invitation from a large tribal council in northern Saskatchewan to work with them in developing a community-sensitive education and training program.

The story of the First Nations Partnerships Program (FNPP), which grew out of the original invitation from the Meadow Lake Tribal Council (MLTC) but continued through ten other partnerships over eighteen years, has been told in many different publications (one of the earliest is Pence et al. 1993; the most comprehensive is Ball and Pence 2006; also see www.fnpp.org for other references), but the relevance of the MLTC for this volume and this preface is its role as a transformative experience that exposed the limitations of positivist and modernist orientations in regard to promoting services for children and especially when attempting to work across cultures. Of particular importance for me was reading an external evaluation of the MLTC program written by an indigenous elder (Jette 1993) that quickly moved beyond the predetermined criteria for success to explore numerous unanticipated outcomes that centred on dramatic intergenerational shifts in interaction patterns and broad capacity building and social development advances at community and tribal levels. Jette's report could not have been written by one who stood fully "outside" the community – in the language of positivism, an "objective" observer. It was only through the combination of insider and outsider – not being from the communities but having cultural and historical links to them – that Jette could look "beyond" the predefined "deliverables" and peer more deeply and perceptively into the complex lives of the communities. Her approach to her work, and the insights she was able to provide, were inspiring and transformative for my own future work.

My experiences working with indigenous communities were supplemented by an invitation to participate in the Childhood in Society project led by European sociologists committed to the establishment of a sociology of childhood not based on precepts of universalism (a strong characteristic of psychology's interest in children – the dominant child discipline in the mid- to late twentieth century). This group's work in defining childhood as a social construction (Qvortrup et al. 1994) complemented my indigenous work and intensified a search for others in the early childhood "branch" of CYC who might share my growing concerns about a field too narrowly bound by restrictive, modernist notions of what constituted "best practice" regardless of context.

That search led me to connect with Peter Moss at the Thomas Coram Institute for Children at the University of London. Peter had a similarly long career in early childhood services and academia, and he too had become increasingly concerned about the narrow and limiting discourses available regarding children, children's services, and concepts of quality care. We shared these concerns with others in the field through an edited volume entitled *Valuing Quality in Early Childhood Services: New Approaches to Defining Quality*, which started with the statement that "quality in early childhood services is a relative concept, not an objective reality" (Moss and Pence 1994, 1) – a position that challenged and continues to challenge the field in North America. With one of the authors from that volume (Dahlberg), we then wrote a book further advancing critical perspectives regarding children's services entitled *Beyond Quality in Early Childhood Education and Care: Postmodern Perspectives* (Dahlberg, Moss, and Pence 1999). That volume became a strong seller and was subsequently translated into eight languages – providing us with some hope that these ideas might resonate broadly (indeed, the book sells much better outside North America).

These various experiences, starting with the FNPP but including others noted above, influenced my subsequent work in Africa and the Middle East, which was in response to requests from UNICEF and the World Bank to address issues of capacity building in the majority ("developing") world. The importance of context and local voices, in interaction with "dominant discourses," became central features of the Early Childhood Development Virtual University (ECDVU; see www.ecdvu. org). Sometimes dramatic advances achieved through the ECDVU approach (made possible in part through completion levels in excess of 95 percent over four African deliveries) have provided a strong platform for critiquing more broadly universalist agendas that remain dominant in the United Nations and international development communities (Pence 2011; Pence and Hix-Small 2007) but that have had significant problems regarding community ownership and sustainability (strengths of the FNPP and ECDVU approaches).

In 2005, I had the opportunity to return to a focus on Canada, with support provided by the BC government to explore issues of "quality." My colleague in this work, Veronica Pacini-Ketchabaw, and I saw this as an opportunity to put into practice approaches that had been explored and discussed in *Beyond Quality in Early Childhood Education and Care* and other sources but that had no Canadian-based funding for operational application and evaluation. With receipt of those funds, we initiated a systemic approach to change reaching from practice-focused work with front-line educators, through college instructors, to government officials and university academics. Ten international forums took place over a five-year period, bringing eminent, scholarly innovators to British Columbia for engagement with the various groups identified above (Pence and Pacini-Ketchabaw 2008).

Facets of these experiences, taking place from 1989 to 2009, were key parts of what I hoped to share and discuss with students in the doctoral seminar as part of a broader exploration of critical perspectives used to positively disrupt established assumptions and approaches in our diverse CYC settings. For some, such critiques were relatively new and somewhat troubling, and for others their practice had already begun to embrace such disruption. All experienced uncertainty and disquietude – places that I had come to understand as being useful indicators of meaningful exploration.

Students took on these disruptive influences to varying degrees, but over time the group became comfortable pushing the boundaries of professional "safety." As the process moved forward, I became increasingly excited by the amount of good academic, professional, and personal work that students were taking on, and the project papers increasingly looked like the basis for a unique contribution to the CYC literature.

I shared my interest in developing such a volume with Jennifer White, a colleague in the school and a fairly recent holder of a doctorate. We decided that we would jointly explore publication possibilities. I had a connection with UBC Press, as it had been a good partner in the 1980s' work that Anglin, Denholm, Ferguson, and I had undertaken in our efforts to help "define and advance the field." Jennifer and I decided that, in addition to the current doctoral cohort, we would reach out to several other colleagues with recent doctorates and to a few other graduate students who shared such interests.

The result of that collaboration is the book that you have in your hands. We are delighted with the collaboration and with the broad range of contexts, issues, and perspectives considered in these pages. It is unlike any other volume in the CYC professional literature. We believe that it not only reflects leading-edge thinking in the field of CYC but also opens up "points of possibility" only imaginable through knowing a place of familiarity "for the first time."

References

Anglin, J., A. Pence, R. Ferguson, and C. Denholm, eds. 1990. *Perspectives in Professional Child and Youth Care*. New York: Haworth Press.

Ball, J., and A. Pence. 2006. *Supporting Indigenous Children's Development: Community-University Partnerships*. Vancouver: UBC Press.

Dahlberg, G., P. Moss, and A.R. Pence. 1999 [2nd ed. 2007]. *Beyond Quality in Early Childhood Education and Care: Postmodern Perspectives*. London: Falmer Press.

Denholm, C., R. Ferguson, and A. Pence, eds. 1987. *Professional Child and Youth Care: The Canadian Perspective*. Vancouver: UBC Press.

Denholm, C., A. Pence, and R. Ferguson, eds. 1983 [2nd ed. 1993]. *The Scope of Professional Child Care in British Columbia*. Victoria, BC: School of Child Care, University of Victoria.

Eliot, T.S. (1942), 1965. "Little Gidding." In *Faber Book of Modern Verse*, ed. M. Roberts. London: Faber and Faber.

Jette, D. 1993. "Meadow Lake Tribal Council Indian Child Care Program Evaluation." Unpublished manuscript, Meadow Lake Tribal Council.

Moss, P., and A. Pence, eds. 1994. *Valuing Quality in Early Childhood Services: New Approaches to Defining Quality*. New York: Teachers College Press, Columbia University; London: Paul Chapman Publishers.

Pence, A. 2011. "Early Childhood Care and Development Research in Africa: Historical, Conceptual, and Structural Challenges." *Child Development Perspectives* 5, 1: 112-18.

–, ed. 1988. *Ecological Research with Children and Families: From Concepts to Methodology*. New York: Teachers College Press, Columbia University.

Pence, A., and H. Hix-Small. 2007. "Global Children in the Shadow of the Global Child." *International Journal of Educational Policy, Research, and Practice* 8, 1: 83-100.

Pence, A., V. Kuehne, M. Greenwood, and M.R. Opekokew. 1993. "Generative Curriculum: A Model of University and First Nations Cooperative, Post-Secondary Education." *International Journal of Educational Development* 13, 4: 339-49.

Pence, A., and V. Pacini-Ketchabaw. 2008. "Discourses on Quality Care: IQ and the Canadian Experience." *Contemporary Issues in Early Childhood* 9, 3: 241-55.

Qvortrup, J., M. Bardy, G. Sgritta, and H. Wintersberger, eds. 1994. *Childhood Matters: Social Theory, Practice, and Politics*. Aldershot, UK: Avebury.

Introduction

ALAN PENCE AND JENNIFER WHITE

Over the past several decades, child and youth care has developed a distinct identity as a unique field of professional practice. Although many allied professions work toward promoting human well-being, CYC has differentiated itself from other human service professions through a focus on children and youth using strengths-based, holistic, and ecological approaches and through active engagement with children, youth, and families across multiple and diverse settings.

Modernist Discourses of Professionalism

In establishing its place, the CYC field has generally been guided by a modernist discourse of professionalism that differentiates its knowledge and practice not only from other professions (Bates 2005; Phelan 2005) but also from lay or "non-professional" perspectives. Among other things, this discourse positions specialized education and training, the creation of standards of expertise, the development of a code of ethics, and the promotion of autonomous decision making as central to the formation of a specific professional identity (Beker 2001; Reinders 2008). While there has been considerable historical debate in the field about whether CYC is an emerging profession, a field of practice, or a craft (Eisikovits and Beker 2001), the development of a professional identity typically means that practitioners are invested with authority and legitimacy from consumers, clients, and other professionals, making it an alluring goal (Prilleltensky, Rossiter, and Walsh-Bowers 1996). Physicians are often held as the exemplars of such professional power. Thus, the path to professionalization that most aspiring professions seek to follow is the one established by the medical profession. Underpinning this inherited and thoroughly modernist project is a belief in an "objective reality" knowable through science, appropriate education, and competency-driven, technical views of practice.

Professionalism as a Contested Idea

In contrast, critical perspectives[1] or postmodern views of professionalism would understand these dynamics differently, calling into question some of the underlying assumptions and beliefs about knowledge, power, and standardized approaches to practice. Through these lenses, a questioning of power and privilege arises as one considers more broadly who is served through the creation of human "services" and for what purpose. Child and youth care, perhaps due in part to its later start on the road to professional status, is somewhat later than some professions in questioning its assumptions, analyzing the forces of power, and considering other paradigms. Education, for example, has a history of approximately two decades of engagement in such critical, reconceptualist activity.

Partially because CYC is an emerging profession and still seeking some of the aspects of power and recognition held by other helping professions, critical and postmodern views are sometimes seen as threatening to the professionalization process. Although this concern is understandable, we believe that a failure to engage with critical perspectives is also potentially problematic for the profession. For example, by not holding our own practices up for critical scrutiny, or by authorizing only a restricted range of methodologies or theoretical perspectives for studying and conceptualizing this work, we run the risk of becoming insular, dogmatic, and hegemonic in our thinking and actions. We believe that a "both/and" position that accommodates diversity, fluidity, and contingency offers a particularly fruitful way forward. We can continue to seek professional recognition through established modernist approaches; we can also increasingly engage with postmodern and critical perspectives so that we can expose the limits of these received vocabularies and transform how we think about practice, policy, and professionalism. This approach has much in common with what others have referred to as a form of double(d) practice, where we do the work and trouble it at the same time (Lather 2007).

Child and youth care, therefore, finds itself within a contested field – the forces of modernity, universalism, individualism, and positivism remain strong, but at the same time new spaces for questioning and reconceptualizing have opened up. For example, there is growing support for more critical, politicized, and discursive conceptualizations of CYC work as well as approaches that centre the agenda of social justice (Skott-Myhre 2003; Smith 2006). By shifting attention away from a primary focus on the individual toward more comprehensive and critically conscious approaches that recognize a range of socio-political influences on child, youth, and family well-being, these critical perspectives, which form the basis of this volume, ask a number of challenging and provocative questions. What is CYC practice? What might it become? Can the ends of CYC practice be separated from the means? Whom are these interventions designed to benefit? How will we decide whether we are making a useful difference? What unspoken understandings regarding child, youth, or family well-being are privileged? Are socio-political and historical contexts adequately accounted for? In bringing this collection together, we hope to provoke, unsettle, invite fresh perspectives, and generate new questions among readers. Ultimately, we want to showcase the exciting and creative work being pursued by an emerging generation of future CYC leaders as well as to recognize the expanded possibilities for pedagogy, policy, and practice that these ways of thinking open up.

Organizational Threads
In reviewing the collection of chapters, we considered various approaches to this introduction. A minimalist approach would have involved a flexible grouping and sequencing of chapters, allowing them to "speak directly" to the reader, who would undertake her own organization. We

also envisioned a more structured and intensive approach that would have included a full additional chapter inspired by the collection, with introductions woven into the new text. Opting for a middle ground, we have instead chosen a particular metanarrative that will run throughout the chapters, leaving many other threads and possibilities for the reader to generate. The organizational metanarrative we have chosen is the notion of "normative" or, more precisely, what constitutes an "acceptable standard." Normative is but one critical metanarrative in the work of CYC; there are others, and these chapters both challenge and comply with them.

Within the West, the source of most research on children and youth (Arnett 2008; Pence and Hix-Small 2007), the "science of child development," is typically promoted as "universal" even though it excludes the vast majority of children and youth living around the world. In other words, it is possible to have normative standards and borders that exclude the majority of child and youth experiences yet are still deemed universally good or right or true. An example from early childhood is the West's elevation of maternal care above all other forms of care, despite the relative rarity of such exclusivity in the majority of societies of the world (Weisner and Gallimore 1977).

CYC is one of several "helping professions" that work in this "borderland" – a site of practice that exists at the border between what is considered "normative" or acceptable and abnormal or not acceptable. Within a traditional, modernist paradigm, the goals of practice are relatively straightforward, at least conceptually: a norm has been identified, and it is the responsibility of the helper to bring those beyond that norm within it or at least closer to it. From a critical or postmodern stance, the work is less clear. Questions we might ask from this perspective include the following. How has this border come into being? Who has established the border? For what purpose? Based on what information? Does the border primarily serve those within it or outside it? Should practitioners be border enforcers or border disturbers? Over the years, many CYC practitioners have found themselves asking such questions. Although the modernist quest for "objectivity" and the promotion of scientific evidence (or "best" practices) often constrain practitioners' ability to ask such questions, critical postmodern perspectives actively invite such questions as a way to recognize complexity, partiality, and contingency, allowing multiple border crossings, transformations, and challenges to occur.

Introduction to the Chapters

The authors of these chapters have practised in a wide array of professional settings and contexts, testifying to the diversity of the CYC field. These contexts include street youth outreach, early childhood care and education, residential care, early intervention, parent support, child and youth mental health, juvenile justice, and post-secondary education. Collectively, the authors have engaged with a range of age groups, social contexts, and cultures. Their practices are located in large urban centres, small cities, rural communities, and the far North. Most authors have more than ten years of experience in the field, and they have completed a wide range of undergraduate and graduate degrees, including child and youth care, education, counselling, sociology, social work, criminology, and psychology. What they have in common is a commitment to promoting the well-being of children, youth, and their families as well as an interest in challenging taken-for-granted understandings and received views of practice, pedagogy, and policy in CYC.

The first section, which includes chapters from J.N. Little, Veronica Pacini-Ketchabaw, and Jennifer White, explores the linked challenges of defining the field and preparing CYC practitioners in higher education contexts in ways that both enable and trouble professional practice in CYC. Little, who describes her own experience as a "CYC-educated" practitioner who has worked in a diverse array of settings, asks this provocative question: "Will the real CYC please stand up?" Meanwhile, Pacini-Ketchabaw describes how child and adolescent development has taken the position of "natural" knowledge in much of the CYC literature, forming one of the foundational bases of the profession. She argues that the problematic history of developmental knowledge needs to be thoroughly investigated and describes some of the pedagogical processes she has engaged in to think and teach child and adolescent development differently. Finally, White describes an approach to teaching professional ethics that challenges the traditional and narrow view of ethics that is tightly tethered to individualist conceptions of morality and dominant discourses of professionalism. She argues for a more expansive, critically reflexive view that invites fresh thinking and reimagined understandings of everyday CYC praxis.

The next section, which includes chapters from Jonathan Morris; Sandrina de Finney, Elicia Loiselle, and Mackenzie Dean; and B. Denise Hodgins, all take up the issue of gender and other dimensions of diversity across a range of CYC policy and practice contexts. Morris describes his experience as a graduate student in a CYC class in which students were invited to engage in a process of collective biography, which included writing and rewriting their first memories of particular experiences, including their first memories of realizing and resisting being gendered. De Finney, Loiselle, and Dean examine structural determinants of well-being in the lives of children and youth. Their intersectional framework maps the role of interplaying processes of racialization, gendering, and sexing (among others) in producing unequal circumstances for some groups of children and youth, with a particular focus on the minoritization of girls in CYC. Finally, Hodgins's chapter explores some of the recent father involvement initiatives in Canada and draws on notions of social inclusion and masculinities to question what these initiatives try to change or uphold and whom they do or do not speak to.

The third section groups together chapters that demonstrate a critically reflective stance toward CYC practice, with a particular focus on challenging individualistic, modernist understandings of what it means to help and to care. Brooke Alsbury, Mark Kelly, and Janet Newbury, though representing very different CYC practice contexts, all exemplify a critical, questioning stance toward practice. Using northern Canada as a context, Alsbury asks the profession and the professional to consider how each can be locally developed and mutually constituted, and she proposes a reconceptualization of CYC professionalization through understanding the socially constructed nature of both profession and professional identity. Drawing from his own experience as a street outreach worker, Kelly examines the structures of Canadian society that impact street-involved youth and provides his current thoughts and understandings of how the interplay of politics, policy, and practice affects youth experiencing street life. Through an exploration of the functions of loss over time, Newbury questions the increasing individualization of human service interventions. Consideration of loss is offered as one avenue through which conceptual shifts can be made from practice that centres predictability to practice that acknowledges contingency and disperses the onus for change (rather than locating it within help seekers).

The final section includes chapters from Lorinda Stoneman and Kathleen Kummen. Although these authors address very different facets and contexts for CYC, juvenile justice and early childhood education, both draw attention to the role of social and policy discourses in shaping current practices with children, youth, and families. Stoneman takes a critical look at the construction of the "young offender" over time and identifies key philosophical changes throughout the past century in Canada, including the implications of the current "managerial" system of youth justice in which actuarial predictions serve to define and identify individual dangerousness. Finally, Kummen explores the concept of readiness as it relates to Canadian early childhood years social policies. She makes visible how readiness can privilege specific ways of knowing for young children and in doing so further maintain the social inequities that are barriers to the development of young children in Canada.

Collectively, these chapters not only challenge and critique various established discourses and ways of understanding in CYC (and other professions and disciplines) but also open up possibilities for CYC practice, policy, research, and education that are not possible through those established understandings. Again, the intent here is not to postulate "right and wrong," an oppositional binary, or to supplant what has come before; rather, it is to seek a place of acceptance that allows diverse understandings to engage with diverse realities to more fully appreciate how child and youth well-being can be understood, engaged, and supported. We see this book as adding to the growing body of knowledge that can contribute to effective CYC practice, policy, research, and education. We hope you find it a good and useful addition!

Note

1 Critical perspectives, as we are using the phrase in this volume, comprise a range of over-lapping theoretical and philosophical paradigms. Some of these perspectives resonate with the diverse and contested intellectual terrain known as postmodernism – or what might be more broadly understood as postfoundational theories (St. Pierre and Pillow 2000). Critically oriented social theories, like some versions of feminism, Marxism, and post-colonial or queer theory, invariably analyze relations of power. Theories that engage with postfoundational thinking, including some versions of social constructionism and post-structuralism, generally concern themselves with analyzing discourses, deconstructing language, exposing plurality and contingency, and unsettling taken-for-granted assumptions. Although each has a rich history and all are taken up in different ways within different disciplines and intellectual traditions, what these perspectives share in common is a skepticism toward objective, value-free, acontextual knowledge or singular truths about reality.

References

Arnett, J.J. 2008. "The Neglected 95%: Why American Psychology Needs to Become Less American." *American Psychologist* 63, 7: 602-14.

Bates, R. 2005. "A Search for Synergy: The Child and Youth Care Educated Child Protection Worker." *Child and Youth Care Forum* 34, 2: 99-110.

Beker, J. 2001, from 1976. "Toward the Unification of the Child Care Field as a Profession." *Child and Youth Care Forum* 30, 6: 355-62.

Eisikovits, Z., and J. Beker. 2001, from 1983. "Beyond Professionalism: The Child and Youth Care Worker as Craftsman." *Child and Youth Care Forum* 30, 6: 415-34.

Lather, P. 2007. *Getting Lost: Feminist Practices toward a Double(d) Science*. Albany: SUNY Press.

Pence, A., and H. Hix-Small. 2007. "Global Children in the Shadow of the Global Child." *International Journal of Educational Policy, Research, and Practice* 8, 1: 83-100.

Phelan, J. 2005. "Child and Youth Care Education: The Creation of Articulate Practitioners." *Child and Youth Care Forum* 34, 5: 347-55.

Prilleltensky, I., A. Rossiter, and R. Walsh-Bowers. 1996. "Preventing Harm and Promoting Ethical Discourse in the Helping Professions: Conceptual, Research, Analytical, and Action Frameworks." *Ethics and Behavior* 6, 4: 287-306.

Reinders, H. 2008. "The Transformation of Human Services." *Journal of Intellectual Disability Research* 52, 7: 544-72.

Skott-Myhre, H. 2003. "Radical Youthwork: Creating and Becoming Everyone." In *Furthering Talk: Advances in the Discursive Therapies*, ed. T. Strong and D. Pare, 217-32. New York: Kluwer Academic/Plenum Publishers.

Smith, M. 2006. "Act Justly, Love Tenderly, Walk Humbly." *Relational Child and Youth Care Practice* 19, 4: 5-16.

St. Pierre, E., and W. Pillow, eds. 2000. *Working the Ruins: Feminist Poststructural Theory and Methods in Education*. New York: Routledge.

Weisner, T.S., and R. Gallimore. 1977. "My Brother's Keeper: Child and Sibling Caretaking." *Current Anthropology* 18, 2: 169-90.

Acronyms

APEC	Asia-Pacific Economic Cooperation
CYC	child and youth care
DSM-IV	*Diagnostic and Statistical Manual of Mental Disorders* (4th ed.)
EBP	evidence-based practice
ECDVU	Early Childhood Development Virtual University
EDI	Early Development Instrument
ELF	Early Learning Framework
FIRA	Father Involvement Research Alliance
FNPP	First Nations Partnerships Program
JDA	Juvenile Delinquents Act
MLTC	Meadow Lake Tribal Council
NACP	North American Certification Project
PAR	participatory action research
PHAC	Public Health Agency of Canada
PIN	personal identification number
SIR	Statistical Inventory on Recidivism
UNICEF	United Nations Children's Fund
WTO	World Trade Organization
YCJA	Youth Criminal Justice Act
YOA	Young Offenders Act

PART 1

Teaching and Theorizing Child and Youth Care

Articulating a Child and Youth Care Philosophy Beyond Binary Constructs

1

J.N. LITTLE

The initial question that prompted this chapter was "what exists between the traditional binary of practice and academia?" Note that I did not ask "what exists *outside* the binary?" I understand that we do not exist outside circulating discourses that favour binary constructs and that we cannot step outside the language that inscribes us. Despite claims that we are now in a postmodern age in which multiplicity is championed, my own experience is that either/or and self/other still permeate institutions, professional discourses, and general conversations. These conversations reflect an inclination toward categorization and hence convenient detours to judgment of worthiness or dismissal. I have sought out interdisciplinary contexts where I erroneously assumed the binary would be erased under the banner of creative practices. For example, at a recent art and social practice symposium, I overheard introductions that included the question "are you studio or gallery?" There appears to be a reluctance to occupy "the space between the lines" (Sandi Wright, personal communication, 12 January 2008) as it suggests professional meandering or, at the least, commitment issues. However, the space between the lines is neither neutral nor static and certainly not easy. Rather, it is a sense of balancing multiple "realities," exploring contradictory passions, and encountering overwhelming potentialities, what Ermine (2007, 193) refers to as "ethical space," which he defines as the electrifying space between two "disparate world views [that] are poised to engage each other." To stand, shift, and shuffle in this space, however, means relinquishing some long-cherished assumptions about professional and personal identities and their articulations. I would like to believe child and youth care is in the process of (re)conceptualizing such spaces as we move our graduates into new career contexts and expand our educational degree-granting capacities. Yet binary and rigid categorizations still block the view of how the space between might be performed.

Various authors have offered up titles for this potential in-between, including transnational feminisms (Mohanty 2003), intersectionality (Anderson 1996; Lee and de Finney 2005), relational politics (Gergen 2006), and appreciative inquiry (Gergen and Gergen 2004). For example, Gergen (2006, 232) speaks eloquently to the idea of ambiguous space as a "new range of poetics." In the realm of CYC writing, White (2007, 226) has argued articulately for a praxis orientation that would promote "conscious reflection both on and in practice." And, though these ideas can move us away from binary thinking in our practices with clients, they appear to be underexplored/-utilized/-developed in the overall field of CYC, where the academic and practitioner divide persists and where certain contexts privilege practice over theory and vice versa. In recent faculty recruitment postings, there is a call for a "strong CYC philosophy" without explicitly saying what is privileged in such a definition. Is the call for academic CYC credentials? CYC certification? A CYC tattoo? My hunch, based on conversations with other CYC practitioners, is that the implicit message is "more practice, less theory." Hence, I want to concurrently trouble and tonic the academy as critical CYC practice. To do this, however, requires playing with existing terms and phrases. Referencing Wittgenstein's "language games," Gergen (2006, 20) says that "games of language are essentially conducted in a rule-like fashion; to make sense at all requires that one play by the rules." But whose rules? I concur with Gergen that "when we can alter the ways in which language is used, develop new forms of talking, or shift the context of usage, we sew [sic] the seeds of human change" (22). I attempt to do this here by arguing for a *theoro-practivist* model that is transdisciplinary and transtheoretical and offering, as Gergen does, "salutary invitations to subverting the traditional binary, and reconceptualizing self and other" (230).

Would the Real CYC Please Stand Up?

Consider this scenario. I swipe my card to the door that divides the waiting room from the offices and invite my client inside. We sit in a grey room in a grey building with a stack of paperwork and the *Diagnostic and Statistical Manual of Mental Disorders* (4th ed.) close at hand. I conduct my assessment, which is filled with "pathologizing questions" that focus on the presenting problem, previous mental health diagnosis, and maladaptive behaviours such as substance abuse and self-harm. There is no section on how clients resist the problem. At the end of the session, I apply a diagnostic label to indicate which eating disorder the client is presenting with to satisfy the requirements of my organization. No diagnostic label equals no service. The client and I then discuss possible treatment options and collaborate on therapeutic goals, with the understanding that these meetings will continue to be one-hour sessions within these four government-approved walls.

Now consider this scenario. I drive to my client's house and sit in the living room, petting the family cat and waiting for the Handi-Dart bus to pull up out front. I chat with the dad and the young woman about the events of the week – what went well, what was challenging. When the Handi-Dart arrives, the young woman and I head off to her volunteer job, where I assume more of a partner role, supporting her to do something she loves. I keep an eye on the clock because she has a different sense of time passing, but otherwise she sets the pace. When we are finished, we ride back to her house, and the shift is done.

Or this scenario. It is the Sunday night before, and I have the familiar butterflies about meeting my new students. My job is to create excitement for change theories, to push the boundaries of what is considered "common sense" or "best practice" despite my decidedly unradical textbook. In the classroom, I am alive, animated, totally in the zone. Some students are elsewhere, despite being physically present – worried about community deaths, money, child care, depression, anxiety, relationship breakups, pregnancy; I can smell the stress. So I am also anticipating the "second shift" of teaching, the emergency interventions, the networking, the "do you have five minutes?" My class is only three hours, but it feels like the shift that never ends.

Given these three examples, which most embodies a CYC philosophy? Or, perhaps more tongue in cheek, a *real* CYC philosophy? My guess is that most CYC practitioners would pick the second as it reflects life-space interventions, strengths-based orientation, and community integration. The first scenario, on the other hand, embodies everything I learned was in opposition to CYC philosophy, especially that notorious axis of evil, the DSM-IV. And the third, of course, is a university classroom, which I argue is a largely unexamined site of critical CYC practice. Yet all are roles I actively engage in, depending on which day of the week it happens to be.

Although I am "purely" CYC on paper, with three degrees from the same school, I am not simply a paper trail of credentials. I have been equally influenced by other life experiences, including shifting geo-social locations, acts of resistance, and a lifetime of joys and sorrows. Although I consider myself a CYC practitioner regardless of which context I practise my skills in, it appears that some of these contexts are considered less authentic CYC practice. For example, Lorde (1984, 110) famously claimed that "the master's tools will never dismantle the master's house," so is it fair to say I hold a CYC philosophy while concurrently holding the DSM-IV? Can I embody an authentic CYC philosophy if I am also beholden to institutional restraint? Although I hold one foot firmly in clinical practice, the other is snug in academia. I need both feet to walk, as it were, just as I need both to inform my practice(s). To assume teaching and research as the culmination of practice, as opposed to practice itself, creates an uneasy tension for those of us who identify the academy as our primary context of critical engagement with young (and not so young) adults. The false dichotomy of practice and research sets in motion a train of identity politics and, ultimately, a spectacular train crash. If the practice train leaves Victoria at 21:00 at 150 kilometres per hour and the theory train leaves Edmonton at the same time but at 200 kilometres per hour, who will reach the national conference first? Or, perhaps more importantly, who will be welcomed as an authentic CYC practitioner with a "real" CYC philosophy?

Binary and Identity Politics

Early in her career, hooks (2000, 113) wrote about division among people working together for an overarching cause (in this case second wave North American feminism):

> The tug-of-war ... has existed within [the] feminist movement between feminist intellectuals and academics ... and participants in the movement who equate education with bourgeois privilege and are fiercely anti-intellectual. This tug-of-war has led to the formation of a false dichotomy between theory (the development of ideas) and practice (the actions of the movement), with one group privileging "practice." As a consequence, there is often little congruity between feminist theory and feminist practice. This intensifies the feelings of some women engaged in activism ... that they are superior to or more "politically correct" than women who concentrate their energies on developing ideas.

I find a parallel in CYC, where, despite our championing of praxis, the theorist/practitioner and academy/community divides still exist. Many years ago, when I was a student engaging in the process of closure with my class colleagues, one student reflected that her biggest fear on graduating was "ending up doing research." Murmurs of agreement swept through the room. In retrospect, that was the beginning of an implicit and condoned silencing of academic CYC practice and the widening gulf between "real" and "academic" CYC engagement. A more recent example was some coaching I received to "tone down" my research focus in a job application, and any mention of theoretical orientation promoting critical interdisciplinary research would be "the kiss of death," especially an orientation with the flavour of feminism or post-structural thought. Both examples speak to the pervading myth that you must align with one side or the other, and no one mentions you can be both. Or something altogether different.

Like the second wave feminist movement in North America, energy is needlessly expended in CYC on drawing an arbitrary line in the sand between what constitutes a legitimate CYC philosophy and whether that philosophy is stronger in community-based practice or teaching/research practice. And, though some readers might argue these conversations are important for critical debate, I witness more identity politics than curious conversations. There is an undercurrent that flows through water cooler conversations, conference themes, and editorials. Some of it is blatant, such as Fewster (2004, 3): "Preference will always be for those with the most impressive academic credentials, not those that possess the personal qualities that reflect the essence of child and youth care." Such circular arguments are not helpful in creating sustainable solidarity. Akin to the rise of third and fourth wave feminisms, essentialist politics cannot thrive in a postmodern world. It seems a shame to me to quest for a singular "truth" of CYC as opposed to the field's possibilities. And, as those of us wrestling with ideas and theories recognize, "most truths are less interesting than the complex and dynamic intercrossing of forces, intensities, discourses, desires, accidents, idiosyncrasies, and relations of power that produce those culminations" (Roy 2003, 1). Although theorists are no strangers to the trade of peddling truth, postmodern critical thinkers also recognize that it shifts based on power, privilege, and dissemination.

But What Camp Are You Really In?
I have been attempting to articulate my own CYC philosophy among varied, and often competing, professional dialogues. As I move into the next phase of my CYC career, many faculty descriptions call for a "strong CYC philosophy." There appears to be an implicit agreement that a so-called strong CYC philosophy is distinct and somehow superior to others (Anglin 1999; Phelan 2005). This is a seductive idea, and, like Thomas (2001), who writes about her experience graduating with a degree in women's studies, and my MA cohort, in CYC we had our fair share of defending our degree choice, creating a self-perpetuating cycle of why CYC was different and unique. To articulate how "we" are ontologically different from "them," however, is extremely problematic. This process is reductive and deeply entrenches the "other" (especially so when in reference to social work, which, frankly, is tired). It also promotes a stagnation of identity. So busy are we trying to illustrate our difference that those cherished traditional concepts do not get taken up critically.

Indeed, we risk reifying a "sociopolitical category [that] is applied to individuals as a reductive agent, circumscribing one's identity, and reducing one's potential to be otherwise" (Gergen 2006, 227).

It might be an issue not of taking up the binary of either/or but of rearranging identity more broadly. Ropers-Huilman (1997, 337) speaks eloquently about this, and thus I quote her at length:

> Identity, then, is a term that is most useful when broadly defined and seen as perhaps not all-encompassing. The "creation" of identity is impossible as there exists no time when a totally new and unchanging being enters a discourse. I cannot distinguish such a point in this research. Rather, the concept of identities is like viewing a borderless map. Many of the landmarks have posted names; indeed, I have lived in places called "White" and "Woman." Once a location, an identity, is a part of me, I cannot disown it. Yet it need not own me. Rather, I can visit, through careful listening, other cities whose characteristics and opportunities provide lessons and insights as well. While some people travel more frequently and enthusiastically than others, this process of travelling is endless. Our identities are multiple, yet enmeshed with each other in a chaotic balance of life choices and struggles for self.

What I understand from her commentary is that, though identity can be conceptualized as "borderless," it is still influenced by previous travels. For example, schools of CYC all across the country have been created by practitioners and scholars representing a range of disciplines and intellectual traditions. Those with tenure have come from several other metaphorical and literal cities, and this diversity enriches dialogue about practice, theorizing, and ethical decision making and introduces a host of potentialities of seeing the world of children, youth, families, and communities. I can head left down the halls for a quantitative perspective or opt right for a social constructionist perspective. I can knock on every door in between for perspectives that have emerged out of allied disciplines but that are housed under the banner of CYC. But this interdisciplinary thrust is at risk of disappearing with the rise of graduate programs that woo those already firmly embedded in the undergraduate discourse of CYC and in turn propagates a field of CYC practitioners who do not critically question the very assumptions therein. This reification of standards, theories, and the apparent urgency for a singular CYC philosophy might actually do us more harm than good. Messer-Davidow (2002, 20) reflects thus:

> Disciplines endure through practice, the continuation of practice depends upon reproduction, and reproduction is accomplished by socializing practitioners. When a discipline trains future practitioners, it doesn't just teach them it's knowing contents; it exercises them in ways of perceiving, thinking, valuing, relating, and acting. Once the discipline has credentialed and employed them, it ensures that they continue to observe its "good subject" practices by subjecting them to ongoing evaluations.

You, dear reader, might be thinking, yes! That is exactly what CYC praxis is! An epistemological and ontological *being*. This is what certification reflects – good practice measures! But this is precisely our strength as well as our challenge and, most importantly, why certain areas of practice such as the academy are rendered "less than" direct practice. Those on the fringes of perceptible CYC practice have eschewed some of the grooming inherent in CYC discourse and as such become risky subjects: "Competent practitioners learn (as inept ones do not) to observe the disciplinary norms, and innovative practitioners learn (as merely competent ones do not) which norms they can transgress in order to generate new knowledge. But woe to the practitioner who violates the disciplinary truth ... because the discipline will regard her as a bad subject to be subdued or expelled" (Messer-Davidow 2002, 20-21).

At the same time, these contexts groom their own subjectivities and performances of authenticity, and I do not suggest that those in the academy are somehow romantic nomads. This brings us back to the vexing subtext of "strong CYC philosophy" embedded in certain employer advertisements, including faculty appointments. As an educator who teaches in a professional school of CYC at a university, I am painfully aware of my role in disciplining subjects in the classroom. At times, it is easier to "speak" CYC discourse than to interrupt it. Phelan (2005) supports the proliferation of this discourse and advocates for a mono-educational curriculum to produce "reflective practitioners." Although I do not disagree with reflective practitioners, indeed I know I have taught and mentored some, I do not believe that project can be accomplished through placing restrictions on what can be reflected on, which is akin to pouring the old wine into new bottles. If we at least concur that the children, youth, families, and communities we work with are complex and ever evolving, then it seems accurate to assume the same for the field(s) of CYC.

As Bloustien (2003, 51) reminds us, "ultimately identities are narratives – stories we tell about ourselves – and they are fictional." The story of what constitutes a "strong CYC philosophy," then, is open to editing and rewriting. At this global juncture, with pressing social and environmental needs, a strong CYC philosophy needs to move beyond the relational and into the political (Bellefeuille, McGrath, and Jamieson 2008). There is an ethical imperative (White, this volume) to do so. What I offer below is my emergent narrative of what constitutes a strong CYC philosophy. I want to be clear that I do not offer this as a static truth, a bundle of essences, or a binary/oppositional argument to the dominant CYC philosophy. Rather, I invite you to consider this a tentative collision of language, ontology, and reflexivity.

Toward a Theoro-Practivist Model

When attempting to articulate my thoughts, I wrestled with familiar word pairings such as scholar-activist, scholar-practitioner, scholar-advocate, social pedagogue, and academic-practitioner. Yet all embody the dichotomous language I seek to dismantle. As I reinvented myself for particular contexts, including job applications, what I created was a theoro-practivist model. Although still a hyphenated word (and I toyed with acapractivist), it holds the three aspects I see as being so critical to my orientation to my work: theory, practice, and activism. In some respects, it plays on the academic catchwords *scholarship, teaching,* and *service* but resides both inside and outside the academy and between the lines of allied disciplines.

Theory

As a scholar, I am deeply embedded in and embodied by the language of theory and happiest while there. Since I often teach a course on theories as they relate to human change processes, this is probably a good thing. My love of theory is multifaceted – I appreciate the social and historical contexts within which ideas reside; for example, I am curious about the parallel between capitalism and "best practice" theories; and theory allows a languaging of ideas and experiences. I love theory because, despite its historical abuses, it can create a more just and inclusive world (Denzin and Giardina 2009). Most importantly, I am resolved that we all operate from a theoretical paradigm, explicitly expressed or implicitly practised. Where we draw our "ontological and epistemological bits" (Messer-Davidow 2002, 189), however, has ethical implications and consequences. From my training in CYC, I had to look elsewhere to queer heteronormative perspectives (Bechdel 2006; Butler 2004; Calfia 1997; herising 2005; Weeks, Heaphy, and Donovan 2001), I needed a language outside CYC to speak to relational interaction and meaning making in a manner that acknowledged their complexity (Denzin 2003; Gergen 2001; McCracken 2008), and I needed a critical race perspective that transcended a multicultural, singular discourse diversity lens (Maracle 1996; Minh-ha 1999). And, given my exposure to developmental theories, I needed theories that would speak to the complexity of youth experience from a postmodern and participatory lens (Bach 1998; Bloustien 2003; Cammarota and Fine 2008; de Finney 2007; Skott-Myhre 2005). And, perhaps most importantly, much of my learning and methodological development has emerged out of feminist fiction and poetry (Allison 1993; Dykewomon 1997; Feinberg 1993; Pratt 1995; Rich 1981, to name too few). You might notice few CYC practitioners in the preceding list. Grant (2005, 91) suggests that many training traditions "often have no sense of the limitations of their practice, and as a result, are not aware of the wealth of wisdom that lies within reach if only they were to ask different questions from those delineated within their own disciplinary canons." As such, different questions reside within, and different temporal answers reside outside, common-sense discourses of CYC. By collaging theories, stories, and narratives from multiple contexts, richer potentials are more easily recognized in terms of interventions and collaborations with co-workers. This cross-contextual curiosity in turn enriches what I can offer in the classroom.

Fewster (2004, 3) remarked once that "no educational courses, training programs or text books can give you what you need in order to be with, understand and guide a young person through the fear, pain, chaos and anger once these demons are at work. We are not dealing with theory and strategic intervention here." I have concerns that the essentialist movement in CYC is akin to what created fissures in North American feminism – that to claim our difference as natural, biologically determined, and developmentally sequential is to further our own imprisonment and foreclose multiple ways of articulating CYC. Essentialism *is* a theoretical perspective. Regardless whether you call CYC a calling, a craft (see Eisikovits and Beker 2001; Maier 2001) or just a job, it cannot be denied that we groom students to be good subjects. In doing so, we rob them of the very gift needed in all areas of CYC work – critical reflection and the theoretical language with which to do it. An example of grooming would be a common lament in my classroom: "Well, the pay sucks, but you couldn't pay me to be one of *them*" (meaning allied disciplines that earn higher wages). Good grooming would be to employ an essentialist argument for heeding one's calling, and one colleague actually had the nerve to say poor wages made CYC practitioners more appealing to institutions and agencies. Drawing on feminist theories, however, illuminates the gendered nature of this work and historical, culturally specific devaluing of child care and youth work.

Practice

As I explicated above, my practice takes place across a spectrum of needs and institutional delivery. In my career, I have done much of what would be considered traditional CYC work, including family support; (dis)ability inclusion; short-term residential, educational, and life skills tutoring; and group and staff training on subjects such as queer inclusion and safer sexual practices. Yet I found myself ending up in the most hinterland CYC contexts, such as office-based counselling and qualitative methodology conferences that had never heard of CYC. I discovered being a heretic was much more liberating than attempting to "translate" my multiple perspectives into CYC dogma. Akin to drawing on multiple literacies to inform my theoretical lens, traversing the practice landscape has challenged how I articulate my practice. Specifically, it has compelled me to step out of the dyadic dance metaphor so popular in CYC discourse and to become politically accountable for my interventions in the community, the classroom, and research.

Activism

I have argued elsewhere (Moen, Little, and Burnett 2005) that an oft-missing component of CYC practice is a radical and political edge that takes up non-essentialist and non-hegemonic positions. Others are certainly involved in this project (Skott-Myhre 2005), but I see little evidence of those willing to name themselves as activists. Others appear to have taken up the scholar-advocate position (Cope 2008; Gunderson 2009; Roysirear 2009; Wilcox 2009, not to mention many who created women's studies programs in North America). Advocacy is not a new concept in CYC, but like practice it needs to be stretched into the realm of political action. Theoro-practivism in the realm of CYC requires teaching as activism. "What is teaching as activism? We believe that our teaching is part and parcel of the anti-globalization demonstrations such as those in Seattle and Quebec City. It includes the teaching that we professors do inside and outside the classroom" (Tripp and Muzzin 2005, 3). So, though I have argued that post-secondary education is overlooked as a viable site of CYC practice, it is also overlooked as a potential site of activism. In some respects, this activism is direct action, such as walking with my students protesting tuition fee increases or demanding state attention to missing indigenous women in British Columbia. Teaching as activism is subversive action on campus as well, for example calling attention to gendered/sexist/heteronormative advertisements on campus for the teaching of feminist theory. Or networking students in a manner that allows space for potentially radical acts. Activism on campus is also the small stuff that counters the commodification of education: letting students know they have one chance to miss tuition and still register (learned in my own undergraduate days), advocating for a reserve copy of the textbook in the library, and supporting students who fall outside dominant CYC discourse and are willing to challenge the status quo. This can be done through institutional routes, such as directed studies, or off-the-side-of-the-desk mentoring. We fail as activists when we embrace ideas of "natural" consequences (too often socially constructed and maintained) and continue to tokenize cultural locations. We fail as activists and CYC faculty when we move inward in our professional associations and publishing circles and continued participation in individualistic and mono-professional discourses. Don't get me wrong: according to my own criteria, I fail every week. However, if our propaganda is self-awareness, then activism as a pedagogue requires vigilance in observing when we slip into dominant discourse and watching for opportunities to resist it.

Where I do see promise of radicalizing CYC through resistance is in the creation of theoro-practivists in the classroom and participatory action research (PAR) methodologies. This is where "your feminist rubber meets your methodological road" (Gergen 2001, 91) and where some historical ideas of what it means to hold a CYC philosophy can be applied. For example, in my own institution, several students and faculty have engaged or are engaging youth voices in dynamic ways. Some projects hold long-term partnerships (see www.antidote.org as an example). Although it is outside the scope of this chapter to explicate the moral, ethical, and revolutionary potential of PAR in CYC research, I believe that it represents a critical juncture at which to ask several important questions. For example, how does milieu get redefined in temporary and collaborative spaces such as research groups and classrooms? How is power made explicit and negotiated? Who decides what constitutes "best practices"? And, most importantly, what don't we know that we thought we did?

Conclusion

It is my sense that, given the proliferation of CYC practice contexts, academic programs, and engaged scholarship, we stand at the beginning of a new decade of possibilities: the possibility of multiple CYC philosophies to emerge. As herising (2005, 142) reflects, "by embracing a queer flexibility, we are better able to let difference live, where we can find pleasures in the ambiguities of multifocaled thresholds. In turn, this openness can create alternative strategies and visions for a radical praxis, where bordered and domesticated claims of knowledge are contested, challenged, decentred in order to engage processes of alteration, regeneration, and transformation."

In many respects, I have travelled varied terrains within this chapter to challenge mono-educational initiatives and to invite the reader to reconceptualize the academic context as a rich site of contesting CYC norms. What I have spoken to is a need for questioning the academic/practitioner dichotomy and the promise of a theoro-practivist orientation. This would, in my opinion, fuse artificially delineated contexts of research, practice, teaching, and activism and challenge us to move the idea of praxis into, well, practice. If we adhere to a mono-educational initiative, we will merely become simulacra. By continuing to delineate practice and academic tracks, the profession becomes potentially embittered and most certainly fractured. How do we avoid this when we secretly believe we are right in our own CYC philosophy? Again, I turn to feminism's experience and end on the words of Yeatman (1994, 50): "The answer lies not in attempting to preempt the differentiation of expert and non-expert feminist theorizing by making all conform to the homogenizing dictates of the feminist community ... Just what this might mean requires rather different models of political accountability, dialogue and democratic participation than those we inherit."

References
Allison, D. 1993. *Bastard out of Carolina*. New York: Plume Fiction.
Anderson, K. 1996. "Engendering Race Research: Unsettling the Self-Other Dichotomy." In *Body Space*, ed. N. Duncan, 197-211. New York: Routledge.
Anglin, J. 1999. "The Uniqueness of Child and Youth Care: A Personal Perspective." *Child and Youth Care Forum* 28, 2: 143-50.
Bach, H. 1998. *A Visual Narrative Concerning Curriculum, Girls, Photography Etc*. Edmonton: Qualitative Institute Press.
Bechdel, A. 2006. *Fun Home*. New York: Houghton Mifflin.
Bellefeuille, G., J. McGrath, and D. Jamieson. 2008. "A Pedagogical Response to a Changing World: Towards a Globally-Informed Pedagogy for Child and Youth Care Education and Practice." *Children and Youth Services Review* 30, 7: 717-26.
Bloustien, G. 2003. *Girl Making: A Cross-Cultural Ethnography on the Processes of Growing Up Female*. New York: Berghahn Books.
Butler, J. 2004. *Undoing Gender*. New York: Routledge.
Calfia, P. 1997. *Sex Changes: The Politics of Transgenderism*. San Francisco: Cleis Press.

Cammarota, J., and M. Fine. 2008. *Revolutionizing Education: Youth Participatory Action Research in Motion.* New York: Routledge.

Cope, M. 2008. "Becoming a Scholar-Advocate: Participatory Research with Children." *Antipode* 40, 3: 428-35.

de Finney, S. 2007. "'It's about Us!' Racialized Minority Girls' Transformative Engagement in Feminist Participatory Action Research." PhD diss., University of Victoria.

Denzin, N.K. 2003. *Performance Ethnography: Critical Pedagogy and the Politics of Culture.* Thousand Oaks, CA: Sage Publications.

Denzin, N., and M.D. Giardina. 2009. *Qualitative Inquiry as Social Justice.* Walnut Creek, CA: Left Coast Press.

Dykewomon, E. 1997. *Beyond the Pale.* Vancouver: Press Gang Publishers.

Eisikovits, Z., and J. Beker. 2001. "Beyond Professionalism: The *Child* and *Youth Care* Worker as Craftsman." *Child and Youth Care Forum* 30, 6: 415-34.

Ermine, W. 2007. "The Ethical Space of Engagement." *Indigenous Law Journal* 6, 1: 193-203. .

Feinberg, L. 1993. *Stone Butch Blues.* Ithaca: Firebrand Books.

Fewster, G. 2004. Editorial. *Relational Child and Youth Care Practice* 17, 3: 3.

Gergen, K.J. 2006. *Therapeutic Realities: Collaboration, Oppression, and Relational Flow.* Chargin Falls, OH: Taos Institute Publications.

Gergen, K.J., and M. Gergen. 2004. *Social Constructionism: Entering the Dialogue.* Chargin Falls, OH: Taos Institute Publications.

Gergen, M. 2001. *Feminist Reconstructions in Psychology: Narrative, Gender, and Performance.* Thousand Oaks, CA: Sage Publications.

Grant, M. 2005. "Professional Ideology and Educational Practice: Learning to Be a Health Professional." In *Teaching as Activism: Equity Meets Environmentalism,* ed. P. Tripp and L. Muzzin, 80-94. Kingston: McGill-Queen's University Press.

Gunderson, M. 2009. "The Virtues of Scholarship and Virtues of Political Action." *Kennedy Institute of Ethics Journal* 19, 2: 171-84.

herising, F. 2005. "Interrupting Positions: Critical Thresholds and Queer Pro/Positions." In *Research as Resistance: Critical, Indigenous, and Anti-Oppressive Approaches,* ed. L. Brown and S. Strega, 127-52. Toronto: Canadian Scholars' Press.

hooks, b. 2000. *Feminist Theory: From Margin to Center.* 2nd ed. Cambridge, MA: South End Press.

Lee, J.A., and S. de Finney. 2005. "Using Popular Theatre for Engaging Racialized Minority Girls in Exploring Questions of Identity and Belonging." *Child and Youth Care Services* 26, 1: 95-118.

Lorde, A.G. 1984. *Sister Outsider: Essays and Speeches.* Berkeley: Crossing Press.

Maier, H.W. 2001. "Should Child and Youth Care Go the Craft or the Professional Route? A Comment on the Preceding Article by Zvi Eisikovits and Jerome Beker." *Child and Youth Care Forum* 30, 6: 435-40.

Maracle, L. 1996. *I Am Woman: A Native Perspective on Sociology and Feminism.* Vancouver: Press Gang Publishers.

McCracken, G. 2008. *Transformations: Identity Construction in Contemporary Culture.* Bloomington: Indiana University Press.

Messer-Davidow, E. 2002. *Disciplining Feminism: From Social Activism to Academic Discourse.* Durham: Duke University Press.

Minh-ha, T.T. 1999. *Cinema Interval.* New York: Routledge.

Moen, K., J.N. Little, and M. Burnett. 2005. "The Earth Is Dying: A Radical Child and Youth Care Perspective." *Relational Child and Youth Care Practice* 18, 1: 7-13.

Mohanty, C.T. 2003. *Feminism without Borders: Decolonizing Theory, Practicing Solidarity.* Durham: Duke University Press.

Phelan, J. 2005. "Child and Youth Care Education: The Creation of Articulate Practitioners." *Child and Youth Care Forum* 34, 5: 347-55.

Pratt, M.B. 1995. *S/he.* New York: Firebrand Books.

Rich, A. 1981. *A Wild Patience Has Taken Me This Far: Poems 1978-1981.* New York: W.W. Norton.

Ropers-Huilman, B. 1997. "Constructing Feminist Teachers: Complexities of Identity." *Gender and Education* 9, 3: 327-43.

Roy, K. 2003. *Teachers in Nomadic Spaces: Deleuze and Curriculum.* New York: Peter Lang Publishing.

Roysirear, G. 2009. "The Big Picture Advocacy: Counsellor, Heal Society and Thyself." *Journal of Counselling and Development* 87, 3: 288-94.

Skott-Myhre, H. 2005. "Captured by Capital: Youth Work and the Loss of Revolutionary Potential." *Child and Youth Care Forum* 34, 2: 141-58.

Thomas, S. 2001. "You're Getting a Degree in WHAT?" *Gender Issues* 19, 2: 16-20.

Tripp, P., and L. Muzzin. 2005. *Teaching as Activism: Equity Meets Environmentalism.* Kingston: McGill-Queen's University Press.

Weeks, J., B. Heaphy, and C. Donovan. 2001. *Same Sex Intimacies: Families of Choice and Other Life Experiments.* New York: Routledge.

White, J. 2007. "Knowing, Doing, and Being in Context: A Praxis-Orientated Approach to Child and Youth Care." *Child and Youth Care Forum* 36, 5-6: 225-44.

Wilcox, H.N. 2009. "Embodied Ways of Knowing, Pedagogies, and Social Justice: Inclusive Science and Beyond." *National Women's Studies Association* 21, 2: 104-20.

Yeatman, A. 1994. *Postmodern Revisionings of the Political.* New York: Routledge.

Rethinking Developmental Theories in Child and Youth Care   **2**

VERONICA PACINI-KETCHABAW

Developmental theories are outlined in child and youth care training documents as a cornerstone of practice and theory in the field. Those preparing to become CYC practitioners are expected to know and apply a wide range of developmental theories in their professional practice with individuals, groups, families, and communities to ensure that the complexities of human behaviour are accounted for (see Rogerson, Shelton, and Hardy 2007). Within developmental psychology, developmental theories are treated as facts about children and their behavioural changes into adulthood. These "facts" lead us to construct certain views about children, and we use these views to interpret observations of the children and youth we encounter in practice. Because developmental psychology sees itself as a science, specifically a sub-discipline of the behavioural sciences, it defines its purpose as objectively observing and measuring age-related changes in human beings. The discipline often perceives itself as being outside political, social, economic, and cultural motives.

In my position as an instructor who teaches developmental theory in a graduate program (see Pacini-Ketchabaw, Kummen, and Thompson 2010), I observe the prevalence of developmental psychology within CYC training. When students come to my class, we analyze the works of influential developmental theorists – Piaget, Freud, Kohlberg,

Vygotsky, and Bowlby, among others. The primary challenge I encounter is that students can describe, some vaguely and some in great detail, the various developmental stages these theorists proposed, but they cannot identify why they produced the work they did or describe the circumstances in which the ideas were developed. For instance, they understand Piaget's stages as truths that objectively represent the children and youth they work with today. They are aware of variability within the stages, but they view the stages as the basis for thinking about who children are (or should be).

This strong hold that developmental psychology has in CYC is problematic given recent developments within two relevant bodies of literature. First, the factual bases of developmental theories have been questioned and seen from a critical standpoint for what they are: frameworks to think about and interpret children's and youths' behaviours. Several scholars propose that these frameworks are in constant interaction with societies' political, economic, and social circumstances (Burman 2008a, 2008b; Lesko 2001; Morss 1996; Rose 1990, 2008). Second, recent literature in the field of CYC calls for a more critical stance to the field that challenges modern constructions of children, youth, families, and communities (Pence 2000; Skott-Myhre 2005, 2008; White 2007). Skott-Myhre (2008), for example, proposes a revolutionary CYC field.

Building on these two strands of the literature, I propose in this chapter that CYC might become a revolutionary profession by decentring developmental theories in CYC training and treating them as frameworks that constantly interact with societal conditions to construct a certain kind of child/youth subject. In other words, I suggest that the study and treatment of developmental psychology in CYC need to be contextually specific, critically embraced, and not necessarily treated as one of the foundations of the field. The spirit of this chapter is, as White (2007, 227) has explained, to critically engage "with a diverse range of resources and intellectual traditions" in the hope that I can provide a "creative, generative and useful" perspective of one aspect of the field of CYC. I join Jennifer White (2007), Hans Skott-Myhre (2005, 2008), and those working within the early childhood part of the field (Dahlberg, Moss, and Pence 1999; Moss and Pence 1994)[1] in bringing a critical stance that opens the field to other possibilities. The chapter expands ideas in the field so that we can better respond, in critical and creative ways, to the trends and shifts that current neoliberal, postmodern, and globalized conditions bring.

To develop my arguments, I outline instances that show how developmental theories and political-societal forms of organization constantly interact to create the child/youth subject. I then describe relevant arguments proposed by critical approaches within the CYC field. In the final section, I link these arguments to elucidate my understanding of revolutionary CYC.

The Context of Developmental Psychology: The Formation of the Subject

My main purpose in this section is to provide a review of the literature that resituates developmental theories as politically positioned and neither neutral nor innocent. Specifically, I show how developmental theories respond and contribute to social movements (Burman 2008a, 2008b). I describe two specific social conditions – modern and postmodern societal circumstances – and link these movements to shifts within developmental psychology.

A few words of caution. These are not the only ways in which developmental psychology can be linked to societal forms of subject formation. Nor do I intend to present a binary between modern and postmodern societies. In fact, not only do other versions of psychology predate modern developmental theories (Burman 2008a), but modern and postmodern conditions also coexist in most Western societies. My analysis presents examples, so its focus is limited to one of a wide range of constellations of practices that create citizen-subjects (Fendler 2001). Furthermore, the connections I draw between societal conditions and the emergence and deployment of developmental theories are not necessarily deterministic, nor do they intend direct causality. Walkerdine (1984, 173) notes that political motivations "should be taken as mutually implicated, making and remaking the other possible, intertwining to produce a discursive and political nexus." Similarly, Fendler (2001, 121) cautions her readers not to imply any sort of determinism when creating relationships between societal organizations and forms of subject formation. Rather, she notes, it is important to "acknowledge the repetitions and reiterations of the status quo" in the work we do every day with children, youth, and families.

Modernity and Developmental Psychology

Modernity emerged during the eighteenth and nineteenth centuries through a set of deep social and intellectual transformations (Bauman 1991; Kumar 1995). Its goal was to develop an objective science and a universal morality that would both foster human emancipation and improve the human condition. In other words, modernity sought the social, political, and cultural freedom of human beings. Systems of thought that offered salvation from what were considered society's evils – specifically myth, religion, and superstition – were developed. Modernity was concerned with classifying and describing things. It brought order to the apparently unordered environment in which people lived. It also provided the basis for discovering the rules, principles, and laws that form and guide men's and women's actions (Kumar 1995; Rose 1990). Modern thinkers believed that science could and should change society for the better; consequently, they postulated a scientific understanding of the human condition (Kumar 1995). The scientific or empirical method was considered the sole rational procedure for attaining progress. Objectivity became the driving idea behind the belief that individuals could detach themselves from their biases and perceptions. This period saw enormous societal changes brought about by technology and industrialization.

This continuous search for the foundations of an ordered world is captured in theories of child development (Morss 1996; Rose 1990, 2008). These theories support the assertion of universal laws and norms, emphasizing issues of normality among *all* children and families. Most child development textbooks, for example, endorse the idea that all children go through common stages of development (Bernhard 1995). Similarly, developmental programs, or programs that apply developmental knowledge, provide guiding principles that underlie acceptable practices and instructions for practical actions that are based on norms (Burman 2008a).

Another example of the influence of modernity in developmental psychology is the development and use of predefined outcomes that measure children's and youths' successes. Many disciplines that base their practices on developmental psychology use developmental norms to help children and youth through their developmental journeys. Burman (2008a) notes that such a journey is much more than a simple or natural progression: it involves the development of the citizen-subject.

> The drive toward rationality in models of development might be a reflection of the rationalization of the capitalism taking place at the level of individual psychic, rather than industrial, processes. The norms and milestones that structure developmental psychology present a picture of orderly, progressive graduation through stages to ever greater competence and maturity. We can see here the modelling of an ideal-typical citizen-subject who is knowable, known, docile, and productive. (Burman 2008a, 26)

Studies on governmentality (e.g., Foucault 1991; Gordon 1991; Rose 1996) have perhaps been the most useful in tracing the links between modernity and developmental psychology. Governmentality studies highlight power-knowledge relations, defined as a network of discursive relations that extends beyond simple coercion (Foucault 1977, 1978). The effects of discursive power relations involve the formation and regulation of meanings and understandings, disciplining how people act. Knowledge creates possibilities and capacities for action (Foucault 1991). Through the concept of governmentality, the ways in which developmental psychology has developed are not assumed to be "natural." Rather, they are thought to be part of discursive relations that involve the productive and reproductive nature of power-knowledge relations. Rose (1999, 20) explains that to "do" a governmentality analysis "is not to start from the apparently obvious historical or sociological question: what happened and why? It is to start by asking what authorities ... wanted it to happen, in relation to problems defined how, in pursuit of what objectives, through what strategies and techniques."

Building on the interpretations of Foucault's writings on governmentality, much has been written about the emergence of psychology and its role within political, social, and cultural contexts. For example, Rose (1996) argues that psychology, in particular developmental psychology, has been used as a political strategy for the purpose of enhancing and regulating a democratic way of life. He suggests that the discourse of psychology has been advanced to support or deny discourses in a wide variety of circumstances, including, but not limited to, those in the social, cultural, political, and economic realms of children (Miller and Rose 1993).

> The psychological sciences are intimately bound up with programs, calculations, and techniques for the government of the soul. The twentieth-century development of psychological sciences opened up new dimensions for our thoughts. Simultaneously, it made possible new techniques of structuring our reality to produce the phenomena and effects that can now be imagined. The translation of the human psyche into the sphere of knowledge and the ambit of technology makes it possible to govern subjectivity according to norms and criteria that ground their authority in an esoteric but objective knowledge. (Rose 1990, 9)

Psychology provided the techniques and tactics for the creation of self-regulated individuals who would act in accordance with government objectives. It granted what Miller and Rose (1993, 79) call the "procedures of inscription" – "particular technical devices of writing, listing, numbering and computing that render a realm into discourse as a knowable, calculable and administrable object."

Psychology made possible the link between individuals' behaviours and political objectives through technologies of government (Miller and Rose 1993): methods of observation, techniques of registration, methods of research and investigation such as surveys and statistics, and regulatory devices such as case work. It was through these subtle forms of power that children and youth became part of government rationalities. These technologies of government represent strategies for disciplining bodies and distributing individuals (Foucault 1977).

Initially, psychology formed as a technology of individualization:

> that is, it emerged as a "positive science" rather than a sub-branch of philosophy when it shifted its concerns from a general theory of

mind to a practical task: the creation of calculable minds and manageable individuals. This occurred within a specific problem space, one formed by the growing demands that individuals should be administered, or distributed to particular regimes, tasks, or treatments, according to their abilities – in school, at work, in the army, in the criminal justice system (Rose 2008, 449).

As Cannella and Viruru (2004) point out, developmental theories can also be linked to the colonial and imperial efforts of the "so-called Enlightened and modern systems of thought" – particularly the Enlightenment beliefs in progress and reason (86). The idea of the developmental child emerges through two primary colonial and imperial ideas. First, we can trace many developmental theories to the idea of human progress, which, to date, places children as subordinated others in relation to adults – in the same way that Western colonial ideology placed colonized peoples as inferior to privileged white European male adults. This value of progression can be seen in the stage theories of Jean Piaget, Erik Erikson, and Laurence Kohlberg. Second, developmental theories embed the "commitment to logic/reason that emerged from the Enlightenment" through their linear, scientific, gendered, and dualistic logic (92). Here we can consider Piaget's theories of logical thought in his construction of the child as a developing scientist.

Nancy Lesko (2001) is interested in this realm. She proposes that the "developmental framework is simultaneously colonial (with privileged, invisible viewers and hypervisible, temporalized, and embodied others) and administrative (ranking, judging, making efficient and productive)" (41). She traces the links between developmental psychology and the evolutionary Tree of Man – "a simple classificatory scheme that easily switched between evolutionary hierarchies within nature and evolutionary progress across human cultures" – and concludes that "younger children and arrested youth were analogous to older and more primitive peoples (lower branches), and each individual child had to climb her own evolutionary tree" (40). The work of G. Stanley Hall and Erik H. Erikson on adolescence follows the evolutionary tree described by Lesko as it ensures that we "attend to progress, precocity, arrest, or decline" (41). Adolescence is not necessarily represented in the form of a tree;

instead, it is mapped through "tables and charts of physical regularities, rates of pubertal change, and psychosocial steps" (42).

To tentatively summarize, the work reviewed above argues that developmental psychology, as a framework to think about children and youth, has contributed to the Western understanding of the human condition – one that privileges the Anglo-US, white, middle-class, masculine subjectivity of modernity (Burman 2008a). Developmental theories, in this way, have emerged in response to and contributed to our current dominant construction of the nature of childhood and adolescence.

Developmental Psychology in Societies of Control

In the previous section, I briefly outlined how psychology, and developmental theories in particular, are located within modernity or what Foucault called *disciplinary societies* (Deleuze 1992). As was evident in the previous section, and as Deleuze notes, disciplinary societies are "environments of enclosure" meant "to concentrate; to distribute in space; to order in time; to compose a productive force within the dimension of space-time whose effect will be greater than the sum of its components" (3). These characteristics of modern or disciplinary societies are reflected in developmental theories that stress normality, logic, and progression. Today, however, according to Deleuze, we live in a different kind of society – a *society of control* that reflects different kinds of strategies within developmental psychology. This shift does not mean that societies of control have entirely replaced disciplinary societies; rather, "discipline does no longer pertain to all aspects of society," and new forms of power relations have emerged (Fendler 2001, 135).

Although disciplinary societies are characterized by enclosures or moulds, societies of control treat control as modulation, "like a self-deforming cast that will continuously change from one moment to the other, or like a sieve whose mesh will transmute from point to point" (Deleuze 1992, 4). Societies of control are inscribed in our current postmodern condition, which, according to Corson (1998, 2), has two main features – "an almost universal trend away from things like centralization, mass production, specialization, and mass consumption; and an almost universal trend towards the development of flexible technologies that are developed and used in smaller and more diverse units." These current social circumstances, Fendler (2001, 119) argues, "call for 'flexible' and 'fluid' ways of being" – so "the conception of a fixed role or position" characteristic of modern organizational structures "has now shifted to a more multifaceted and response-ready capacity."

Developmental psychology in societies of control has changed its strategies. According to Fendler (2001), the social technologies deployed and inscribed by developmental psychology are different from previous technologies, so a different child/youth subject is constructed. Whereas modern developmental theories were primarily concerned with intellect, moral behaviour, discipline, management, and social responsibility, current approaches in developmental psychology attempt to get at desires, fears, wishes, aspirations, attitudes, inclinations, and pleasures. Fendler notes that in societies of control "the multiplication and discovery of new aspects of human being that can be described, measured, evaluated, and improved are celebrated as indications of scientific progress and advances in knowledge" (129). Developmental psychology in disciplinary societies focused on cognition and behaviour, as illustrated in Piaget's work, but the more recent versions of developmentalist constructions rely on desire – the subject herself desires to be normal.

Following Deleuze (1992), Fendler (2001) describes three interrelated ways in which societies of control work. First, they involve constant and frequent monitoring of individuals. An interesting example is how developmental testing is now deployed in Canada for young children. They are not tested by developmental psychologists in a laboratory; rather, the test comes to them – to the environments they inhabit. Teachers, using tests such as the Early Development Instrument, now perform continuous monitoring of children's development every year in their kindergarten classrooms. Through this constant monitoring, Deleuze (1992, 5) notes, "we no longer find ourselves dealing with the mass/individual pair. Individuals have become '*dividuals*,' and masses, samples, data, markets or '*banks*.'" We can see this in the context of British Columbia, where children are provided with a personal identification number (PIN) in kindergarten and their development is tracked toward high school through testing every three to four years. Second, the standards in a control society are no longer centralized; they are diverse and change quickly. In the case of young children, educators are to ensure they are answerable to developmental and educational standards set by ministries of education and health, school boards, local health authorities, psychologists, local community groups, and parents. Third, in societies of control, there is no completion or closure, resulting in the need for perpetual training. Current discussions about lifespan development – development that is continual and never ends – are characteristic of societies of control. The individual now begins to monitor her own ever-changing life. She is invited to accept new challenges, embrace new stages of life. Deleuze (1992, 7) notes that "many young people strangely boast of being 'motivated'; they re-request apprenticeships and permanent training. It's up to them to discover what they're being made to serve, just as their elders discovered, not without difficulty, the telos of the disciplines."

Skott-Myhre (2008) outlines the ways in which youth work is deployed differently in disciplinary societies and societies of control. In a disciplinary society, the goal of youth work "was either to accommodate or normalize youth to the regimes of discipline or to assist them in avenues of resistance. The focus was on the development of singular identities that could either accommodate or resist" (148-49). In a society of control, the youth worker does not necessarily focus on "elements of confinement in the school, the workplace, or the family" (149). More importantly, a fragmentation of identities begins to proliferate, and "the role of desire is joined with that of consumption, bringing youth whose desiring discourse is deeply laden with metaphors of capital" (149). Within this context, "problems and solutions become linked to an unstable field of shifting identity and desire, resulting in youth with a changing multiplicity of problems" (149).

Revolutionary Child and Youth Care and Developmental Theories

The foregoing review was not intended to include every possible convergence between developmental psychology and societal forms of organization and subject formation. Rather, I presented examples to illustrate the need to problematize, from a political standpoint that unpacks power relations, the deployment of developmental knowledge in child and youth care as "rationalistic, a priori truths upon which a [practice] can be designed or evaluated" (Fendler 2001, 125). In this section, then, I bring the foregoing overviews to bear on new movements in the CYC field.

I propose that the field begin a conversation about the consequences of seeing developmental psychology as a pillar of CYC practice. To do this, we might start by placing developmental psychology in its own context of emergence. These conversations are proposed in the spirit of recent developments in CYC that ask for a different kind of CYC practice and theory (e.g., Skott-Myhre 2005, 2008; White 2007). These new calls in the field can be considered revolutionary. Pence (2000, viii) notes the difference between evolutionary and revolutionary approaches to practice: evolutionary approaches are concerned with the progression toward "a relatively more sophisticated understanding of children [and youth] and their development and appropriate care," representing "an incremental step on the upward spiral" of a field's knowledge. Revolutionary approaches, in contrast, are "capable of stimulating a discussion" of how the field is constructed, capable of challenging the basic assumptions on which a field is created to appreciate the diversity that constitutes the field (viii).

Skott-Myhre (2008) specifically calls for revolutionary CYC practice and theory that, to my mind, would require an approach to developmental theories that differs from that currently outlined in training documents (e.g., CYC competencies). Revolutionary youth work, he argues, requires rethinking the concepts of the subject and subjectivity itself. Rethinking subjectivities requires thinking of the subject as *subjectum* rather than *subjectus*. The subjectus, he explains, refers to submission or subjection – "a subject whose goal it is to be defined clearly and finally as a coherent set of descriptions and actions without any loose ends or unexplained aspects of character" (4). This is the humanist, rational, and coherent subject of developmental psychology. A revolutionary CYC field requires working with the concept of the subjectum that moves beyond sovereign authority. It is defined "through its ability to creatively produce itself," not constrained by any social category or by the boundaries of time and evolution embedded in psychological accounts of the subject (4).

Following the idea of the subjectum, Skott-Myhre (2008) argues that a revolutionary CYC field "is not concerned with accommodation, assimilation, integration, or compromise" in young people's lives (181). It is instead "an active praxis or proposal that suggests, if not demands, that youth [and child] work explore a radical alterity to the state and all other axiomatic processes. It is human service no longer concerned with 'healing' within capital, but rather the 'healing' entailed in the alternative ontology of the minority" (181). Revolutionary CYC is thus "purely creative as sheer affirmation" (182).

From this understanding of revolutionary CYC, engaging with developmental psychology as the basis for CYC practice without acknowledging its interactions with its processes of emergence runs the great risk of working within the confinements of the state. Developmental theories work in constant interaction with social and political motives toward the appropriation of subjectivities that revolutionary CYC particularly challenges. A revolutionary CYC requires that we question how subjects are formed, and questioning the emergence and deployment of developmental psychology is key for unpacking the formation of the child/youth subject (as I attempted to demonstrate in the examples above). CYC can perhaps engage with the subjectum by liberating children from the scientific and political traps of developmental theories.

Finally, and to clarify, my argument is not that child development not be taught in CYC programs. All knowledge is useful but also incomplete because it has been separated from its full potential (Skott-Myhre 2008). What we need instead is a different kind of approach to developmental theories. In a revolutionary CYC field, child and youth development cannot be thought of as the basis that, in later stages of the educational ladder, can be critically analyzed and deconstructed. This is an evolutionary approach. But, in the spirit of a profession that values context in the lives of children and youth (White 2007), developmental theories also need to be politically contextualized. As bodies of knowledge, they need to be extended. As Skott-Myhre (2008, 183) proposes, "the praxis of such teaching is to connect backwards, forwards, and to the side without closure or repetition." By politically contextualizing and extending developmental psychology, we can also politically contextualize the processes of subject formation and allow spaces for revolutionary work and new subjectivities to emerge. For example, rather than reading and considering texts that have already digested the "facts" about child development (e.g., Berk 2008; Santrock 2001), a revolutionary practice could engage with the original texts of developmental theorists and analyze them in relation to how current views of childhood and adolescence have emerged, what the reasons were for their emergence, and how the child/youth subject is inscribed and deployed in those texts.

It seems to me that CYC, as a profession that cares about ecologies, is well situated to bring greater emphasis to the conditions through which ideas about children are constructed and, more importantly, to work with/through/against them in practice. This approach would challenge the idea of the unitary or multiple selves and allow us to engage with the creative aspect of the self, therefore reimagining the revolutionary aspect of CYC.

Note

1 The early childhood education field has a long history of reconceptualization, beginning in the early 1990s. The field has benefited from the adoption of critical perspectives.

References

Bauman, Z. 1991. *Modernity and Ambivalence.* Cambridge, UK: Polity Press.
Berk, L. 2008. *Child Development.* 8th ed. Boston: Allyn and Bacon.
Bernhard, J. 1995. "Child Development, Cultural Diversity, and the Professional Training of Early Childhood Educators." *Canadian Journal of Education* 20, 4: 415-36.
Burman, E. 2008a. *Deconstructing Developmental Psychology.* New York: Routledge.
–. 2008b. *Developments: Child, Image, Nation.* London: Routledge.
Cannella, G.S., and R. Viruru. 2004. *Childhood and Postcolonization: Power, Education, and Contemporary Practice.* New York: RoutledgeFalmer.
Corson, D. 1998. *Changing Education for Diversity.* Philadelphia: Open University Press.
Dahlberg, G., P. Moss, and A.R. Pence. 1999. *Beyond Quality in Early Childhood Education and Care: Postmodern Perspectives.* London: Falmer Press.
Deleuze, G. 1992. "Postscript on the Societies of Control." *October* 59: 3-7.
Fendler, L. 2001. "Educating Flexible Souls: The Construction of Subjectivity through Developmentality and Interaction." In *Governing the Child in the New Millennium,* ed. K. Hultqvist and G. Dahlberg, 119-42. New York: RoutledgeFalmer.
Foucault, M. 1977. *Discipline and Punish: The Birth of the Prison.* New York: Vintage Books.
–. 1978. *The History of Sexuality.* New York: Pantheon Books.
–. 1991. "Governmentality." In *The Foucault Effect: Studies in Governmentality,* ed. G. Burchell, C. Gordon, and P. Miller, 87-104. Chicago: University of Chicago Press.

Gordon, C. 1991. "Governmental Rationality: An Introduction." In *The Foucault Effect: Studies in Governmentality,* ed. G. Burchell, C. Gordon, and P. Miller, 1-52. Chicago: University of Chicago Press.

Kumar, K. 1995. *From Post-Industrial to Post-Modern Society: New Theories of the Contemporary World.* Cambridge, MA: Blackwell.

Lesko, N. 2001. "Time Matters in Adolescence." In *Governing the Child in the New Millennium,* ed. K. Hultqvist and G. Dahlberg, 35-67. New York: RoutledgeFalmer.

Miller, P., and N. Rose. 1993. "Governing Economic Life." In *Foucault's New Domains,* ed. M. Gane and T. Johnson, 75-105. London: Routledge.

Morss, J.R. 1996. *Growing Critical: Alternatives to Developmental Psychology.* London: Routledge.

Moss, P., and A. Pence. 1994. *Valuing Quality in Early Childhood Services: New Approaches to Defining Quality.* New York: Teachers College Press.

Pacini-Ketchabaw, V., K. Kummen, and D. Thompson. 2010. "Becoming Intimate with Developmental Knowledge: Pedagogical Explorations with Collective Biography." *Alberta Journal of Educational Research* 56, 3: 335-54.

Pence, A. 2000. "Foreword." In *Authentic Childhood: Experiencing Reggio Emilia in the Classroom,* by S. Fraser, viii-xiii. Scarborough, ON: Nelson Thompson Learning.

Rogerson, J., C. Shelton, and B. Hardy, eds. 2007. "A Model for Core Curriculum for Child and Youth Care Education in British Columbia." Paper developed in consultation with the Standing Committee on Curriculum, British Columbia Child and Youth Care Education Consortium.

Rose, N. 1990. *Governing the Soul: The Shaping of the Private Self.* New York: Routledge.

–. 1996. "Governing 'Advanced' Liberal Democracies." In *Foucault and Political Reason: Liberalism, Neo-Liberalism, and Rationalities of Government,* ed. A. Barry, T. Osborne, and N.S. Rose, 37-63. Chicago: University of Chicago Press.

–. 1999. *Powers of Freedom: Reframing Political Thought.* Cambridge, UK: Cambridge University Press.

–. 2008. "Psychology as a Social Science." *Subjectivity: International Journal of Critical Psychology* 25: 446-62.

Santrock, J. 2001. *Life-Span Development.* 8th ed. Boston: McGraw-Hill.

Skott-Myhre, H. 2005. "Captured by Capital: Youth Work and the Loss of Revolutionary Potential." *Child and Youth Care Forum* 34, 2: 141-57.

–. 2008. *Youth and Subculture as Creative Force: Creating New Spaces for Radical Youth Work.* Toronto: University of Toronto Press.

Walkerdine, V. 1984. "Developmental Psychology and the Child-Centred Pedagogy: The Insertion of Piaget into Early Education." In *Changing the Subject: Psychology, Social Regulation, and Subjectivity,* ed. J. Henriques, W. Holloway, C. Urwin, C. Vener, and V. Walkerdine, 153-202. London: Methuen.

White, J. 2007. "Knowing, Doing, and Being in Context: A Praxis-Oriented Approach to Child and Youth Care." *Child and Youth Care Forum* 36: 225-44.

Re-Stor(y)ing Professional Ethics in Child and Youth Care

Toward More Contextualized, Reflexive, and Generative Practices

JENNIFER WHITE

3

> The hegemonic tendency of North American professional ethics is to position itself as the only story: we in North America have a difficult time entertaining the idea that professional ethics may not be universal, and that our version grows from our particularity.
>
> – ROSSITER, WALSH-BOWERS, AND PRILLELTENKSY (2002, 534)

Child and youth care has evolved into a unique field of practice that promotes young people's flourishing by engaging with children and youth in their social contexts. It emphasizes strengths-based, relational, collaborative, socially just, and empowering practices (Gharabaghi 2008; Smith 2006; White 2007). With these trademark emphases, CYC has emerged as a distinct helping profession that has often positioned itself *in opposition to* models of helping that privilege expert-driven, deficit-oriented, narrowly specialized approaches (Anglin 1999; Ferguson, Pence, and Denholm 1993; Little, this volume). Over the course of its evolution, those writing in the field of CYC have enthusiastically promoted the benefits of practitioner self-awareness (Fewster 1990), extolled the qualities of curiosity, critical reflection, and discovery (Ricks and Bellefeuille 2003), and underscored the value of direct care and "life space interventions" when working with children, youth, and families (Anglin 1999).

More recent formulations of CYC practice recognize the emergence of social problems and identities within specific discursive, historical, institutional, and socio-cultural contexts (Alsbury, this volume; Ball and Pence 2006; Hoskins and White 2010). Scholars in early childhood care, development, and education (Dahlberg and Moss 2005; Dahlberg, Moss, and Pence 2007; Pacini-Ketchabaw, this volume; Taguchi 2007) have often been at the forefront of efforts dedicated to "think[ing] outside of the neoliberal framework" (Davies 2009, 4). In these intellectual endeavours, deconstruction is often embraced as an important analytical and ethical resource. For example, Taguchi (2007, 276) writes that "deconstruction as a process of *re*doing by *un*doing, *re*formulating by *un*formulating, and *re*theorizing by *un*theorizing, is crucial to that which I will theorize as an ethic of 'resistance,' affirmation and becoming."

Meanwhile, critically oriented, feminist, and post-structural theorists and activists challenge depoliticized views of the work and call attention to the unjust, inequitable social arrangements that perpetuate certain groups' marginalization (de Finney, Loiselle, and Dean, this volume; Little 2005; Reynolds 2002; Skott-Myhre 2003). Other postmodern approaches highlight the constructed nature of professional knowledge and invite a deconstructive, questioning stance toward taken-for-granted mainstays such as codes of ethics, practice standards, professional competencies, and evidence-based practices (Newbury 2009; White 2007). Each of these recent conceptualizations has significant implications for how we think about and "do ethics" in CYC.

In this more recent rendering, CYC has much in common with other caring professions drawing from critical, feminist, constructionist, post-structural, post-colonial, decolonizing, and discursive theories as a way to reflect and respond to the social complexities, pluralities, and indeterminacies that characterize the current global context (Aldarondo 2007; Holmes and Gastaldo 2004; Sinclair 2007; Stronach et al. 2002). It is from these broadly interpreted, postmodern epistemological locations that I would like to explore some of the key challenges and opportunities for teaching and learning about ethics in CYC and invite a reconceptualized view of professional ethics in our field.

More specifically, with this chapter I seek to animate and extend current conversations about ethics in CYC by critically interrogating the relationship between ethics and dominant discourses of professionalism, which will include deconstructing prevailing understandings of knowledge, identities, and selfhood within CYC. To do this, I will engage with a range of critical and postmodern texts from within and outside CYC.

In the sections that follow, I will briefly describe the current state of professional ethics within the mainstream CYC literature. I will then describe the complex, constantly shifting, and thoroughly ethical character of everyday CYC practice. Next I will explore two prominent and interrelated discourses within CYC: professionalism and liberal humanism, both of which are typically indexed to individualist conceptions of morality and modernist notions of ethics. Working within and against these traditions, I will describe one approach to teaching a graduate-level ethics course in CYC that is designed to unsettle predetermined, universalist, rule-based orientations to support an enlarged, more complex view of ethics; one that is characterized by relationality, multiplicity, generativity, accountability, and critical reflexivity (Dahlberg and Moss 2005; Davies and Gannon 2009; Prilleltensky, Rossiter, and Walsh-Bowers 1996; Sellick, Delaney, and Brownlee 2002). While honouring the contributions of previous CYC scholars, I also seek to open up new horizons and stimulate fresh lines of inquiry for the future, making space for new stories to emerge regarding the meaning and doing of professional ethics in CYC. Borrowing from Sinclair (2007, 149), it is "in an inviting spirit" that I write this chapter.

Professional Ethics in Child and Youth Care

Several CYC scholars have made significant contributions to deepening our understanding of professional ethics, many of which resonate with the position I am taking here. Practitioner self-awareness (Garfat and Ricks 1995), the role of moral reference points and principles in guiding ethical practice (Magnuson 1995), and the creation of a formal code of ethics (Mattingly 1995) were important themes discussed in a special issue of *Child and Youth Care Forum* published in 1995. More recently, a participatory inquiry process for working ethically with families (Ricks and Bellefeuille 2003), a feminist approach to ethical practice in CYC (Little 2005), and a discussion of values, critical reflection, and ethics (Gharabaghi 2008) have all been explored in the CYC literature. A virtues-based approach to ethics (Greenwald 2008) and an examination of boundary recognition and management (Stuart 2008) are just two of the chapters of ethical significance published in the edited book *Standing on the Precipice: Inquiry into the Creative Potential of Child and Youth Care Practice* (Bellefeuille and Ricks 2008).

Meanwhile, within the North American context of CYC practice, we have two professional documents that articulate, among other things, the ethical vision for the profession. First, the Ethics of Child and Youth Care Professionals (Association for Child and Youth Care Practice 1995, 1) provides an ethical framework "to guide thinking and practice for all Child and Youth Care Professionals." Second, the Competencies for Professional Child and Youth Work Practitioners (CPCYWP) document (Mattingly, Stuart, and VanderVen 2010) articulates the expected competencies for professional youth work practitioners in North America.

Despite the intentions of the architects of the CYC Code of Ethics to produce a "living document" to be revisited and revised over time, it appears that the original code developed in 1995 has been adopted by many national and state organizations with few, if any, changes. Importantly, the original Code of Ethics drafted by a small group of CYC leaders in 1995 currently stands as the primary reference point on ethical practice within the CPCYWP document. In this document, to be considered "competent" within the ethical domain, CYC practitioners must be able to

1   describe the functions of professional ethics
2   apply the process of ethical decision making in a proactive manner
3   integrate specific principles and standards from the relevant Code of Ethics to specific professional problems
4   carry out work tasks in a way that conforms to professional ethical principles and standards. (12)

Within the CPCYWP document, the ethically competent CYC practitioner is thus positioned as someone who is capable of correctly reading what is at stake, knowing which "specific principles" from the relevant Code of Ethics apply, and implementing a course of action that conforms to predetermined standards and principles. In sum, the traditional approach to conceptualizing professional ethics as exemplified in the CPCYWP document sits in contrast to more critical, expansive, and participatory (Prilleltensky, Rossiter, and Walsh-Bowers 1996), constructionist (Cottone 2004; Guterman and Rudes 2008), and postmodern and discursive approaches (Dahlberg and Moss 2005). I will discuss these ideas in more detail in a later section. First, though, I will highlight the complexity of everyday CYC practice. By recognizing its thoroughly ethical, political, ambivalent, and contingent character, I aim to set the stage for the promotion of a more expansive, postmodern, and relational view of ethics.

Human Caring Practices Are Ethical Practices

Securing general agreement on the publicly stated aims and values of CYC practice is not difficult. Who, for example, can argue against strengths-based practices, inclusion, best interests of the child, collaboration, or social justice? Where agreement starts to break down and cracks start to show is when we try to decide on the *meanings* of these abstract principles and attempt to figure out what enacting and embodying them might look like within actual, local contexts. As Carr (1999, 38) notes, "though no sane person could seriously doubt that it is a bad thing to be diseased, oppressed or ignorant, very sane and sensible people do debate about what constitutes genuine or adequate education, justice or healthcare."

In a similar manner, conflicting opinions, uncertainties, and pluralistic understandings about what constitutes "genuine or adequate" child and youth care are constantly in play – though often unspoken – setting the stage for complex ethical questions, challenges, and dilemmas to emerge. In other words, ethics permeate every aspect of human caring practices, and what is considered to be good or right in one context might be quite different in another, casting suspicion on individualist, universalist, predetermined approaches to ethics and professional practices.

Ethical dilemmas do not occur in some suspended or discrete zone outside the day-to-day practice context (Gharabaghi 2008). CYC work is inherently relational, value laden, and often undertaken with vulnerable young people and their families in a range of diverse socio-political and -cultural contexts. The ethical dilemmas that practitioners face are often much more ambiguous, unprecedented, nuanced, and complex than those commonly presented in professional ethics textbooks (Carr 1999; Prilleltensky, Rossiter, and Walsh-Bowers 1996).

Challenging Individualistic Understandings
To illustrate some of this complexity, I draw from my own work in youth suicide prevention. Within the mainstream practice context, the predominant, taken-for-granted understanding of suicide is that it is an individual, private act linked to mental illness. When faced with the ethically challenging yet relatively common situation of the young person who is contemplating suicide and who does not want his parents to be told, it is customary to reference the ethical principles of trust, privacy, autonomy (self-determination), and protection from harm.

Codes of ethics and professional competencies clearly provide some important reference points to guide deliberation in such a situation, yet the analyses they engender typically perpetuate the status quo by framing the dilemma in individualistic terms. In the specific case of suicide, these professional resources do a good job of focusing attention on balancing rights to privacy with protection from harm, but typically they do little to invite a broader consideration of the oppressive social, political, and historical conditions that might have given rise to hopelessness, despair, isolation, or loss of dignity in the first place. Nor do they enable practitioners to consider forms of activism and practices of solidarity – what Reynolds (2008) calls an "ethic of resistance" – as legitimate, ethical responses to the emergence of suicidal despair among young people. In a related passage, Butler (2004, 16) writes that "to take the self-generated acts of the individual as our point of departure in moral reasoning is precisely to foreclose the possibility of questioning what kind of world gives rise to such individuals ... What social conditions help to form the very ways that choice and deliberation proceed?"

Ambiguity and Uncertainty

Recognizing the limits of codified, universal rules for guiding ethical action, many postmodern theorists have argued for an approach to ethics that rests less on the "individualized decision-making subject" and more on the "ongoing openness of each to the other, and the recognition each bestows on the other, moment-by-moment" (Davies 2009, 28). Taking responsibility for the other depends on care, creativity, openness, engagement, recognition, and relational accountability. These orientations have much in common with many ethics of care theories (Held 2006) yet are generally incommensurable with a traditional rule-based, universalist approach to ethics (Dahlberg and Moss 2005; Davies and Gannon 2009). Reflecting a distinctly postmodern view of ethics, Bauman (1995, 3) writes that

> Dilemmas have no ready-made solutions; the necessity to choose comes without a foolproof recipe for proper choice; the attempt to do good is undertaken without guarantee of goodness of either the intention or its results. The realm of responsibility is frayed on all sides; it is equally easy to underdo and to overdo what "acting responsibly" may ideally require. Moral life is a life of continuous uncertainty. It is built on the bricks of doubt and cemented with bouts of self-deprecation. Since the dividing lines between good and evil have not been drawn before, they are drawn in the course of action; the outcome of these efforts at drawing lines is akin to a string of footprints rather than a network of charted roads. And thus loneliness is as permanent and unevictable a resident of the house of responsibility as is ambivalence.

Such loneliness, doubt, and uncertainty are rarely, if ever, reflected in codes of ethics or other professional documents. Yet the complexities and irreconcilable tensions that we as human caring professionals grapple with on a daily basis remind us that these qualities and experiences are inevitable features of moral life. As I argue in the next section, CYC, like many emerging professions, has patterned itself after other professions to gain the recognition and legitimacy it rightly deserves. Codes of ethics, which are cultural products, implicitly convey a rational and knowable social world and are typically considered a key marker of professional status. By uncritically adopting potentially narrow and "received understandings" of professionalism, CYC might be unwittingly and unnecessarily limiting its ethical vision and imagination.

Discourses of Professionalism in CYC

Dominant discourses are social practices that actively construct meaning and reflect prevailing ideologies. They refer to "those cultural ideas that have a privileged and dominant influence on our behaviour in the world ... and are so persuasive in a community that they are completely taken-for-granted about how life should be lived" (Sinclair 2007, 157). Our deep embeddedness within the modernist discourses of professionalism and liberal humanism in CYC frequently becomes unhinged from discussions of ethics. Yet, as I argue below, their influences on how we think about and do our work have far-reaching ethical significance.

Restrictive Ethical Frameworks

Typically, helping professions are guided by what Prilleltensky, Rossiter, and Walsh-Bowers (1996) call a "restrictive ethical framework." In these approaches, the orientation is largely individualistic, and harm is typically conceived of in only the most blatant of forms (e.g., gross violation of clients' rights). What often gets obscured from view in these ethical frameworks are the socio-economic, historical, and political structures and social practices that perpetuate and reproduce oppressive relations of power, including, for example, the harmful effects of policies of colonization and assimilation on Indigenous peoples.

The dominant discourse of professionalism is also predicated on the idea of a clear separation between clients and professionals, with specialized expertise and authority clearly lodged with the professional who enjoys socially sanctioned power to address various social needs, often with minimal input from those who seek such services. In other words, professionals "are entrusted with the task of maintaining social order and reproducing the societal status quo" (Prilleltensky, Rossiter, and Walsh-Bowers 1996, 291).

We see evidence of this in many ethical decision-making models, including those initially developed to support ethical practice in CYC. For example, Garfat and Ricks's (1995, 397) "self-driven ethical decision making model" clearly centres the practitioner and privileges her professional knowledge and agency: "The model for practicing ethics that emerges from this thinking is one within which a responsible, self-aware helper critically evaluates available options in a values-conflicting situation. The worker then makes and acts upon the most appropriate decision for this client, at this time."

Although the model has several strengths, including, for example, the focus on process and critical reflection, it often resembles a monologue more than a dialogue. Reflecting this theme, Magnuson (1995, 405) argues that "ethical practice is not a self-referential conversation with the self; it is a 'conversation' between the self and the 'other(s)."

A more recent example of a critical and collaborative way of thinking about ethics in CYC comes from Ricks and Bellefeuille (2003), who have described some of the ethical hazards and limits of certainty and "knowing" when working with families. Despite these and other more critical and expansive contributions to conceptualizing ethics in CYC (Little 2005; Skott-Myhre 2003; Smith 2006), the CPCYWP document outlined above still exemplifies a traditional and restrictive approach to ethics. For example, the "competent" CYC practitioner is expected to "integrate specific ethical principles and standards from the relevant Code of Ethics to specific professional problems" and "conform to professional ethical principles and standards" (12).

Ethics as Product

In a trenchant analysis of professional education and professional ethics, Carr (1999) highlights the dangers of assuming a neutral, technical orientation to practice, which many competency-driven models of professionalism implicitly condone. For example, when skills, attitudes, and knowledge are treated as neutral and uncontroversial, debate about the ultimate aims of practice is circumvented, and ethical obligations and responsibilities become unproblematically systemized and codified. As Carr notes, such competency-based approaches position professionals as "mere deliverers of a body of knowledge pre-determined by others" (45).

Within CYC, Stuart (2008, 138) suggests that "the formation of professional codes is a marker of the development of the profession, because having a professional code of behaviour is a criterion for a legitimate profession." The uncritical acceptance of this assumption is common among occupational groups seeking professional recognition (Carr 1999) but can inadvertently support a "checklist approach" to professional practice – specialized body of knowledge, check; code of ethics, check. This tendency to treat ethics as a product was well articulated by Levy in 1974 (cited in Freeman, Engels, and Altekruse 2004, 163), who observed that, in the "zeal for respectability," professional codes of ethics often function as an "arbitrarily prepared shortcut to prestige and status."

With the CPCYWP document's emphases on conformity and standardization, combined with the promotion of a predominantly instrumentalist view of ethics (i.e., "integrating specific principles from the relevant Code of Ethics to specific problems"), the epistemological foundations become visible. In this modernist paradigm, "ethics are viewed as depoliticized concepts which produce a strong attachment to such abstract ideals as 'respect' and 'duty.' These concepts are derived from a taken-for-granted, quasi-legal framework and have become standardized in codes of ethics" (Philp, Guy, and Lowe 2007, 57).

Liberal Humanist Foundations

Such taken-for-granted orientations to ethics and professionalism within CYC reflect the mainstream humanist "ideal of the autonomous and sovereign subject" (Dahlberg and Moss 2005, 69), where a "self-aware" practitioner reads the practice dilemma in an unambiguous way and then *applies* the correct ethical principle. Generally taken to be self-evident, a liberal humanist approach has "traditionally identified the individual as the central agent of all social phenomena, and has celebrated the self as independent, stable and knowable, emphasizing an individual's capacity for choice, freedom and self-development ... Liberal humanism has tended to locate human problems within individuals as distinct and separate from social, cultural and political contexts in which they live" (Sinclair 2007, 149).

Ethics, in such models, are typically conceptualized as taking place "inside the mind of the practitioner" (Cottone 2004, 7). On closer scrutiny, we also see that the professional is typically constructed in terms of a core identity that is singular, stable, definitive, and essential. This is in sharp contrast to the unstable, pluralist, "fragmented possibility" and contradictory "narratives of identification" that characterize other professional groups, including teachers and nurses (and likely CYC practitioners), which "belie the professional as 'type'" (Stronach et al. 2002, 116).

Prevailing approaches to professional development in CYC also reflect traditional liberal humanist assumptions. For example, the field's whole-hearted and unproblematic embrace of self-awareness as a cornerstone of ethical and professional practice has largely gone unquestioned. In a relevant article, Hansen (2009, 186) revisits the construct of self-awareness for the counselling profession, which, much like CYC, "has placed an extraordinarily high value on the construct of self-awareness." He notes that the concept of self-awareness is tenable only if certain underlying assumptions are accepted as givens: "(a) the self must exist, (b) this self must be available for introspection, (c) the self must have an enduring essence, and (d) the self must be able to be represented by language." Each assumption is deeply rooted in a humanist philosophy.

As one way to overcome the limits of the essentialist, singular self that occupies such a prominent place in liberal humanism, Hansen (2009) suggests replacing the static concept of self-awareness with the more dynamic notion of self-storying. In this way, the notion of the one "true" or "real" self is called into question, making room for multiple, fluid, ongoing, emerging, and narrated identities and becomings. Building on this theme, I argue that singular, essentialist, or final descriptions of the field of CYC as a whole should also be strongly resisted. Early childhood educators (Davies and Gannon 2009; Pacini-Ketchabaw, this volume) as well as scholars in other professional fields such as nursing (Holmes and Gastaldo 2004) exemplify multiplicity and plurality in theorizing practice and have borrowed on Deleuze and Guattari's symbol of the rhizome to support this shift in thinking:

> The rhizome is open at both ends. It has no central or governing structure; it has neither beginning nor end. As a rhizome has no centre, it spreads continuously without beginning or ending and

> basically exists in a constant state of play. It does not conform to a unidirectional or linear reasoning. The rhizome challenges the sense of a unique direction because it emerges and grows in simultaneous, multiple ways. (Holmes and Gastaldo 2004, 261)

Such shifts have significant implications for professional development and ethics education in CYC.

Toward More Reflexive and Generative Approaches to Teaching Ethics

I have had the opportunity to teach the graduate-level ethics course in the School of Child and Youth Care, University of Victoria, for the past five years. In this section, I describe some of the ways that I have attempted to respond to some of the limits of a traditional, individualistic view of ethics in constructing and teaching this course.

Enlarging the View

First, I explicitly support an enlarged view of ethics. I take inspiration from the critical contributions of Prilleltensky and his colleagues, who have been at the forefront of promoting a broad view of ethical practice and have explicitly centred social justice as a primary ethical concern. More specifically, Prilleltensky, Rossiter, and Walsh-Bowers (1996, 288) have recognized ethics as a discursive practice and have called for the promotion of ethical discourse in the helping professions as a way to address subtle forms of harm, including "suffering caused by unexamined practices and assumptions of clinicians." Referencing practice with children specifically, Prilleltenksy, Walsh-Bowers, and Rossiter (1999) have called attention to the ways in which organizational and system-level requirements, like narrow mandates or the practices of labelling and categorization, create numerous ethical challenges and constraints for child- and youth-serving professionals. Their work thus invites a form of ethical activism that includes challenging unjust organizational structures, resisting oppressive societal conditions, and disrupting hegemonic relations of power.

As one example of supporting this enlarged view, I include readings from Indigenous scholars, such as Ermine (2007) and Tait (2008), who draw from Indigenous knowledge and political philosophy to situate their discussions of ethics. Tait calls attention to the pernicious effects of short-sighted planning, the lack of secure funding, and the imposition of Eurocentric models of health and healing on Indigenous peoples and communities. She usefully draws on Ermine's concept of "ethical space" – the space between Indigenous and Western worldviews – to argue for a greater commitment to ethics in program planning when conceptualizing and delivering mental health and addiction services for First Nations, Inuit, and Métis peoples in Canada.

Promoting Ongoing Critical Engagement

Second, I believe ongoing reflection, critique, and ethical debate contribute to the advancement of our field as a whole, and I aim to support the development of students' critical reflexivity. Far from being a threat, the process of critically deliberating across a range of intellectual traditions, disrupting taken-for-granted notions, and collectively reflecting on the appropriate ends of practice are what keep the moral character of this work in constant view (Prilleltensky, Rossiter, and Walsh-Bowers 1996). On this point, we can learn a lot from allied organizations, such as the National Youth Agency (2004, 10) in the United Kingdom, which recently recommended that youth workers make a commitment to "foster and engage in ethical debate in youth work" as a matter of ethical principle.

As others have convincingly argued, "for growth and movement to occur, we believe that all paradigms should be subjected to critique. One has to free her/himself from authority and tradition which are still rooted in a 'received view' of the world" (Holmes and Gastaldo 2004, 260). In keeping with this spirit, the graduate course I teach, like this chapter and all other writings and teachings in CYC, should be subject to close reading, debate, and critique.

Embracing Postmodern Ideas

Third, throughout the course, I draw on critical and discursive theories and practices, including narrative, post-structural, and collaborative approaches to working with individuals, groups, and families. To a varying degree, each of these postmodern approaches critiques the limit of the dominant discourse of liberal humanism, a modernist orientation that has occupied a central role in the helping field (Reynolds 2002; Sinclair 2007), including CYC, for many decades. Although not always made explicit in the CYC literature, many of our cherished ideas, including "self-awareness," "developmentally appropriate approaches," and various constructions of "at-risk youth," bear the traces of a distinctly humanist approach.

Valuing Multidisciplinarity
Fourth, I do not believe we can embrace the value of diversity in practice without simultaneously embracing diversity in our scholarship and pedagogy, which in my view requires maintaining a commitment to multi/interdisciplinarity (Minnich 2004). As I argue here, a questioning stance toward our knowledge and practice serves as an important form of ethical accountability to the people we serve (Sellick, Delaney, and Brownlee 2002).

Throughout the course, students are exposed to a range of intellectual and professional resources. I have attempted to construct the course in a way that introduces students to historical and contemporary viewpoints as well as relevant articles and professional resources from within the CYC field, including the Competencies for Professional Child and Youth Work Practitioners and the Code of Ethics for CYC. At the same time, I include texts from moral and political philosophy, Indigenous ethics, feminist theory, critical and community psychology, education, and other allied social care professions. I also include codes of ethics that exemplify open, relational, and critical orientations to everyday CYC practice (see, for example, the Code of Ethics for Youth Work in Aotearoa/New Zealand at http://www.youthworkers.net.nz/).

In Support of Big Questions
Fifth, and finally, big, agonizing ethical questions often get brushed aside in discussions of professional ethics in favour of a focus on the "micro-ethics of the therapeutic relationship" (Prilleltensky, Rossiter, and Walsh-Bowers 1996, 293). These deeply contested questions, many of which have been preoccupying philosophers for centuries, are important to invite students to take seriously. What does it mean to live a worthwhile life? Who gets to decide? Whose version of human flourishing should

prevail? What do we mean by dignity? How can we support its emergence within diverse social, cultural, and historical contexts?

Other questions that are typically given minimal attention in discussions of professional ethics pertain to the constructed nature of professional knowledge. For example, how do our professional practices, intellectual traditions, and available vocabularies shape our understandings of children, youth, families, and communities? What unspoken vision of the ideal or normal or well-adjusted human being are our models of practice predicated on? Which meanings and identities do our practice frameworks and theories make available to practitioners and clients? How can we think more critically and deeply about our professional interventions in CYC, such that we attend to individual well-being and social justice concerns, to both *what* and *how* we know? Finally, how do we strike a balance between enacting practices that preserve social harmony with those that disrupt, challenge, and radically transform the status quo (Dokecki 1996)?

In summary, by explicitly valuing multidisciplinarity (Minnich 2004), critical reflection (Fook, White, and Gardner 2006), as well as "responsibility, relationships, situatedness and otherness" (Dahlberg and Moss 2005, 69), I aim to stimulate an enlarged perspective on professional ethics. Students are supported to recognize the value-laden quality of CYC, discern morally relevant issues, critically reflect on their own social and cultural situatedness and professional assumptions, practise articulating moral positions, anticipate and respond to ambiguity and uncertainty, engage in critical debate, generate creative responses, and recognize that taking ethically responsible action is much more demanding than simply conforming to standards or consulting a code of ethics. Borrowing from Minnich (2004, 145), who makes a helpful distinction between knowledge and thinking, it is my hope that ethics education in CYC can support students to become better thinkers:

> On the most basic level, knowledge is comprised of the answers to questions posed and pursued to their conclusion in ways that are legitimated by an intellectual tradition as "sound." Thinking is what we are doing as we pose and pursue those questions, but it is also, and more basically – and more freely, creatively, and responsibly – the

capacity we have to question the acceptable questions, to imagine other ways of pursuing and responding to them, to be open to answers that are not compatible with those already established, and throughout, to keep reflecting on what anything and everything means.

Concluding Remarks

Educators who are charged with preparing new practitioners for the field must paradoxically support students to learn about the values and aims of the profession and provide them with opportunities to deepen their knowledge and develop practical skills, all the while recognizing that human caring practices cannot be easily specified in advance. Ethical dilemmas cannot be solved by "applying specific principles to specific problems." Moreover, knowing what to do and how to be in particular moments cannot be easily taught through models that conceive of practice in instrumental, depoliticized terms (Smith 2006; White 2007).

Ethics education, in this particular view, has much in common with what Stronach and colleagues (2002, 125) refer to as an "uncertain theory of professionalism." They suggest that, "if professional lives are to be understood in their complexity, plurality, and inconsistency, then one requirement may be that of a 'narrative adequacy', the possibility of a 'good story.'" To build on this theme and conclude this chapter, I suggest that we might want to consider re-storying our own relationship to ethics and professionalism in a way that makes space for multiple, alternative, ongoing, and open-ended conceptualizations of CYC. These new narratives might invite ways of thinking about ethics that place less emphasis on competencies, codes, conformity, and standardization. By giving increased attention to multiplicity, generativity, solidarity, and creativity, a renewed emphasis on contextual understandings, emergent processes, relational and political engagement, and critical reflexivity might emerge. Such an approach supports students and practitioners to be ethically accountable and prepares them to take responsible action, even in the midst of ambiguity and uncertainty.

References
Aldarondo, E., ed. 2007. *Advancing Social Justice through Clinical Practice.* Malwah, NJ: Lawrence Erlbaum Associates.

Anglin, J. 1999. "The Uniqueness of Child and Youth Care: A Personal Perspective." *Child and Youth Care Forum* 28, 2: 143-50.

Association for Child and Youth Care Practice. 1995. "Ethics of Child and Youth Care Professionals." http://www.acycp.org/standards/CYC%20Ethics%20Code%20Rev%20 9.2009.pdf.

Ball, J., and A. Pence. 2006. "Turning the World Upside Down." In *Supporting Indigenous Children's Development*, ed. J. Ball and A. Pence, 3-16. Vancouver: UBC Press.

Bauman, Z. 1995. *Life in Fragments: Essays in Postmodern Morality*. Oxford: Blackwell.

Bellefeuille, G., and F. Ricks. 2008. *Standing on the Precipice: Inquiry into the Creative Potential of Child and Youth Care Practice*. Edmonton: MacEwan Press.

Butler, J. 2004. *Precarious Life: The Powers of Mourning and Violence*. London: Verso.

Carr, D. 1999. "Professional Education and Professional Ethics." *Journal of Applied Philosophy* 16, 1: 33-46.

Cottone, R. 2004. "Displacing the Psychology of the Individual in Ethical Decision-Making: The Social Constructivism Model." *Canadian Journal of Counselling* 38: 5-13.

Dahlberg, G., and P. Moss. 2005. *Ethics and Politics in Early Childhood Education*. London: RoutledgeFalmer.

Dahlberg, G., P. Moss, and A. Pence. 2007. *Beyond Quality in Early Childhood Education and Care: Languages of Evaluation*. 2nd ed. London: Routledge.

Davies, B. 2009. "Introduction." In *Pedagogical Encounters*, ed. B. Davies and S. Gannon, 1-16. New York: Peter Lang.

Davies, B., and S. Gannon, eds. 2009. *Pedagogical Encounters*. New York: Peter Lang.

Dokecki, P. 1996. *The Tragi-Comic Professional: Basic Considerations for Ethical Reflective-Generative Practice*. Pittsburgh: Duquesne University Press.

Ermine, W. 2007. "The Ethical Space of Engagement." *Indigenous Law Journal* 6, 1: 193-203.

Ferguson, R., A. Pence, and C. Denholm. 1993. *Professional Child and Youth Care*. Vancouver: UBC Press.

Fewster, G. 1990. *Being in Child Care: A Journey into Self*. Binghampton, NY: Haworth Press.

Fook, J., S. White, and F. Gardner. 2006. "Critical Reflection: A Review of Contemporary Literature and Understandings." In *Critical Reflection in Health and Social Care*, ed. S. White, J. Fook, and F. Gardner, 3-20. Berkshire, UK: Open University Press.

Freeman, S., D. Engels, and M. Altekruse. 2004. "Foundations for Ethical Standards and Codes: The Role of Moral Philosophy and Theory in Ethics." *Counseling and Values* 48: 163-73.

Garfat, T., and F. Ricks. 1995. "Self-Driven Ethical Decision-Making: A Model for Child and Youth Care." *Child and Youth Care Forum* 24: 393-403.

Gharabaghi, K. 2008. "Values and Ethics in Child and Youth Care Practice." *Child and Youth Services* 30, 3: 185-209.

Greenwald, M. 2008. "The Virtuous Child and Youth Care Practitioner: Exploring Identity and Ethical Practice." In *Standing on the Precipice: Inquiry into the Creative Potential of Child and Youth Care Practice*, ed. G. Bellefeuille and F. Ricks, 169-203. Edmonton: MacEwan Press.

Guterman, J., and J. Rudes. 2008. "Social Constructionism and Ethics: Implications for Counseling." *Counseling and Values* 52: 136-44.

Hansen, J. 2009. "Self Awareness Revisited: Reconsidering a Core Value of the Counseling Profession." *Journal of Counseling and Development* 87: 186-93.

Held, V. 2006. *The Ethics of Care: Personal, Political, and Global*. New York: Oxford University Press.

Holmes, D., and D. Gastaldo. 2004. "Rhizomatic Thought in Nursing: An Alternative Path for the Development of the Discipline." *Nursing Philosophy* 5: 258-67.

Hoskins, M., and J. White. 2010. "Processes of Discernment When Considering Issues of Neglect in Child Protection Practice." *Child and Youth Care Forum* 39, 1: 27-45.

Little, N. 2005. "Feminist Ethical Development: From Wonder Woman to Wondering Woman." *Child and Youth Care Forum* 34, 2: 111-26.

Magnuson, D. 1995. "Essential Moral Sources of Ethical Standards in Child and Youth Care Work." *Child and Youth Care Forum* 24, 6: 405-11.

Mattingly, M. 1995. "Developing Professional Ethics for Child and Youth Care Work: Assuming Responsibility for the Quality of Care." *Child and Youth Care Forum* 24, 6: 379-91.

Mattingly, M., C. Stuart, and K. VanderVen. 2010. "Competencies for Professional Child and Youth Work Practitioners." Association for Child and Youth Care Practice, http://www.historyconference.org/Documents/2010_rev_professional_competencies.pdf.

Minnich, E. 2004. "Reflections on the Wellspring of Interdisciplinary Studies and Transformative Education." *Issues in Integrative Studies* 22: 141-54.

National Youth Agency. 2004. *Ethical Conduct in Youth Work*. Leicester, UK: National Youth Agency.

Newbury, J. 2009. "Theory, Policy, and Practice Entwined: Exploration through a Case in Point." *Relational Child and Youth Care Practice* 22, 3: 52-56.

Philp, K., G. Guy, and R. Lowe. 2007. "Introduction to Social Constructionist Supervision or Supervision as Social Construction: Some Dilemmas." *Journal of Systemic Therapies* 26, 1: 51-62.

Prilleltensky, I., A. Rossiter, and R. Walsh-Bowers. 1996. "Preventing Harm and Promoting Ethical Discourse in the Helping Professions: Conceptual, Research, Analytical, and Action Frameworks." *Ethics and Behavior* 6, 4: 287-306.

Prilleltensky, I., R. Walsh-Bowers, and A. Rossiter. 1999. "Clinicians' Lived Experience of Ethics: Values and Challenges in Helping Children." *Journal of Educational and Psychological Consultation* 10, 4: 315-42.

Reynolds, V. 2002. "Weaving Threads of Belonging: Cultural Witnessing Groups." *Journal of Child and Youth Care* 15, 3: 89-105.

-. 2008. "An Ethic of Resistance: Frontline Worker as Activist." *Battered Women's Support Services Newsletter* 19, 1: 5.

Ricks, F., and G. Bellefeuille. 2003. "Knowing: The Critical Error of Ethics in Family Work." *Child and Youth Services* 25: 117-30.

Rossiter, A., R. Walsh-Bowers, and I. Prilleltensky. 2002. "Ethics as a Located Story: A Comparison of North American and Cuban Clinical Ethics." *Theory and Psychology* 12, 4: 533-56.

Sellick, M., R. Delaney, and K. Brownlee. 2002. "The Deconstruction of Professional Knowledge: Accountability without Authority." *Families in Society: The Journal of Contemporary Human Services* 83, 5-6: 493-98.

Sinclair, S. 2007. "Back in the Mirrored Room: The Enduring Relevance of Discursive Practice." *Journal of Family Therapy* 29: 147-68.

Skott-Myhre, H. 2003. "Radical Youthwork: Creating and Becoming Everyone." In *Furthering Talk: Advances in the Discursive Therapies*, ed. T. Strong and D. Pare, 217-32. New York: Kluwer Academic/Plenum Publishers.

Smith, M. 2006. "Act Justly, Love Tenderly, Walk Humbly." *Relational Child and Youth Care Practice,* 19, 4: 5-16.

Stronach, I., B. Corbin, O. McNamara, S. Stark, and T. Warne. 2002. "Towards an Uncertain Politics of Professionalism." *Journal of Education Policy* 17, 1: 109-38.

Stuart, C. 2008. "Shaping the Rules: Child and Youth Care Boundaries in the Context of Relationship. Bonzai!" In *Standing on the Precipice: Inquiry into the Creative Potential of Child and Youth Care Practice,* ed. G. Bellefeuille and F. Ricks, 135-68. Edmonton: MacEwan Press.

Taguchi, H. 2007. "Deconstructing and Transgressing the Theory-Practice Dichotomy in Early Childhood Education." *Educational Philosophy and Theory* 39, 3: 275-90.

Tait, C. 2008. "Ethical Programming: Towards a Community Centred Approach to Mental Health and Addiction Programming in Aboriginal Communities." *Pimatisiwin: A Journal of Aboriginal and Indigenous Community Health* 6, 1: 29-60.

White, J. 2007. "Knowing, Doing, and Being in Context: A Praxis-Oriented Approach to Child and Youth Care." *Child and Youth Care Forum* 36: 225-44.

PART 2

Critically Interrogating Gender in Child and Youth Care

Doing "Sissy" and "Tomboy"

Exploring Childhood Participation in and Resistance to Discourses of Gender and Sexuality

JONATHAN MORRIS

4

The call to complexify contemporary understandings and appreciations of how gender and sexuality are constructed in the context of childhood is becoming louder. Questioning taken-for-granted constructions of gender is fuelled by research explicating the agentic nature of children's participation in, resistance to, and regulation of their own and others' performances of gender, *within* the conventional boundaries of the static and fixed male/female dualism (Blaise 2005a; Davies 1989a, 1989b; MacNaughton 2006). A developing body of research at the nexus of childhood and gender has challenged the current gendered social order and its predication on the reified male/female dualism. This work in-terrogates long-standing gendered power relations that promote inequity, oppression, and marginalization (Blaise 2005a). Examples of oppressive and marginalizing practices continue to show up on the playground, in the classroom, and in the home, despite efforts to eliminate stereo-typing, bias, and discrimination. Many argue that a paradigm shift away from the continuing oppressive gendered social order is contingent on efforts to problematize regimes of truth that cast gender as "two oppos-ing social categories – masculine and feminine which are linked seam-lessly with the two equivalent biological categories of sex – male and female" (MacNaughton 2006, 128; see also Blaise 2005a). Others have also suggested that there is a need to better account for how gender is bound up with practices of "heterosexualization" (Robinson 2005, 19). In other words, attention needs to be paid to how constructions of gender (male/female) become entwined with dominant discourses of heteronormalization, which in turn construct children as heterosexual beings, subject to "compulsory heterosexuality" (Butler 1990, 18).

With this chapter, I plan to extend and contextualize these ideas by drawing from my recent experience as a graduate student in a child and youth care course called Child and Adolescent Development in Context. My experience in this graduate course included participation in a process called "collective biography" (Davies and Gannon 2006), which we used as a means to explore the embeddedness of everyday experiences in complex relations of power. Using methods of collective biography, we were able to generate a series of rich and vivid memories of particular experiences that each of us had while growing up. Through the lens of feminist post-structuralism, these memories served as a site for analysis of notions of power and knowledge and processes of subjectification. I will first provide an overview of the process of collective biography. Following that, I will sketch out the theoretical perspectives that helped to guide my analysis of the memories generated during the class. I will then highlight some of the major themes produced by my analysis of the memories as they relate to "gender," concluding with an overview of potential implications for CYC teaching and practice.

Collective Biography

Eighteen graduate students, including me, were enrolled in the Child and Adolescent Development in Context course with Dr. Veronica Pacini-Ketchabaw. Most of the students in the class were in the first year of their graduate programs with a range of training and experience in developmental theories. Fifteen students self-identified as female, and three students self-identified as male. During the course of the semester, we all engaged in the process of collective biography while simultaneously reading works by Erica Burman and Bronwyn Davies. While engaging in the process of collective biography, we worked "together on a particular topic, drawing on [our] own memories relevant to that topic, and through the shared work of telling, listening, and writing, [we moved] beyond the clichés and usual explanations to the point where the written memories come as close as [we could] make them to 'an embodied sense of what happened'" (Davies and Gannon 2006, 3).

Several topics provided the focus for our collective biography, including our first memories of "mastering theories of child and adolescent development *and* being mastered by them" and "realizing and resisting being gendered." During our telling, listening, and writing of our memories, we were not interested in uncovering reliable or factually correct memories. Indeed, we were not trying to establish the "truth" of our memories. Rather, we used the practice of telling, listening, and writing as a means to "produce, through attention to the embodied sense of being in the remembered moment, a truth in relation to what cannot actually be recovered – the moment as it was lived" (Davies and Gannon 2006, 3). The discursive work of telling, listening, writing, and retelling memories made space to contest the naturalness and certainty of particular experiences, creating room to manoeuvre and the potential for negotiating change. Our memories also presented a site to examine the production of particular kinds of "subjects," such as "sissy," that were in turn maintained by dominant discourses.

Practices of Collective Biography
The first step in our process of collective biography was to break into smaller groups of five to six students. The smaller groups meant that students had enough time to both tell their memories and respond to questions from their classmates. We had already received a list of topics for the entire semester, each starting with "what is your first memory of ... ?" Topics included "first memories of being teenaged" and "first memories of becoming a biological subject and being made a biological subject." We were asked to come to each class with a written memory corresponding to the week's particular topic. The memories had to be written in a way that avoided clichés, romanticism, and explanations. Words such as *excited, anxious,* and *angry* had to be used at an *embodied* level, situating the body as the object of our descriptions. Where in our bodies did we notice anger? Were we able to discern a particular smell? A particular taste?

Students read their memories aloud to their group mates, who in turn responded with questions if they had any difficulty imagining elements of the memories. The key was to be able to listen deeply to a memory being told while simultaneously imagining being there with the narrator. This process helped to "thicken up" the memories and render them less opaque. As we narrated together, newer memories would present themselves, layering and weaving into previously told memories. Students who initially had difficulty conjuring up a related memory quickly found themselves remembering and ready to share with their peers.

After the telling, listening, writing, and retelling of memory after memory, our similar and dissimilar experiences of "being teenaged" or "being gendered" became more apparent, emphasizing the "discourses in which we have constituted others and have ourselves been constituted as particular kinds of subjects" (Davies and Gannon 2006, 11). Contradictions and overlaps among memories of the entire class became strikingly apparent as we collated the texts into each topic grouping. After almost ten weeks of collective biography, we had a vibrant and rich series of texts ready for analysis using feminist post-structural notions of discourse, power-knowledge, and subjectification (Davies 2000; Weedon 1997).

Feminist Post-structuralism

Before I explain the steps taken in the analysis of the memories and present some of the themes of the findings, it is useful to contextualize what I mean by "feminist post-structuralism." An important place to start is with the intellectual tradition of post-structuralism itself. The following discussion is a rough sketch of a contested and complex intellectual tradition.

In their work exploring post-structuralism and education, Peters and Burbules (2004) provide a broad survey of the theoretical tenets underlying post-structuralist thinking. First, they explain how post-structuralist thinkers, including Foucault, have emphasized in different ways how *meaning* is contingent on *context*. Such contingency has helped to rupture the universality of truth claims. A simple example of a truth claim in the context of gender is "boys should never wear pink." Second, post-structuralism has disassembled the humanist, rational, and autonomous self, describing the subject as *"embodied* and *engendered,* physiologically speaking, as a *temporal* being ... yet ... also malleable, infinitely flexible, and subject to the practices of normalization and individualization" (19). I will return to the "subject" when discussing subjectification later in this section. Third, post-structuralism seeks to disrupt the dominance of "scientific" knowledge and its production of "grand narrative" truths, produced by the rational, autonomous, and objective humanist self. For example, Veronica Pacini-Ketchabaw (this volume) pays attention to the dominance of developmental psychology in CYC and its produc-tion of "developmental facts" in relation to young people. Fourth, post-structuralism seeks to explore the construction and reification of particular essentialized identities (e.g., gender, citizenship, and race) and tries to understand the formation of identity binaries and how they are regulated and maintained. This particular focus of poststructuralism has been taken up in the work of feminist post-structural scholars such as Davies (2000) and Weedon (1997).

A strand of post-structuralism – feminist post-structuralism – often seeks to examine processes of "gendered subjectification." Davies and Gannon (2004) describe subjectification as a process that reflects how relations of power can force us into assuming particular subject positions and make those subjectivities "desirable" to the point where we end up taking particular positions as our own. Davies and Gannon use the language of "inscription," in which an individual is simultaneously in-scribed by discourses from the outside while "actively taking up the values, norms, and desires that make her into a recognizable, legitimate member of her social group" (318). Based on the post-structuralist rup-turing of the rational and coherent humanist subject, there is an assump-tion here that individuals are being constituted and are constituting themselves, leading to contradictory, fragmented, and multiple ways of existing in the world. Taking these ideas further, Davies (2000) suggests that "discursive positioning" is another important aspect of the subjecti-fication process. In other words, discourses help to position people into an array of subject positions in which their actions can be constrained or enabled. Feminist post-structuralism helps to "disrupt that which is taken as stable/unquestionable truth" (Davies and Gannon 2004, 320), in turn generating questions such as how does developmental psychology produce and reproduce the male/female binary? Which subject positions are available or not available as a result?

Performativity

The notion of "performativity" suggests that gender exists in a socio-political, cultural, and geo-spatial context that is actively constructed through children's talk, actions, and interactions with each other and the social world (Jagger 2008; Thorne 1995). Applying this lens to gender helps to reveal the ways in which power circulates through dominant discourses of gender, in turn sanctioning and monitoring "appropriate" gendered performances. Intersectionality theory helps to explain how these discourses intersect with other identity locations, resulting in a multiplicity of power relations and shifts in the discourses available to be taken up: that is, different power relations exist at the intersections of white/heterosexual/male and racialized/queer/transgendered. Power constitutes gender performances, and these performances are constitutive of power, creating a "normal" that subjects desire, subsequently granting more power to particular gendered locations over others, such as male over female over transgendered (Robinson 2005). These ideas have allowed for the identification of "hegemonic masculinity" (Connell, cited in Blaise 2005b), which subordinates other discourses of masculinity and femininity and is imbued by processes of hetero-sexualization, further shaping the gendered social order. In the current gendered social order, there is no space provided for hegemonic femininity. Instead, using Connell's term, there is "emphasized femininity," which is symbolized by subordination, compliance, and accommodation of the desires of hegemonic masculinity. Butler's (1990) idea of compulsory heterosexuality scaffolds hegemonic masculinity and emphasized femininity, sanctioning the male/female dualism in sexual relationships while dividing and disordering other sexualized combinations of gender. Conceptualizing gender is contingent on conceptualizing heterosexuality.

Analysis

The theoretical perspectives discussed so far offer some useful analytical tools in exploring how gender showed up in the context of the memories generated through the collective biography process. Specifically, feminist post-structuralism and performativity were helpful in exploring (a) the relational aspects of performing and regulating gender; (b) children's maintenance of and resistance to dominant discourses of gender; and (c) the constituting and constitutive relationship between gender and sexuality and the circulating power and regulation associated with compulsory heterosexuality (Butler 1990). The following questions helped to guide my analysis.

1   Which discourses of gender and sexuality are in operation throughout the memories?
2   How do the children in the memories talk and perform gender?
3   How do the children in the memories maintain or resist the discourses of gender and sexuality available to them?
4   How do heteronormativity and heterosexualization impact children's construction of gender?

The memories corresponding to the topic of "first memories of being and resisting being gendered" were compiled and closely read multiple times. Using the questions above as an analytical strategy, I analyzed the memories to identify corresponding themes. Figure 4.1 displays the written talk contained in the memories. The words that featured most prominently in the discursive productions of gender are represented in a larger type size. I will now turn to highlighting several themes across the memories, followed by a discussion of potential implications for child and youth care practice.

Wearing Gender

Blaise (2005b) noticed several gender discourses in her study of kindergarten children "doing gender" in the classroom. She demonstrated how power, specifically as it manifests in hegemonic masculinity, maintains a particular gendered social order in the classroom. She identified

Figure 4.1   Memories word map

"wearing femininities" as a gender discourse positioned in relation to hegemonic masculinity (61), and she discussed how one of the most explicit ways in which children play and perform gender is how they wear gender and present themselves during their everyday lives through clothing and other fashion choices. This discourse also showed up across several of the collective biography memories.

She looked up at the boy in front of her, who faced her straight on. "You kind of look like a boy. I mean ... you could be pretty if you grew your hair long. You should totally grow it," he said to her. Her stomach flipped, her cheeks burned hot, and her heart thumped loudly, resonating through her neck and throat. Feeling angry and hurt, she remembered back to the power and excitement that she had felt as she had watched the long locks of hair fall to the floor. She had felt different and energized. She reached up and ruffled her hand through her newly cut hair; it felt reassuringly fuzzy and soft. She could feel him looking at her as if he was evaluating her, and she felt raw and exposed like he could see straight through her. She adjusted the wet towel under her armpit and clutched at it with her cold hands, wishing that she could somehow cover herself up. As thoughts spun through her mind, her body felt heavy, her shoulders slumped, and though her throat ached with the want to speak she could not muster up a response. (G4)

Through the boy's words "you kind of look like a boy," the girl is being "hailed as a transgressive" in that she is being read as not having
"unremarked or obvious membership" in either side of the male/female
dualism (Davies 2000, 27). Furthermore, the girl's "transgression" based
on the length of her hair has positioned her as a less desirable subject,
as emphasized by the boy's words "you could be pretty if you grew your
hair long. You should totally grow it." The effects of surveillance and
objectification are experienced through the narrator's embodied memory of experiencing what is named as "raw" and "exposure," while the
matrix of compulsory heterosexuality is clearly maintained: that is, male
subject desiring female subject. It is striking how the girl appears to
have experienced the "power[ful]" and "energizing" effects of accessing
alternative discourses of gender but simultaneously succumbs to the
processes of maintaining the current gendered social order as her "shoulders slumped" and "her throat ached with the want to speak." This
particular memory fits well with Davies's (2000, 27) explication of
subjectification: "The process of subjectification, then, entails a tension
between simultaneously becoming a speaking, agentic subject and the
corequisite for this, being subjected to the meanings inherent in the
discourses through which one becomes a subject."

The following memory clearly illustrates the gendered social order
as maintained by hegemonic masculinity and "wearing femininities" in
the restrictions on the girl's ability to play:

> She looked longingly out the window at her brothers romping around
> in the back yard, feeling an unfamiliar ache in her bones. Ties thrown
> off. Sleeves rolled up. Their bare feet experiencing the pleasure of the
> cool welcoming grass beneath their feet. How come nobody seemed
> to care if they got their clothes dirty? Stupid dress. Hot blood coursed
> through her veins and up into her pounding temples. As her anger
> then faded into resignation and she sunk lower into her chair, she
> glanced over at her Gram with pleading eyes, as if willing her to utter
> the words she so desperately wanted to hear. (G5)

Clothing enforces a different set of rules for the girl versus the boys
playing outside. Hegemonic masculinity is maintained by the ability of

the boys to participate in play that is unrestricted by clothing. The dualisms of male/female, independent/dependent, and free/contained continue to persist and succeed in quashing any resistance "as her anger then faded into resignation and she sunk lower into her chair." The gendered social order is also exhibited in the following girl's decision to "do gender" by wearing the same amount of clothing as boys: "Honey, only boys are allowed to do that. Girls need to wear shirts, okay, why don't you come with me, and we will put your shirt back on" (G11). Another narrator puts it this way,

> The little girl looks down at her chest searching for clues as to why it must be covered. She has no answer but feels the squeamishness in her stomach in response to the woman's tone of voice. She notices people watching her and bursts into tears (G16).

There is a clear set of rules in this discourse for boys and a competing set for girls. Which discourse might have imbued the adult's decision to regulate the girl's lack of clothing? Given the modernist discourses that position children as innocent/pure, asexual, and undeveloped (Robinson 2005), there seems to be a noteworthy contradiction in heterosexualizing the girl in her state of undress in conjunction with a desire to protect her from unknown forces by disciplining her to cover up. Poignantly, one of the narrators relays her confusion: "How could her mom make her feel ... this way? So ashamed. Why did she need to be covered up? What was so special about dad and her brother ...? But she and her brother looked the same" (G11).

Discourses of femininity and the surveillance of dress also manifest in this experience of pain as the girl is regulated into a subject position of passive/weak:

> The boys were laughing and play fighting, and Mrs. K had informed the class no one was entering the school until there was order. Her legs hurt from the cold, and she could feel the pin pricks of frost bite on her knees. The boys, wearing their pants, played in the line up. As a girl, she was required to wear a dress to school and only had tights to keep her legs warm. (G6)

The agentic nature of children's maintenance of and resistance to gender discourses is clearly illustrated in the following memory, in which the girl's "wearing of gender" is a site of resistance:

> She walked into the classroom wearing her jeans, gazed around the room, and saw all the other girls in dresses. She felt strong, standing tall with both feet firmly planted to the ground ... She waited, standing firm but with a tension rising in her body. The teacher continued to look, released her gaze, and went back to the work on her desk. The girl relaxed just enough for the tension to ease, but the feeling of strength solidified. (G18)

Weedon (1997) asserts that resisting the dominant discourse is an initial step to producing alternative knowledges. It is also important to underscore how children become agentic, speaking subjects when resisting dominant discourses and accessing counterdiscourses. In the case of this memory, the girl resists emphasizing femininity's offering of a compulsory form of gender (having to wear a dress) and instead empowers herself to perform or speak in her own right, challenging normal and circulating power relations (Blaise 2005b). The girl's choice to employ a counterdiscourse creates a third space, and new knowledges are produced in the relational context of the girl, other girls, and boys. Furthermore, the girl's hard work in performing gender is plainly evident, challenging another dominant discourse that positions children as innocent sponges that soak up everything around them. Subversion is possible and accessible.

One other sub-theme that emerged in the analysis is related to the intimate linkages between gender and sexuality, specifically processes of heteronormativity and the construction of children as heterosexual beings. As Robinson (2005, 9) states, examining gender outside a constituting/constitutive relationship with heterosexuality is akin to reading Cinderella "without considering the construction of heterosexual desire as a major subset of the story."

Processes of the construction of children as heterosexual beings, without space for alternative locations of sexuality, are evident in the following memory:

I approach my uncle and begin to lean in for a hug and a kiss on the cheek, just as I had previously done with my aunt and cousins. At this point, my body is warm and flowing. He stops me by raising his hand and in a stern voice says, "I'm okay with the hug, but men don't give kisses." He laughs. I feel the warm, flowing energy disappear from my body. (G14)

The uncle positions the boy within a hegemonic discourse of "compulsory heterosexuality" (Butler 1990) stipulating that kissing is a behaviour expected of individuals of the opposite sex in this particular cultural context. The boy is positioned as normal/abnormal in that he participates in "gender-inappropriate" behaviour, though arguably he resists heterosexual gendered norms. Gender is performed within a "heterosexual matrix" that "designates that grid of cultural intelligibility through which bodies, genders, and desires are naturalized" (Butler 1990, 151). In sum, he is disciplined for deviating from the norm of being a boy.

Implications for Child and Youth Care Practice
Feminist post-structural analysis opens up another space to consider how children participate in the maintenance of and resistance to discourses of gender and sexuality. These ideas open up possibilities for reimagining CYC pedagogy and practice in the context of children's gendered worlds. The themes within the collective biography memories also help to explicate children's *active participation* in the construction and regulation of gender discourses. Exemplars in this analysis relate to the performance of gender on the body through the wearing of clothing and the embeddedness of "compulsory heterosexuality" within discourses of gender. All of this represents a contesting of the singularized "truth effects" of developmental psychology on gender and sexuality, but how might this richer account manifest in CYC pedagogy and practice?

Challenging the current gendered social order can gain momentum at the site of CYC curricula. Developmental psychology and its conceptualization of gender as a process of biological determinism and social learning are often at the core of child and adolescent development

courses in CYC undergraduate programs, as evidenced by the dominance of mainstream developmental psychology texts and readings.
Furthermore, the North American Certification Project contains a series
of basic professional competencies expected of all CYC practitioners
working with children, youth, families, and communities. The document
clearly emphasizes a developmental-ecological perspective requiring
practitioners to be "well-versed in current research and theory in human
development ... including life-span ... and psycho-sexual development"
(Mattingly and Stuart 2002, 12). I argue that, through these modernist
ideas, the male/female dualism and long-standing gendered power relations continue to be reproduced and reified. These singularized "truth
effects" of gender can then show up in the context of interactions between CYC workers and young people. What would it look like if the
CYC classroom became a space where pedagogies were employed in
order for learners themselves to take up, resist, and transgress discourses
of gender and sexuality? What if CYC educators and learners were explicit
in identifying and discussing hegemonic discourses of gender and sexuality and how young people actively participate in them to take up power
and be desired?

Such a lively pedagogy could make available multiple discourses of
gender and sexuality for discussion and contestation, could help to interrogate the effects of hegemonic discourses such as heterosexualization,
and could help to deepen both educators' and learners' discursive rep-
ertoires for constructing gender and sexuality. Practically, this might be
achieved through educators and learners being intentional in their use
of language, using curriculum materials in ways that encompass fuller
and richer ways of understanding gender and sexuality without privileging developmental psychology, and implementing learning activities
and assignments designed to disrupt what Blaise (2005b, 186) identifies
as "categorical thinking." It would also be useful for curricula to offer
opportunities to engage with theory and research that help to demonstrate children's participation in and choice making with discursive
practices of gender (see, e.g., MacNaughton 2006). Finally, it would also
be important for educators and learners to acknowledge their own
participation in gendered power relations within the heterosexualized

classroom space (Blaise 2005b). As an educator of undergraduate students, I feel reassured to realize my own agentic capacity especially in my own experiences of subjectification. I notice this in particular at the level of my own performance of gender and my own implication and participation in gendered power relations. Troubling taken-for-granted ideas about gender and sexuality in the undergraduate CYC classroom offers opportunities for educators and learners to notice, engage with, and contest discourses of gender and sexuality, with the intended effects of supporting the flourishing of curricula committed to social justice and the dismantling of power relations oppressive to individuals of *all* genders.

Conclusion

Collective biography is a powerful tool when applied to the project of translating abstract concepts into concrete events of everyday lives. The process of remembering, telling, writing, retelling, and rewriting helps to bring into relief the idea of the body as a site of inscribing and reading discourse. The analytical process serves to hold a space for contradiction, fluidity, volatility, and fragmentation amid circulating discourses and power relations.

In sum, the process of collective biography and the theoretical concepts of feminist post-structural analysis can help to contest the singularized "truth effects" of developmental psychology. These kinds of analyses can help to clarify the idea of subjectivity and illuminate how discourse and power have both restricted and freed. Furthermore, feminist post-structuralism has relevance for both pedagogy and practice in its invitation for CYC to adopt a critical stance toward dominant discourses of developmental psychology, in turn revealing the power and multiplicity of discourses that both constitute and are constitutive of ourselves and our relationships with others.

References

Blaise, M. 2005a. "A Feminist Poststructuralist Study of Children 'Doing' Gender in an Urban Kindergarten Classroom." *Early Childhood Research Quarterly* 20: 85-108.
–. 2005b. *Playing It Straight: Uncovering Gender Discourses in the Early Childhood Classroom.* New York: Taylor and Francis.

Butler, J. 1990. *Gender Trouble: Feminisms and the Subversion of Identity.* New York: Routledge.

Davies, B. 1989a. *Frogs and Snails and Feminist Tales: Preschool Children and Gender.* Sydney: Allen and Unwin.

–. 1989b. "The Discursive Production of the Male/Female Dualism in School Settings." *Oxford Review of Education* 15, 3: 229-41.

–. 2000. *A Body of Writing 1990-1999.* Walnut Creek, CA: Altamira Press.

Davies, B., and S. Gannon. 2004. "Feminism/Poststructuralism." In *Research Methods in the Social Sciences,* ed. B. Somekh and C. Lewin, 318-26. London: Sage.

–, eds. 2006. *Doing Collective Biography.* New York: Open University Press.

Jagger, G. 2008. *Judith Butler: Sexual Politics, Social Change, and the Power of the Performative.* New York: Routledge.

MacNaughton, G. 2006. "Constructing Gender in Early-Years Education." In *The SAGE Handbook of Gender and Education,* ed. C. Skelton, B. Francis, and L. Smulyan, 127-38. Thousand Oaks, CA: Sage.

Mattingly, M., and C. Stuart. 2002. "The North American Certification Project: Competencies for Professional Child and Youth Work Practitioners." *Journal of Child and Youth Work* 17: 16-49.

Peters, M., and N. Burbules. 2004. *Poststructuralism and Educational Research.* Lanham, MD: Rowman and Littlefield.

Robinson, K. 2005. "'Queerying' Gender: Heteronormativity in Early Childhood Education." *Australian Journal of Early Childhood* 30, 2 19-28.

Thorne, B. 1995. *Gender Play: Girls and Boys in School.* New Brunswick, NJ: Rutgers University Press.

Weedon, C. 1997. *Feminist Practice and Poststructural Theory.* Oxford: Blackwell.

Bottom of the Food Chain
The Minoritization of Girls
in Child and Youth Care

SANDRINA DE FINNEY, ELICIA LOISELLE,
AND MACKENZIE DEAN

5

> Girls like me, we're not real high on the government priority list ...
> the racism, sexism, mental health effects, colonialism, how First
> Nations women were treated in history. We're basically the bottom
> of the food chain.
>
> — RIANNA, SIXTEEN, FIRST NATIONS ACTIVIST,
> SPEAKING AT A FORUM ON RACISM

Media headlines ("Girls Gone Wild!"; "Gurl Power"; "Tween Super Shoppers"; "Girl Gangs"; "Mean Girls") reveal our growing fascination with girls as socio-cultural producers, consumers, sexualized bodies, and recipients of social intervention. But despite its vernacular ubiquity, "girlhood" is a contested space, deeply fissured by a multitude of perspectives and debates. Griffin (2004, 32) stresses that "there is nothing 'essential' about girlhood; it is always produced and negotiated (by us, but especially by girls) in particular historical and political moments." Given that our current historical and political moment is characterized by the growth of neoliberalism as a dominant social order, there is a need to map the changing conditions under which contemporary girlhoods are crafted. Increasingly complex local and global intersections have brought to the fore an ideologically charged debate about how girls are constituted, and how they constitute themselves, at the nexus of competing claims about their bodies, identities, social locations, and political and economic roles. In this context, girl-centred research, policy, and practice have gained saliency. Girls have become the focus of new scholarship, with the growing terrain of girlhood studies undergoing dramatic conceptual shifts in the past thirty years. At a geo-political level, the need to make girls' concerns more visible and to infuse their voices into policy development was highlighted by the United Nations's declaration of the 1990s as "the decade of the girl child." In 2007, the UN Commission on the Status of Women made girls the focus of its international talks. The UN definition of the "girl child" as a female under the age of eighteen has become a global marker of girlhood, with paradoxical effects. On the one hand, a globally accepted definition reifies the notion of a universal girl, abstracting girls from their complex socio-cultural milieus and obscuring the impacts of structural barriers such as poverty, racism, and sexism in shaping unequal outcomes for marginalized girls. On the other hand, a global focus on girls has garnered much-needed economic and political support for girl-centred initiatives. One thing is certain: as rapid global change reconfigures girls' local realities, our traditional models and discourses of girlhood must be expanded.

In this chapter, we draw on our practice and research experience with diverse girls in Canada[1] to map the terrain of girlhood studies with a view toward applications for the field of child and youth care.[2] We review conceptualizations and gaps in the emerging girlhood studies field as it has evolved in Euro-Western contexts. Our focus is the minoritization of girls who fall outside white, heterosexual, abled, middle-class norms and as a result are chronically overrepresented in indicators of social exclusion yet underrepresented and underserved in child- and youth-related research, policy, and practice. As we demonstrate, the omission of minoritized girls from research and practice creates critical gaps in our ability to serve them while excluding them from avenues for advocacy among their peers, communities, and with service providers, policy makers, and researchers. These omissions call for a much more critical, politicized approach to girl-centred practice in the CYC field. The reconceptualization we propose here makes visible the impacts of structural relations of power[3] and the intersecting effects of gender, race, class, sexuality, (dis)ability, and age formations, among others, in shaping unequal girlhoods. In order to apply a trans-theoretical, intersectional gender analysis to Foucauldian (1978, 1980) notions of power relations and subject formation, we weave together diverse theoretical strands, including sexuality studies and queer theory (Charles 2010; Renold and Ringrose 2008; Robinson and Davies 2007; Youdell 2005), Indigenous studies (Laenui 2002; Lawrence 2004; Smith 2001), and post-colonial and transnational feminisms (Anzaldúa 2002; Hernández and Rehman 2002; Minh-ha 1997; Mohanty 2003; Narayan and Harding 2000). In presenting this framework, we hope to uncover how dominant social discourses such as those related to gender, sexuality, race, (dis)ability, class, and age circulate under neoliberalism and come to be accepted as normal and natural while their roles in the production of social inequities remain hidden. Like other analyses in this volume, ours is critical of master narratives that take positivist, Eurocentric representations as unproblematic and universally applicable.

Minoritized Girls in Child and Youth Care

> Girls Night was part of the mandatory programming at the group home. I knocked on her door to tell her it was about to start. She stood in the doorway – her shaved head, boyish appearance, and sadeyes. I could sense her discomfort as she anticipated my words. I struggled to find a way to explain to her why this was important and why pedicures, popcorn, and boy talk would be good for her.
>
> – MACKENZIE DEAN, CYC PRACTITIONER

Girls are the focus of diverse CYC interventions. As CYC practitioners, we provide girl-centred programs, run groups and camps for girls, manage girls-only group homes and residential settings, and engage in research with girls. Many of these interventions are intended to address gender-specific issues and vulnerabilities. For instance, girls are three times more likely than boys to experience depression and four times more likely to be sexually assaulted (Girls Action Foundation 2009). But even when research and practice interventions address the constituting effects of gender structures in shaping girls' lives differently than boys' lives, critical conceptual and practice gaps remain. Girl-centred spaces and programs are not transformative in and of themselves; when they do not employ a critical gender analysis that addresses the inner workings of intersecting relations of race, class, (dis)ability, and sexuality, to name a few, they can reproduce the exclusion of minoritized girls who fall outside normative girlhood.

It is to name this process of "being made" as irrevocably outside the norm that we use the term "minoritization," because it conveys the effects of social relations of power in producing hierarchical subject positions for girls.[4] In this context, neither the meaning of "girlhood" nor that of "minoritization" can be taken as essential, neutral, or fixed; both terms must be understood as socially constituted and constituting, meaning that minoritized girls "do not occupy the position of minority by virtue of some inherent property (e.g., of their body shape, culture or religion), but acquire this position as an outcome of a socio-historical process" (Chantler and Smailes 2004, 34). Pereira (2008, 349) explains that in these processes the "dominant group uses recognition to control and discipline minority groups." Individuals who identify and/or are identified as part of a marginalized group are positioned as outsiders or others to the dominant norm. Minoritized groups consequently find themselves compared to, and often falling short of, the standards of the dominant status quo. Here difference is the basis for exclusion, and a social context is created where certain identities are privileged and others subjugated or minoritized based on their positioning in a normative social hierarchy (Harley et al. 2002). These exclusions produce drastically unequal outcomes for certain groups of girls.

Consider, for example, the following:

- Aboriginal girls face the highest rates of incarceration, sexual exploitation, and involvement with child welfare agencies (Girls Action Foundation 2009; Moore, Morrison, and Glei 1995).
- The rate of sexual abuse and assault of girls with disabilities is four times greater than the national average (National Clearinghouse on Family Violence 2004).

- Lesbian and bisexual girls run away from home and attempt suicide at over four and three times (respectively) the rate of heterosexual girls (Saewyc et al. 2007).
- Racialized girls experience multiple forms of racial, religious, and cultural discrimination yet face more barriers when accessing services than do white girls (Lee 2005; Suarez-Orozco 2001).

These unequal girlhoods point to an urgent need for further CYC-specific theorizing and practice innovations related to girls' minoritization. A focus on gender alone obscures how other constituting relations, such as race, class, (dis)ability, and sexuality, intersect to shape the experience of gender, with real impacts on structural inequities among girls. Importantly, these dimensions cannot be assumed to be fixed or mutually exclusive. For instance, a First Nations girl can also have a disability and identify as queer. Furthermore, not only are minoritized girls overlooked in debates about girlhood, but we must also emphasize that the very notion of girlhood is problematic. The reproduction of artificial gender dichotomies between "girls" and "boys" in social sciences research takes as natural and mutually exclusive differences that are complex and structurally produced and excludes, for example, transgender, gender queer, and gender non-conforming youth.

Girlhood and Girlhood Studies

> In our girls' groups, we talk about gender as a spectrum – not just "girl" versus "boy." But it's hard to subvert dominant language and constructions. When we speak about gender queer, we often resort to some sort of equally problematic term like "youth" or "young adult." And funders may not understand the nuances of "gender spectrum services" or "socially constituted categories programming," which makes it difficult to get support from mainstream institutions.
>
> – SANDRINA DE FINNEY, CYC PRACTITIONER

To examine the implications of minoritization for CYC practice with girls, a brief history of girlhood studies is in order. Although cursory, our overview echoes those who call for a new, more critical phase of girl studies, stressing that minoritized girls are underrepresented and often problematically characterized in psycho-social theories that inform applied youth and girl work (Harris 2004; Tolman and Brydon-Miller 2001; Weaver 1990).

First, however, a conceptual disclaimer: we know that in our attempt to interrogate the notion of "girlhood" we stand to reify a concept we wish instead to problematize. As we are immersed in language that re-asserts dominant discourses, we have been limited in our ability simul-taneously to write about minoritized girlhoods and contest gender norms and dichotomies.

We are limited too by the confines of this chapter, so our overview must generalize within and among dynamic fields of study and practice. Terminology related to sexuality, disability, queer studies, racialization, and feminism is diverse, deeply contested, and always evolving, but a comprehensive discussion of these nuances exceeds the chapter's scope. We choose to write through these tensions as transparently as possible precisely to demonstrate how contradictory and messy they are. Therefore, despite conceptual and linguistic limitations, we focus on girlhood because other terms (e.g., "youth" and "young people") are equally limited and loaded and because we believe there is value in unpacking a concept that holds such power in constituting not only identities and daily realities but also the research, policies, and services developed to serve young people. To avoid doing so might result in an even more damaging intellectual paralysis. Therefore, in taking up girl-hood as our conceptual focus, our intentions are to unpack the very notion of "girl," to foster critical dialogue about girlhood, and to make an analysis of minoritization more visible and relevant to CYC.

A Brief History of Girl Studies

The past thirty years have seen a proliferation of literature mapping the changing conditions under which contemporary girlhoods are crafted.[5] The field of girl studies, dominated by Euro-Western scholarship, arose from a need to theorize girls' experiences in response to two construc-tions: as other than boys, and as in the process of becoming women.

First, theories of youth development have traditionally assumed the inherent and unproblematic nature of biological sex categories, taking up the male-centred "youth" category as their main focus of analysis and ignoring the role of patriarchy in shaping gender (Carlson 2000; Hey 1997; Ward and Benjamin 2004). Second, Western feminists have positioned girls as de facto beneficiaries of women-centred theorization and activism, undertheorizing age as a constituting force of girlhood (Fine 2004).

In response to the erasure of girls in youth and women-centric studies, in the mid-1970s feminist scholars inserted girl-centred theories and practices into feminism and introduced a structural analysis of gender and patriarchy into youth studies (Chesney-Lind and Irwin 2004). Thus, despite its pitfalls (e.g., its reproduction of a problematic gender binary), girlhood has become a strategic conceptual and political position from which to advocate for girl-centred language, policies, and social services.

Competing Concepts of Girlhood

Contemporary discourses of girlhood constitute girls in multiple and often contradictory ways: as voiceless victims of patriarchal culture; as aggressive and explicitly sexualized; as feminist countercultural agents; and as feisty, empowered, pop cultural icons. These competing conceptualizations provide powerful scripts for public and academic discourses about girls. But Griffin (2004, 30) disputes the assumption that the push for girl-centred studies has made girls' lives equally visible: "If girls and young women have been and remain relatively invisible in most youth research, then some girls have been more invisible than others." Since the 1980s, some girlhood scholars have criticized universal normative psycho-social perspectives that understand girlhood as a developmental transition from childhood into adulthood, experienced by all girls in similar ways based on white, middle-class, heterosexual, able-bodied norms (Amos and Parmar 1981; Griffin 2004; Hernández and Rehman 2002).

To explore these gaps, we focus next on two prevalent constructions of girls within contemporary girlhood studies: powerful and vulnerable girls. These conflicting discourses have dominated debates of girlhood and thus the development of girl-centred research, policy, and programming, including in the field of CYC. We incorporate some perspectives of girls we have worked with to shed light on how these constructions are enacted by girls in their everyday lives and in their interactions with service providers and institutions.

Girl Power

Girl Power is one of the most recognizable discourses shaping public conceptualizations of girlhood. Service providers, agencies, and funders that serve girls find its message of girl empowerment compelling. Many of the programs we run as CYC workers are rooted in some iteration of this discourse, so it warrants a critical overview.

The Girl Power discourse is fissured by two competing interpretations: the anti-establishment, explicitly politicized "riot grrrls," and the mainstream, marketable "power girl" (Aapola et al. 2005). Riot grrrls emerged from the punk rock scene in a movement involving mainly white middle-class young women, many identifying as queer, who problematized the heteronormativity and gender conformism embedded in the notion of "girl."[6] As the riot grrrl movement grew in visibility, its liberatory message was appropriated and commodified into a depoliticized iteration of girl power. The now ubiquitous feisty, sexy, "power girl" icon is exemplified by the Spice Girls or, more recently, Pink. Constructing girls as empowered agents and significant cultural and economic producers and consumers, the "can do" and "you go, girl!" brand of Girl Power has catapulted marketing campaigns that target the rapidly growing teen and "tween" girl markets.

Girl Power has had the positive effect of popularizing feminist concerns for girls' voices and engagement, enhancing access by community-based organizations to girl-focused research and program funding. However, Mikel-Brown (2005, 147) stresses that neoliberal representations of the "self-made," "can do" girl subject have also engendered a "relentless overpsychologising of girls that has served to render invisible the social and material conditions of girls' lives." Fine (2004, xvii) concurs:

Rising rates of arrest, incarceration and un and under-employment among young women are a troubling counterpoint to images of over-achieving, consumer-oriented girlpower. While some privileged young women are indeed reaping the benefits of new opportunities, those without economic or social capital are slipping through the ever-widening holes in what remains of our social safety nets. Young women appear to have it all, and yet many constitute those hardest hit by the effects of the new global political economy on jobs, resources and economy. How do they survive and flourish in a world of greater choices and opportunities, but fewer structures of support?

Although girls' ability to resist or subvert systems of domination is often deeply creative, as Fine asserts, it is also constrained by powerful social forces that are amplified under neoliberalism. Girls we work with are familiar with the contradictions between the dominant discourse of opportunity and minoritized girls' lived realities. Ruthie, a seventeen year old who lives independently while attending an all-girls' alternative high school, articulates how such a discourse erases working-class girls' resilience in dealing with experiences of poverty:

> Maybe you're a sixteen or seventeen year old going home to a place where you live by yourself. Or maybe after school you have to go to work, because you have to pay your bills. And maybe that's causing you to be behind on your school work, you know ... Or maybe you don't even have a place to live. There's lots of situations where people wouldn't really take that into consideration in a regular school. It wouldn't be valued as a life experience.

As Ruthie observes, because their experiences do not fit into the neoliberal definitions of individualized success espoused by Girl Power discourse, poor and working-class girls are often excluded from access to this particular brand of social capital and thus cast even further toward the margins. In fact, "girl power's popularity is credited to its very lack of threat to the status quo for the ways in which it reflects the ideologies of white middle-class individualism and personal responsibility over collective responses to social problems" (Aapola et al. 2005, 30). Fine (2004, xv) observes that "the cumulative constraints on [girls'] lives masquerade as freedom and autonomy. Such well-crafted moments of both/and/between, domination and resistance, force us to retheorize 'choice' within conditions of enormous constraint glamorized with neoliberal commodification." A more nuanced unpacking of the limitations of empowerment-based discourses and programs in the CYC field would make visible the constraining effects of neoliberalism on minoritized girls.

Vulnerable Girlhood

Although Girl Power focuses on girls' empowerment, a growing preoccupation with girls' vulnerability has created three competing "girl in crisis" scripts: the *voiceless girl,* the *mean girl,* and the *party girl.* These representations of girls' agency support the psychological imperative that, to effect changes in their lives, girls at risk require expert outside intervention, a representation that also often informs girl-centred programming.

The voiceless girl discourse was most famously articulated in Mary Pipher's *Reviving Ophelia: Saving the Selves of Adolescent Girls* (1994). Pipher argued that girls lose voice and experience a process of self-splitting as they enter adolescence – consequences of the challenges inherent in a girl-hostile patriarchal society. Pipher's "loss of self" discourse importantly focused attention away from psychological explanations and onto the socio-cultural pressures placed on girls, naming the effects of patriarchy, sexism, and capitalism in robbing girls of their voices. However, constructing girls as voiceless and disempowered problematically assumes they are passive vessels for relations of power and ignores their agency in naming and resisting their minoritization.

Following in the footsteps of the voiceless girl, the mean girl and the party girl appear as new manifestations of the crisis discourse of girlhood (Jiwani, Steenbergen, and Mitchell 2006). The party girl is the latest iteration of a growing glamorization of seemingly empowered, highly sexualized, economically privileged girl consumers, exemplified by young Hollywood celebrities such as Paris Hilton and Britney Spears. Girls we work with are quite aware of these limiting representations of girlhood. As Sanaa emphasizes, the commodification of the party girl icon reproduces normative constructions of gender, sexuality, and race: "That whole skinny, straight, blonde girl, it's pretty impossible for most girls to look like that, you'd drive yourself crazy trying to be that." It also ignores the role of patriarchal formations in shaping girls' sexuality as suspect and inappropriate, as observed by Beckie and Starr: "Girls are always called whores or sluts or something, and then guys are just players. I don't get why it's like that." "Yeah, it's so not fair."

In addition to the exclusive party girl, the image of the mean girl has gained currency. This mean girl construct is eclipsing the image of the victimized, voiceless girl, revealing an emerging preoccupation with girls' perceived social, physical, and sexual aggression. This aggression has become a focus of concern and surveillance, resulting in the increasing criminalization of girls' offences. But here again the mean girl image remains steeped in race and class stereotypes; Chesney-Lind and Irwin (2004, 50) argue that it is those young women "who lack the resources to stay out of view of the criminal justice system who are targeted and criminalized, resulting in spiraling arrest rates for girls of colour." Particularly in a post-9/11 world, racialized girls experience increased racial profiling and are pathologized for structural inequities over which they have little control: "The omission of racism as a debilitating social ingredient in girls' lives is curious ... [when] race continues to be the single most important factor in determining the life chances of young people. The suggestion seems to be that ... the lives of young white women are assumed to represent all of American girlhood" (Aapola et al. 2005, 45). Here again the criminalization of minoritized girls results in a lack of policy and programming focus on other important issues, such as sexualized and racialized violence.

The Problem with Normative Girlhood

Both powerful and vulnerable girl representations have the paradoxical effect of popularizing exclusive conceptualizations of girlhood. As Harris (2004) points out, the vulnerable girl discourse assumes that an upper-middle-class white heterosexual girl, despite the privilege afforded her, is as vulnerable as one who is socially and economically marginalized. In turn, the neoliberal Girl Power subject, which assumes that determination and style are all one needs to achieve success and social belonging, presumes that girls are free to create themselves outside the constraints of social disparities. Such a perspective, Griffin (2004, 31) argues, "does not reflect the diversity of girls' lives [or] the complexity of the contemporary constitution of girlhood."

We argue instead for a reconceptualization of girlhood that makes visible the following erasures. First, dominant psycho-social conceptualizations of gender, race, sexuality, (dis)ability, and age as fixed, innate, and comparable units of analysis reveal little about their fluid, overlapping effects in girls' lives and position minoritized girls as perpetual others in relation to dominant norms. Second, the representation in girlhood studies of girls as a homogeneous group erases the uneven impacts of social forces in shaping structural inequities that impact minoritized girls. Third, the positioning of minoritized girls as only problematic and at risk ignores their complex negotiations of power relations and limits the infusion of their diverse voices into research, policy, and practice.

Rethinking CYC Practice

> I was born here. My parents were born here. But that doesn't seem to matter. A few times a week somebody asks me where I am from. When Canadians see me, they see an outsider, not fully Canadian, who will always be "from somewhere else."
>
> – HARPREET, EIGHTEEN

Because youth- and girl-related policies, practice standards, and programs flow from conceptualizations of girlhood, they inevitably suffer from the same weaknesses we have identified. These omissions help to explain why minoritized girls are chronically underserved in so many areas of importance to CYC practitioners. The construction of minoritized girls as permanently "at risk" reveals misplaced anxieties about their bodies and their social, political, and economic roles while ignoring the strategies girls develop to negotiate and speak back to limiting girlhood discourses. Ormond (2004; 249) stresses that risk factors facing girls must be "continually situated within their daily experiences of oppressive institutional and social silencing." As we have demonstrated, the minoritization of girls has consequential, material effects on every aspect of their development, yet this does not result in their being adequately served by youth- and girl-centred programming. As facilitators of therapeutic interventions, CYC practitioners should understand how structural inequities *produce* the risk factors in which we intervene while paradoxically maintaining barriers to transformative social services.

For instance, immigrant girls of colour often report they do not seek help for physical, emotional, and mental health issues because service providers, even when supportive, are too often unable to grasp the complexities of their lives (Lee 2005). When girls do seek help, experiences of marginalization are often interpreted as cultural or adaptive risk factors rather than as symptoms of systemic racism, as Prisha, sixteen, articulates: "I went to see the counsellor because of racism, and all she focused on was like my home life, like I'm getting abused by my culture, like they don't want to hear about racism or anything, they just want to know if my parents abuse me because we're Muslim." Because psychological conceptualizations of risk often focus on the individual or family level, girls are pathologized for the impacts of structural inequities in their lives, and they become the focus of inappropriate or inadequate interventions. For instance, Varcoe (2002) finds that girls of colour who experience violence are subjected to increased scrutiny and are even denied services because health care providers commonly attribute incidents of violence against racialized women and girls to their culture rather than to vulnerabilities created by systemic sexism and racism. Similar patterns have been found when girls with disabilities report sexual abuse or assault (DAWN Ontario, n.d.). Whereas other children might be taught to be "risk savvy" or "street smart," girls with disabilities are more often socialized to be compliant with and passive to authority. They might also be constructed as non-sexual, thus excluded from sexual education and sexual health services that would provide them with tools for self-advocacy (DAWN Ontario, n.d.).

Equally concerning is how dominant discourses marginalize minoritized girls' diverse sexualities. McClelland and Fine (2008) problematize the limiting language of risk and prevention that precludes multifaceted discussions of girls' sexuality. For instance, calls for more effective pregnancy prevention initiatives reflect a widespread social anxiety over the consequences young "misguided" women's sexuality will have on the public purse. Proweller (2000, 101) notes that "teenage pregnancy has been politically constructed as a 'social problem' principally aimed at singling out poor, single mothers as convenient scapegoats for moral denigration." The effects are felt by the young women marginalized by this social agenda. Take, for instance, the experience of Leah, eighteen:

> [My friend] was young and had a baby. She didn't know what to do, and she went to [an education program for teen moms], and she learned how to be a great mother. But if you say "oh, I go to [this program]," [people] automatically give you this look like you're a fuckin' loser, you're a bad parent because you're a young mother. Like, you know, if you were to go up to that same person and ... say, like, yeah, "I'm married to this older man, and he has a good job," they would look at you totally different than if you say "I'm a single parent. I'm independent. I work my ass off and go to school." They would look at you like you're fucking struggling and you obviously aren't a good parent.

The pathologizing of young mothers as described by Leah is often reinforced through interactions with service providers who reproduce dominant middle-class values that position young mothers as powerless (Rutman et al. 2002). A lack of training on the impacts of minoritization leads to institutional and programmatic blindness that curtails practitioners from responding to their effects, leaving minoritized girls further marginalized and isolated.

As we have illustrated, processes of minoritization are simultaneously constituted and ignored by the ecological systems in which girls are embedded. Walkerdine (1988, 228) argues that "the voices of the oppressed are not simply left out of the system. Rather, [the system] regulates what a child is, and children of outsider groups (and all girls) respond in a number of contradictory ways. The critical educator has to understand how particular children live those multiple positionings." The need to understand multiple positionings is precisely why we argue for a trans-theoretical, intersectional feminist framework. As underscored by Girls Action Foundation (2009), such an analysis facilitates a more accurate understanding of the diversity of girls' experiences and recognizes that girls' experiences of life occur in multiple and compounding spheres. Such a framework holds open a vision of new possibilities and might enable more critical collaborations and advocacy.

Yet, despite calls for more politicized, change-centred programming for diverse girls, common understandings of "diversity in practice" in applied fields such as CYC too often remain superficial.[7] Diversity competencies that "celebrate" difference demonstrate a lack of structural analysis that disconnects CYC practice from political contexts and limits our ability to address minoritization in a critical manner. Chantler (2005, 244) argues that "racism, sexism, and class inequalities are overlooked by focusing on culture rather than power, thereby presenting a more exoticised and rose tinted view of the world than that experienced by minoritized people." CYC practitioners need more critical tools to intervene in structural inequities that perpetuate minoritization: interventions that require multiple levels of advocacy. In the sections that follow, we explore two important areas of intervention for a more critical approach to practice: reconceptualizing and supporting girls' agency, and creating critical spaces that promote diverse strategies of social change.

Reconceptualizing and Supporting Girls' Agency

To explore strategies for critical advocacy with or by girls, it is important to clarify how we conceptualize girls' agency. A popular buzzword, *agency* has become apoliticized through Girl Power discourses and heavily implicated in the production of normative girlhood. In its dominant usage, agency is the domain of the illusive neoliberal "self-made girl" discussed earlier, whose choices are constructed as universal, democratic freedoms. Within this frame, girls' empowerment is tied to individual decision-making processes abstracted from the complex social contexts and structural barriers that limit the choices available to some girls.

From our trans-theoretical feminist framework, girls' diverse strategies for engaging with dominant and alternative discourses of girlhood constitute "another kind of agency" (Davies 2000, 60). Engaging girls in discussions about how they negotiate power in their daily lives reveals the skills and advocacy strategies that they are already always enacting and opens up space for alternative ways of understanding and (re)constituting minoritization. Davies explains that through this kind of reformulated agency girls "can move within and between discourses, can see precisely how they subject her, and can use the terms of one discourse to counteract, modify, refuse, or go beyond the other, in terms of both her own experienced subjectivity and how she speaks in relation to the subjectivities of others" (60).

CYC practitioners might therefore support girls' agency in naming and contesting structural inequities so that they can "refuse the established story of a white, middle-class heterosexual woman's life, a story all girls in this culture – whether they are white or of colour, rich or poor, heterosexual or lesbian – struggle against, albeit in different ways" (Brown and Gilligan 1992, 15). This support is important because monolithic discourses of powerful and at-risk girls do not account for the complex and uneven ways in which minoritized girls engage as knowledge producers and advocates in contexts that impede their politicization and social inclusion.

Endeavours to understand how girls negotiate the discourses, practices, and policies that constitute them as racialized, gendered, classed, (dis)abled, sexed subjects are integral to developing a more radically engaged and social change-centred CYC practice. Many of the girls we work with stress not knowing where to begin their engagement in social action due to the pervasive silencing that surrounds minoritization: "I always wanted to do something about it, but I just didn't know where to start" (Jillien, sixteen); "Yeah, like our school doesn't teach about this stuff, you just think you're alone dealing with it" (Lili, seventeen). Others report that, when they do speak back against institutional power structures, far from being rewarded for their advocacy, they face silencing, denial, and backlash – not only from peers but also from service providers:

This one group for girls was like pretty racist against Native girls, like lots of harsh comments against us all the time, and every time I said something to the counsellor she was like "you just have to be patient with them." And after that she was weird with me, like avoiding me and stuff. (Hannah, seventeen)

Yeah, and like if you say anything to all the comments they all roll their eyes, like, "oh, there they go again, those Native girls are always mad." (Lianna, fifteen)

The systemic lack of supports for girls' diverse and creative forms of advocacy is concerning. In 2005, the Canadian Women's Foundation completed an extensive scan of girl-centred programming in Canada. Although it noted "a wide-ranging and diverse offering from neighbourhood-based activity groups, to innovative social action projects, to national networks that support and network with local girls' empowerment programs" (55), it raised concerns that "very few programs ... were geared to advocacy by and for girls including more marginalized girls in Canada" (60). The foundation also noted that, though programs focus on girls' strengths, "few promote an expressed feminist perspective or purport to use an analysis of gender, race, class and sexuality in their implementation" (61). CYC practitioners could take a leadership role in bridging this gap by more consistently providing information, space, and support for girls to engage in a spectrum of advocacy, including self-advocacy, political activism, community building, grassroots organizing, and more formal participation in shaping policy, research, and practice agendas.

Critical Spaces and Social Change Advocacy

There are certainly examples of innovative feminist initiatives for and by girls that offer insights into the challenges and benefits of such work.[8] What can be gleaned from them is that girl-centred spaces that are critical and responsive are integral to generating solidarity among minoritized girls, shifting power away from normative constructions and toward girls' own articulations of their complex experiences. Girls we work with have expressed the importance of such spaces in their lives:

I thought I couldn't be friends with girls because they're all bitches, and then I came here [to a girls' alternative program]. And, yeah, I made a lot of strong relationships with other women. Now I don't try to be a badass anymore. I'm not getting into fights every other week. I have ambitions and goals and self-worth, and I have a new-found feminism, and I am a stronger woman by coming [here]. (Leah, eighteen)

All of us, I'm pretty sure, are sick and tired of being judged. So you put a bunch of judged people together, and it creates a good community, I think, just because, like, you all have a common pain of being judged by society ... And then you come here, and it's like there is no judging, there is no accepting, you just are. (Sarah, eighteen)

Critical spaces are those in which practitioners engage with girls in naming intersecting relations of power and explore and support girls' strategies for resisting their impacts. Although no one practitioner, group, or program can speak to all of these complexities, in our experience, when they are successfully critical (and self-critical), such spaces share important commonalities by providing the following:

- critical tools and knowledge;
- supportive, ongoing mentoring that facilitates deep engagement with and mobilization of girls' marginalized knowledges and skills;
- inclusive structures, procedures, and languages that do not assume that "we're all equal here" and instead model how to respectfully and productively name gaps at every level despite the discomfort or conflict doing so might cause;
- opportunities to unpack and subvert the very category of "girl"; and
- explicit advocacy, social action, and intervention into problematic institutional practices and policies.

This list is certainly not exhaustive, and we do not intend it to be a prescriptive formula but rather a starting point for a creative reimagining of girl-centred practice. It is important to note that critical and politicized practice with girls is necessarily concerned with reflecting deeply on how dominant and alternative discourses are taken up within, and constructed through, girl-centred spaces. As we discussed earlier, girl spaces are not transformative in and of themselves, and practitioners and programs that lack a critical analysis and take such spaces as inherently safe and unproblematic risk reifying dominant discourses of girlhood that silence minoritized girls' complex realities. Lili stresses this point:

> This one youth worker was doing a health workshop about safe sex and that, and this girl who's gay, she's like pretty open about it, ... she was like "what about girl-on-girl sex?" And the worker ... was all un-comfortable, she never said anything, like she was all focused on just girl-to-boy, and it had nothing to do with like how we are ... It was just such a waste of time. (Lili, seventeen)

As Lili notes, health interventions embedded in dominant constructions of sexuality obscure the experiences of many girls and negate the complex intersections among socially constituted and constituting categories of sexuality, sexual orientation, racialization, gender identity, class, citizen-ship, ability, and so on. Thus, providing uncritical programs for diverse groups of girls might even be dangerous if some girls are further mar-ginalized within spaces purported to be safe.

Additionally, however critical girl-centred spaces might be, they overwhelmingly take up a dichotomized gender structure, potentially excluding gender non-conforming youth such as seventeen-year-old Taylin: "Well, I kind of knew early on I didn't really identify as a girly-girl, I guess not a boy but not a girl, like somewhere in between I guess, it's hard to describe." A lack of critical language to capture experiences that fall outside the girl/boy dichotomy reinforces the need for CYC practitioners to be flexible and responsive and to complicate concep-tualizations of girlhood. We reiterate how much we struggle with this binary even as we seek to write differently about girl-focused studies and practice. Although we know that critical, girl-centred spaces are necessary to unpack intersecting gendered oppressions, we must also unsettle the structural barriers that we might be reproducing for those who face gendered minoritization but do not identify as girls.[9] As we have emphasized, since there are no perfect, all-encompassing terminologies, formulas, or programs that neatly resolve these complexities, it is integral that we work alongside young people to interrogate power as it operates within the spaces we create together.

On a final note, we also wish to put forward the idea of broader social change advocacy as integral to our roles as CYC practitioners and advocates. Advocacy that targets the effects of minoritization requires practitioners to disrupt the status quo, not only within girl- and youth-centred spaces (alongside the young people with whom we work) but also within spaces, institutions, and systems most heavily entrenched in dominant discourses and practices. Far beyond superficial representations of diversity competencies, such advocacy requires that we examine our complicity in relations of power and our responsibility to intervene in structural inequities. A comprehensive discussion of such interventions is beyond this chapter's scope, but we mention it here to highlight the importance of systemic change. In addition to working with and through critical theories in our front-line practice with children, youth, and families, CYC practitioners are well positioned to take a leadership role in our field and in the political, economic, and socio-cultural systems that perpetuate minoritization.

Conclusion

How could the girls and I do this critical work together without trying to change the systems that marginalize them? We can't just sit around deconstructing the inequalities they negotiate without also creating spaces for them to turn their resistance into social action. When we recognize that these problems are systemic, it doesn't make sense to try to change things in a room by ourselves.

– ELICIA LOISELLE, CYC PRACTITIONER

Minoritization is political, complex, and painful – and that is precisely what makes critical practice so necessary and so messy. There is no easy formula. But if we use this as an excuse to avoid engaging in critical advocacy, we run the risk of giving the appearance to the minoritized children, youth, families, and communities with whom we work that we accept structural inequities, thus sending the inevitably harmful message that "it is their 'responsibility' that they happen to be subjugated" (Waterhouse, cited in Chantler 2005, 247). The CYC field and its practitioners are ideally positioned to model strategies that address the silencing surrounding minoritization by modelling a critical, intersectional analysis and by engaging in difficult conversations and actions through our practice and research. As we specified in our disclaimer at the beginning of this chapter, such advocacies can never neatly and simply resolve the complexities of historical, overlapping social inequities. Rather, the ability to engage fully and transparently with – not despite – these many asymmetries can form the basis of our efforts to validate to our peers and the children, youth, families, and communities with whom we work that resisting minoritization and social inequality constitutes a viable, healthy, and supported possibility. Resistance sends a powerful message because, even though it takes us, as a field and as practitioners, to difficult, complicated places, it is work that is driven by an ethic of care and a shared desire for change.

Notes

1   Throughout this chapter, we draw on quotations from girls we have worked and researched with in two settings: Project Artemis (http://www.artemisplace.blip.tv/) and antidote: Racialized Minority and Indigenous Girls and Women's Network (http://www.antidote network.org/). These are examples of advocacy-focused programming and research by and with girls. We hope that the quotations bring to light girls' diverse negotiations of minoritization and related experiences.

2   We believe it is valuable to speak to CYC as a site of shared history, language, conceptual frameworks, and practice standards, but we are also cognizant that the field is inherently diverse and shifting, with no homogeneous perspective with respect to the issues discussed.

3   Under a neoliberal order, structural inequities are embedded in socio-cultural, economic, and political structures (i.e., social institutions, governmental discourses and policies, human services, family systems, etc.) that are enacted in girls' everyday lives. Rather than operating simply at an individual level, these inequities take hold as social reality and have deep-seated, systemic effects on minoritized groups.

4   We bring a trans-theoretical gender analysis to minoritized subject formation, but related concepts are also relevant. See, for example, conceptualizations of the subaltern (Spivak 1996) and minoritarian (Deleuze and Guattari 1986, 1987).

5 See Bettis and Adams (2005); Gonick (2003); Handa (2003); Harris (2004); Jiwani et al. (2006); Lalik and Oliver (2005); Mikel-Brown (2005); Torres (1999).
6 Also rooted in the riot grrrl movement is an emerging anti-colonial, anti-racist feminism to which many of the girls we work with contribute. See, for example, *Colonize This! Young Women of Color on Today's Feminism* (Hernández and Rehman 2002); *Girlhood: Redefining the Limits* (Jiwani, Steenbergen, and Mitchell 2006); and *Yello-Oh Girls! Emerging Voices Explore Culture, Identity, and Growing up Asian American* (Nam 2001).
7 For North American diversity competencies in CYC, see the North American Certification Project (Mattingly and Stuart 2002).
8 See, for example, Fed Up Honeys, http://www.fed-up-honeys.org/mainpage.htm; Girls Action Foundation, http://www.girlsactionfoundation.ca and http://www.kickaction.ca/node/1499; and the Young Feminist Activism program, http://www.awid.org/.
9 Important work in queer and transgender studies rethinks sex or gender categories (Bornstein 1998; Nestle, Wilchins, and Howell 2002; Wilchins 1997) and introduces terms to subvert dominant gender constructions, including gender-neutral pronouns such as *ze* and *hir* (Bornstein 1998). See also Wilchins's *Read My Lips* (1997). Because this alternative language is always in flux, it is useful for CYC practitioners to scan the Internet to explore the range of young people's gender queer experiences.

References

Aapola, S., M. Gonick, and A. Harris. 2005. *Young Femininity: Girlhood, Power, and Social Change*. New York: Palgrave Macmillan.

Amos, V., and P. Parmar. 1981. "Resistance and Responses: The Experiences of Black Girls in Britain." In *Feminism for Girls: An Adventure Story*, ed. A. McRobbie and T. McCabe, 129-48. London: Routledge and Kegan Paul.

Anzaldúa, G.E. 2002. "(Un)natural Bridges, (Un)safe Spaces." In *This Bridge We Call Home: Radical Visions for Transformation*, ed. G.E. Anzaldúa and A. Keating, 1-6. New York: Routledge.

Bettis, P., and N. Adams, eds. 2005. *Geographies of Girlhood: Identities In-Between*. New York: Lawrence Erlbaum.

Bornstein, K. 1998. *My Gender Workbook*. New York: Routledge.

Brown, L.M., and C. Gilligan. 1992. *Meeting at the Crossroads: Women's Psychology and Girls' Development*. New York: Ballantine.

Canadian Women's Foundation. 2005. *Girls in Canada 2005*. http://www.cdnwomen.org/PDFs/EN/CWF-GirlsCanada-Report05.pdf.

Carlson, C. 2000. "Ethnic Differences in Processes Contributing to the Self-Esteem of Early Adolescent Girls." *Journal of Early Adolescence* 20, 1: 44-67.

Chantler, K. 2005. "From Disconnection to Connection: Race, Gender, and the Politics of Therapy." *British Journal of Guidance and Counselling* 33, 2: 239-56.

Chantler, K., and S. Smailes. 2004. "Working with Differences: Issues for Research and Counselling." *Counselling and Psychotherapy Research* 4, 2: 34-39.

Charles, C.E. 2010. "Complicating Hetero-Femininities: Young Women, Sexualities, and 'Girl Power' at School." *International Journal of Qualitative Studies in Education* 23, 1: 33-47.

Chesney-Lind, M., and K. Irwin. 2004. "From Badness to Meanness: Popular Constructions of Contemporary Girlhood." In *All about the Girl: Culture, Power, and Identity*, ed. A. Harris, 45-58. New York: Routledge.

Davies, B. 2000. *Body of Writing 1990-1999.* Walnut Creek: AltaMira Press.

DAWN Ontario. N.d. *Family Violence against Women with Disabilities.* http://dawn.thot.net/violence_wwd.html.

Deleuze, G., and F. Guattari. 1987. *A Thousand Plateaus: Capitalism and Schizophrenia.* Minneapolis: University of Minnesota Press.

Fine, M. 2004. "Foreword." In *All about the Girl: Culture, Power, and Identity,* ed. A. Harris, xi-xvi. New York: Routledge.

Foucault, M. 1978. *The History of Sexuality Volume I: An Introduction.* New York: Vintage Books.

–. 1980. *Power/Knowledge.* Brighton, UK: Harvester.

Girls Action Foundation. 2009, September. *Racialized Girls Research Review: A Compilation of Research on Racialized Girls' and Young Women's Issues.* http://www.girlsaction foundation.ca/.

Gonick, M. 2003. *Between Femininities: Ambivalence, Identity, and the Education of Girls.* Albany: SUNY Press.

Griffin, C. 2004. "Good Girls, Bad Girls: Anglocentrism and Diversity in the Constitution of Contemporary Girlhood." In *All about the Girl: Culture, Power, and Identity,* ed. A. Harris, 29-44. New York: Routledge.

Handa, A. 2003. *Of Silk Saris and Mini-Skirts: South Asian Girls Walk the Tightrope of Culture.* Toronto: Women's Press.

Harley, D.A., K. Jolivette, K. McCormick, and K. Tice. 2002. "Race, Class, and Gender: A Constellation of Possibilities with Implications for Counselling." *Journal of Multicultural Counseling and Development* 30: 216-38.

Harris, A., ed. 2004. *All about the Girl: Culture, Power, and Identity.* New York: Routledge.

Hernández, D., and B. Rehman. 2002. *Colonize This! Young Women of Color on Today's Feminism.* New York: Seal Press.

Hey, V. 1997. *The Company She Keeps: An Ethnography of Girls' Friendships.* Buckingham, MA: Open University Press.

Jiwani, Y., C. Steenbergen, and C. Mitchell, eds. 2006. *Girlhood: Redefining the Limits.* Montreal: Black Rose Books.

Laenui, P. 2002. "Processes of Decolonization." In *Reclaiming Indigenous Voice and Vision,* ed. M. Battiste, 150-60. Vancouver: UBC Press.

Lalik, K., and L. Oliver. 2005. "'The Beauty Walk' as a Social Space for Messages about the Female Body: Toward Transformative Collaboration." In *Geographies of Girlhood: Identities In-Between,* ed. P.J. Bettis and N.G. Adams, 95-107. New York: Lawrence Erlbaum Associates.

Lawrence, B. 2004. *"Real" Indians and Others: Mixed-Blood Urban Native Peoples and Indigenous Nationhood.* Vancouver: UBC Press.

Lee, J.A. 2005. "Talking about 'Us': Racialized Girls, Cultural Citizenship, and Growing Up under Whiteness." In *Gendered Intersections: A Collection of Readings for Women's and Gender Studies,* ed. L. Biggs and P. Downe, 164-69. Halifax: Fernwood Press.

Mattingly, M., and C. Stuart. 2002. "The North American Certification Project (NACP) Competencies for Professional Child and Youth Work Practitioners." *Journal of Child and Youth Care Work* 17: 16-49. See also http://www.acycp.org/childcarecompr.pdf.

McClelland, S.I., and M. Fine. 2008. "Rescuing a Theory of Adolescent Sexual Excess: Young Women and Wanting." In *Next Wave Cultures: Feminism, Subcultures, Activism,* ed. A. Harris, 83-102. New York: Routledge.

Mikel-Brown, L. 2005. "In the Bad or Good of Girlhood: Social Class, Schooling, and White Femininities." In *Beyond Silenced Voices: Class, Race, and Gender in the United States Schools*, ed. L. Weis and M. Fine, 147-62. Albany: SUNY Press.

Minh-ha, T.T. 1997. "Not Like You/Like You: Postcolonial Women and the Interlocking Questions of Identity and Difference." In *Dangerous Liaisons: Gender, Nation, and Postcolonial Perspectives*, ed. E. Shohat and X. McClintock, 415-19. Minneapolis: University of Minnesota Press.

Mohanty, C.T. 2003. *Feminism without Borders: Decolonizing Theory, Practicing Solidarity.* Durham: Duke University Press.

Moore, K.A., D.R. Morrison, and D.A. Glei. 1995. "Welfare and Adolescent Sex: The Effects of Family History, Benefit Levels, and Community Context." *Journal of Family and Economic Issues* 16, 2-3: 207-37.

Nam, V. 2001. *Yell-Oh Girls! Emerging Voices Explore Culture, Identity, and Growing Up Asian American.* Berkeley: Harper Paperbacks.

Narayan, U., and S. Harding. 2000. "Introduction." In *Decentering the Center: Philosophy for a Multiculturalist, Postcolonial, and Feminist World*, ed. U. Narayan and S. Harding, vii-xv. Indianapolis: Indiana University Press.

National Clearinghouse on Family Violence. 2004. *Violence against Women with Disabilities.* Ottawa: Government of Canada.

Nestle, J., R. Wilchins, and C. Howell, eds. 2002. *Gender Queer: Voices from Beyond the Sexual Binary.* Los Angeles: Alyson.

Ormond, A. 2004. "Beneath the Surface of Voice and Silence: Researching the Home Front." In *All about the Girl: Culture, Power, and Identity*, ed. A. Harris, 29-44. New York: Routledge.

Pereira, A. 2008. "Does Multiculturalism Recognise or 'Minoritise' Minorities?" *Studies in Ethnicity and Nationalism* 8, 2: 349-56.

Pipher, M. 1994. *Reviving Ophelia: Saving the Selves of Adolescent Girls.* New York: Grosset/ Putnam.

Proweller, A. 2000. "Re-Writing/-Righting Lives: Voices of Pregnant and Parenting Teenagers in an Alternative School." In *Construction Sites: Excavating Race, Class, and Gender among Urban Youth*, ed. L. Weis and M. Fine, 100-20. New York: Teachers College Press.

Renold, E., and J. Ringrose. 2008. "Regulation and Rupture: Mapping Tween and Teenage Girls' Resistance to the Heterosexual Matrix." *Feminist Theory* 9, 3: 313-39.

Robinson, K., and C. Davies. 2007. "Tomboys and Sissy Girls: Young Girls' Negotiations of Femininity and Masculinity." *International Journal of Equity and Innovation in Early Childhood* 5, 2: 17-31.

Rutman, D., S. Strega, M. Callahan, and L. Dominelli. 2002. "'Undeserving' Mothers? Practitioners' Experiences Working with Young Mothers in/from Care." *Child and Family Social Work* 7, 3: 149-59.

Saewyc, E., C. Poon, N. Wang, Y. Homma, A. Smith, and McCreary Centre Society. 2007. *Not Yet Equal: The Health of Lesbian, Gay, and Bisexual Youth in BC.* Vancouver: McCreary Centre Society.

Smith, L.T. 2001. "Constituting Spaces for Countering the Stories of Encounter and Encountering the Counter Stories." *Under the Covers: Theorizing the Politics of Counter Stories*, special issue of *Critical Psychology: International Journal of Critical Psychology* 4: 167-82.

Spivak, G.C. 1996. *The Spivak Reader: Edited Works by Gayatri Chakravorty Spivak.* New York: Routledge.

Suarez-Orozco, M. 2001. "Afterword: Understanding and Serving the Children of Immigrants." *Immigration and Education*, special issue of *Harvard Educational Review* 71, 3: 579-89.

Tolman, D., and M. Brydon-Miller, eds. 2001. *From Subjects to Subjectivities: A Handbook of Interpretive and Participatory Methods*. New York: New York University Press.

Torres, S., ed. 1999. *That Body Image Thing: Young Women Speak Out!* Ottawa: CRIAW.

Varcoe, C. 2002. "Women, Inequality, and Violence." In *Health, Illness, and Health Care in Canada*, 3rd ed., ed. B.S. Bolaria and H. Dickenson, 211-30. Scarborough: Nelson Thomson Learning.

Walkerdine, V. 1988. The Mastery of Reason: Cognitive Development and the Production of Rationality. London/New York: Routledge.

Ward, J., and B. Benjamin. 2004. "Women, Girls, and the Unfinished Work of Connection: A Critical Review of American Girls' Studies." In *All about the Girl: Culture, Power, and Identity*, ed. A. Harris, 5-28. New York: Routledge.

Weaver, G. 1990. "The Crisis of Cross-Cultural Child and Youth Care." In *Choices in Caring*, ed. M. Krueger and N. Powell, 67-103. Washington, DC: Child Welfare League of America.

Wilchins, R.A. 1997. *Read My Lips: Sexual Subversion and the End of Gender*. Ithaca: Firebrand.

Youdell, D. 2005. "Sex-Gender-Sexuality: How Sex, Gender, and Sexuality Constellations Are Constituted in Secondary Schools." *Gender and Education* 17, 3: 249-70.

Father Involvement Initiatives   6
Social Inclusion or the (Re)Construction of Hegemonic Masculinity?

B. DENISE HODGINS

Over the past forty years, the focus on fatherhood and fathering practices within the social sciences has grown tremendously. Empirical studies demonstrate that father involvement has significant implications for "men on their own path of adult development, for their wives and partners in the coparenting relationship and, most importantly, for their children in terms of social, emotional, physical, and cognitive development" (Allen and Daly 2007, 1). Findings such as these have contributed to an increased attention to fathers from research and practice-based activities as well as from political and policy perspectives. Using various critical lenses, this chapter questions how current Canadian father involvement initiatives foster the social inclusion of fathers in parenting discourses and practices and whether such initiatives (re)construct a narrow vision of father involvement based on dominant discourses of masculinity.

Historical and Cultural Context of Father Involvement Initiatives
The maternal focus within the history of the Western modern family has meant that fatherhood has not received a significant amount of attention (Broughton and Rogers 2007; Comacchio 1997). Most of the published literature has focused primarily on urban-industrial cultures

of the past 200 years (Hewlett and Lamb 2005), often neglecting particular groups of fathers in the discussion (e.g., indigenous fathers in North America; see Pleck and Pleck 1997). Although there has always been a range of diverse fathering styles and ideals of fatherhood, it is the image of father based on a Western view of family and parenting practices that has dominated the literature and the popular imagination (Broughton and Rogers 2007; Lupton and Barclay 1997; Pleck and Pleck 1997). Iconic images such as the stern colonial father (Pleck and Pleck 1997), the detached Victorian *paterfamilias* (Broughton and Rogers 2007), and the breadwinner-playmate of the late twentieth century obscure the multiple, and often contradictory, experiences and meanings of fatherhood that have existed over time and across cultures.

The current North American dominant image of the "involved father," particularly as portrayed through the media, is one of a nurturing co-parent who provides both emotional and financial support for his family. Canadian newspaper and website articles describe this "new" father as one who participates in prenatal classes, takes part in the daily care of his children from infancy, and remains involved throughout his children's schooling (e.g., Beck 2005; Canadian Press 2003; "Involved Dads Feeling Invisible" 2006; Lorinc 2002; Nyhan 2006; Owens 2006). Fathers are heralded as "more involved with their children than fathers from generations past" (Beck 2005), and articles espouse how important it is for fathers to "be there" for their children (Beck 2005; Brott 2006; Hoffman 2005; "Involved Dads Feeling Invisible" 2006). Anthropologist Barry Hewlett (2000, 66) has observed that today's prescribed role for fathers as parenting partners is "relatively unique in human history." Although some researchers have questioned whether the conduct of fathers has actually changed as much as the image of fathers, most adults *believe* that fatherhood has changed dramatically from their childhood experiences of fathering (LaRossa 1988).

Drawing on the theories of Griswold (1993) and reflecting the theoretical contributions of Hondagneu-Sotelo and Messner, Catlett and McKenry (2004, 183) point out that the highly involved father acts as a marker for class status: "The 'new fatherhood' is viewed as a sign that one has knowledge, time, and an inclination to embrace more positive, inclusive visions of parenthood." Caragata and Miller (2008, 22) propose that "men balancing a breadwinner role with a more active caregiver role have the opportunity to model a different notion of citizen that extends beyond the labour force to include the nurture and care of future generations." Is this "different notion of citizen" intended to be an expectation of all fathers or an opening up of possibilities for what diverse fathering can look like? Is the message that fathers are "good citizens" only if they are involved with their families (Bergman and Hobson 2002; Miller 2006), and is the notion of involvement open to multiple conceptualizations from families, service providers, and policy makers? Although the plea for active paternal engagement is reported as new, in her review of American fatherhood Pleck (2004, 52) points out that there have been calls for father involvement throughout that history: "What is striking is how many and various are the claims about why fathers should be involved. These rationales reflect the prevailing beliefs and anxieties of the age."

Fathers of the Past

By the nineteenth century, within North America and Western Europe, industrialization resulted in a decline in farming and artisanal work and an increase in factory work outside the home (Broughton and Rogers 2007; Pleck and Pleck 1997). With that change came profound changes in familial roles, including those of gender relationships (Broughton and Rogers 2007), as male labour moved away from the house and as women became more tied to the home and to children in the home. Men's primary identity became linked with the shop/factory/office away from the home and the role of provider for the family. Although fathers were still encouraged to be involved in childrearing for the good of their children (Pleck and Pleck 1997), mothers became the primary target for household literature and advice about parenting, which previously had been aimed at fathers (Broughton and Rogers 2007; Lupton and Barclay 1997). Drawing on the work of Donzelot, Foucault, and Urwin, Lupton and Barclay (1997, 38) write that "mothers were encouraged to engage in self-surveillance and self-regulation by monitoring their own activities and those of their children and comparing them to 'norms' of behaviour, growth and development that had been instituted by expert discourses." Mothers' care of their children in the home was deemed essential to the children's well-being, though the reality was that many working-class women at this time did paid work outside the home (Lupton and Barclay 1997). Tosh suggests that, "for much of the nineteenth century, the 'cult of the home,' underpinned by evangelical beliefs and practices, was a key component of [the] bourgeois family ideal, and as such was as central to hegemonic understandings of masculinity as it was to femininity and childhood" (cited by Broughton and Rogers 2007, 7).

The middle-class father of the mid-nineteenth century was to be both a playmate for his children and the lead source of Christian nurturance and guidance to counter the dangers of immoral influences outside the family (Pleck 2004). Broughton and Rogers (2007, 8) suggest that, within Victorian England, as the middle-class ideal of fatherly involvement and authority was ebbing at the end of the nineteenth century, working-class families were being urged to conform to this middle-class ideal, "to new standards of respectability hinging on marriage and the bread winner norm." By the late nineteenth century, calls for father involvement were less religious in nature and increasingly came from physicians, health reformers, and scientists (Pleck 2004). Citing Frank, Pleck (2004) points out that this literature had little to say about the tasks of fatherhood; instead, it celebrated the fertility of men and reinvested the paternal role with masculine meaning.

Citing Griswold (1993), Pleck and Pleck (1997, 78) suggest that, though it was the magazine writers and home economists at the turn of the twentieth century who invented the fatherhood ideal, it was the psychologists, sociologists, social workers, home economists, and family service counsellors beginning in the 1920s who "propagated" it. A class of men now had the means and leisure to be involved with their children, and they were joined by "a group of intellectuals and social scientists who gave this relationship intellectual meaning and academic responsibility." Comacchio's (1997, 404) review of the new fatherhood ideal during the interwar years in Canada states that "the urban, middle-class, Euro-Canadian focus of most of the advice literature is apparent. However inappropriate its class and racial assumptions or inapplicable its directives, it was intended to cut through barriers of class, race, and ethnicity, as its mass production and dissemination by state agencies indicate."

Although the call for fathers to be at home and involved in child-rearing was sounded in the United States (Griswold 1993; LaRossa 1997) and Canada (Comacchio 1997), this does not mean that the perception of the father's role as provider for the family diminished. In her review of the American good-dad/bad-dad complex, Pleck (2004, 52) comments that the "long history of concern about the deadbeat dad is an indirect way of revealing the centrality of the breadwinner role to American fatherhood." She goes on to say that, "not only was a father seen as having this responsibility, but the government also staked out a role to play in requiring a father to fulfill his breadwinner responsibility." In Canada, fathers' breadwinner role was sanctioned by the state through interventionary legislation and regulatory agencies such as welfare and public health. "During the Great Depression, relief was unwaveringly premised on the principle of male breadwinner rights" (Comacchio 1997, 394). Drawing on Griswold (1993), Pleck and Pleck (1997, 43) write that "the central lesson of the depression was that paternal involvement was never the main goal of fathers or their children: money was." With the advent of World War II, men's breadwinning abilities were restored (Griswold 1993, 161).

Beginning in the 1920s, calls for increased paternal involvement were partly an antidote to maternal overprotection and what Pleck (2004, 39) refers to as "the manly father's effort to make his son more masculine." Comacchio (1997, 395) cites the Council on Child and Family Welfare, Canada's central social welfare agency in the 1930s, as writing that "'in the average home the fathers contribute too little to the family life, the mothers too much,' and that this was not 'a healthy or desirable arrangement for the family.'" Through the council, fathers were encouraged to "become involved in playful activities, in providing moral support, and as masculine role models." Bolstered by the increased academic interest during and after World War II in father absence, calls for increased paternal involvement came more vehemently than before (Pleck 1998). Fathers were deemed necessary as sex role models to help promote socially sanctioned gender roles. Children needed their fathers because of the differences it was believed they brought to the parenting relationship (Lupton and Barclay 1997). "What family experts envisioned was the injection of male presence into the family, not a fundamental reassessment of male and female gender roles" (Weiss, cited by Pleck 2004, 41).

It was not until the 1970s and the rise of feminism that the call for increased father involvement became a push for egalitarian parenting. Pleck (2004, 42) describes Lamb et al.'s (1985, 1987) typology of father involvement as "an academic response to feminist demands that husbands and fathers share equally in the responsibilities of child raising." There have been two contradictory interpretations of this increased attention to the "role played by men in the domestic realm and the maintaining of inequalities between men and women" (Lupton and Barclay 1997, 3). On the one hand, that men are taking a more equal share has been hailed as progressive; on the other, this development can be seen as reactionary in the sense that men are competing with women and taking over the one sphere where women have traditionally held some limited power and acknowledged expertise (Burman 2008, 163).

Conceptualizing Father Involvement

When Lamb et al. (1985, 1987) introduced the term "father involvement" into social science research, their typology was characterized by interaction, availability, and responsibility. Since that time, the field of fatherhood research has grown a great deal (Cabrera et al. 2000; Lamb and Tamis-LeMonda 2004). But how much has this research, which has acted as a guide for better strategies and interventions in parenting, "provide[d] a highly normative perspective on fatherhood by advocating appropriate behaviours in men and identifying those who fail to fit the ideal of the involved father" (Lupton and Barclay 1997, 51)?

One of the major criticisms of Lamb et al.'s (1985, 1987) typology of father involvement has been that it did not sufficiently account for the impacts culture, religion, and economics have on a father's involvement with his children (Palkovitz 1997). As Hewlett (2000, 61) asserts, "cultural assumptions about the roles of fathers and why paternal involvement is highly desirable" must be taken into account. Lupton and Barclay (1997, 51) suggest that, in terms of father involvement, culture still tends to be represented "as an external influence, shaped predominantly via social structures such as the family, education, ethnicity, economic and workplace issues." Alternatively, they suggest that fatherhood needs to be explored as a cultural construct for dominant Western culture, to investigate the roles of language, discourse, and representation in the cultural construction of fatherhood.

Although interest in father involvement from researchers, policy makers, and family program developers has increased, what has prompted this interest to a large degree differs across nations. In the United States, initiatives have been driven by perceived problems associated with the rise in the number of "single mothers," non-marital births, "absent fathers," and a lack of child support – what Hawkins and Dollahite (1997) refer to as a deficit perspective on fatherhood. The growth in fatherhood research in the United States has paralleled the development of government policies aimed at fathers (Gavanas 2004) and a strong increase in the number of programs designed to promote father involvement (McBride and Lutz 2004). In 1995, the US federal government introduced the Father Initiative, which resulted in an increase in programs aimed to improve father responsibility, particularly financial responsibility (Gavanas 2004). Targeted approaches to "problems with fathers" have also led to the growth of general interest in fathers and the complexity and diversity of their experiences (Lero, Ashbourne, and Whitehead 2006).

In Canada, though we have not developed as large a body of scholarship or as rich a portrait of fatherhood as researchers in the United States (Dubeau 2002), fatherhood initiatives have increased. Scholars across Canada explore various aspects of fatherhood from a range of social science disciplines (Dubeau 2002), and, with the establishment of the Father Involvement Research Alliance (FIRA) in 2003, academic and community-based research related to fatherhood has grown. Federally, the government has supported several father-focused initiatives, including the National Project on Fathering, funded in 1999 through Health Canada; the My Daddy Matters Because project, funded through the Public Health Agency of Canada (PHAC) from 2002 to 2005; and the FIRA community-university partnership research from 2003 to 2008. Calls for increased government support of, and consolidated action for, father involvement continue (e.g., Father Involvement Initiative Ontario Network, n.d.; Long 2008).

Raising the Profile of Fathers' Importance

A common theme underlying father involvement initiatives in North America is the intention to raise awareness and acknowledgment of the importance of fathers' participation in parenting their children. For example, the Canadian federally funded project My Daddy Matters Because ran between 2002 and 2005 and aimed to increase community mobilization in "promoting the place and role of father" (My Daddy Matters Because 2004, 7). This project (n.d.c) included a social marketing campaign with print, radio, and television advertisements. Research demonstrating that father involvement has a significant impact on children's development often provides the empirical evidence that supports initiatives designed to raise the profile of fathers' importance to children (see Allen and Daly 2007, and Marsiglio et al. 2000, for summaries of research evidence as well as a recent meta-analysis of twenty-four long-term studies by Sarkadi et al. 2008). This research has been an important focus for those who advocate for more just and equitable standards of child custody, access, and parental responsibility within separation and divorce (Kruk 2008). It has also been used to rationalize why family program and service providers should assess the extent to which they include fathers (Bolté et al. 2001; Devault et al. 2005; My Daddy Matters Because 2004, n.d.a, n.d.b). One of the problems, however, with the children's development discourse is that it "render[s] invisible class, gender and other structures of inequality among adults" (Dobrowolski and Jenson 2004, 155).

Changing Fathering Behaviour

Father involvement initiatives might aim to increase the public consciousness of and appreciation for the importance of father involvement in parenting, but they are also purposeful attempts to change attitudes and behaviours related to father involvement. In their overview of the status of parenting programs in the United States designed specifically for fathers, McBride and Lutz (2004, 447) cite several researchers (Levine and Pitt; McBride and Rane 1997; Palm) who believe parenting programs developed for fathers "may be one way to help men more effectively live up to the changing societal expectations for fatherhood." These changing expectations are often described in terms of a more "hands-on" approach to parenting, where fathers are increasingly engaged in the daily care of their children. Many of the government-funded father involvement initiatives in Canada have been directed at the behaviour and attitude of service providers so that they might better support paternal engagement (Bolté et al. 2001; My Daddy Matters Because, n.d.a). Parent education advocates assert that more research in Canada is needed to better understand how to attract fathers to family resource programs and how to engage and sustain their involvement (Russell 2003a, 2003b).

A recent study of formal parenting education programs in British Columbia (Hodgins 2007) found that, though four of the participating programs purposefully included father involvement content, generally aimed at increasing fathers' care-giving behaviours, paternal engagement was not an integral theme in most of the programs. Fathers were often sidelined as support persons or helpers for primary caregivers (mothers) or were absent altogether from the course material. Similar findings have been presented in terms of parenting guide books (Fleming and Tobin 2005) and Canadian newspaper articles about parenting (Wall and Arnold 2007). The lack of acknowledgment that fathers can be (and indeed want to be) effective primary caregivers to young children is problematic in that it further embeds mothers as the *natural* caregivers of children. However, the active attempt to change fathering behaviour can be equally problematic.

Doucet (2006, 247) cites the work of American sociologist Scott Coltrane that "illuminates well the unexpected link between promoting active fathering and the dangers of it being used to promote a particular narrow model of *the family.*" Gavanas (2004) explores this kind of "moral enterprise" most evident in the US Father Responsibility Movement. Miller's Foucauldian examination of the Barbershop Fatherhood Organization, a small branch of the larger umbrella non-profit organization called the Birthing Project, is an excellent example of how father promotion efforts through an organization can also "serve as a function of State control to construct and regulate responsible and fatherly subjectivities" (2006, 4). Lupton and Barclay (1997, 51) caution that most interventions in parenting draw on a body of research that "provides a highly normative perspective on fatherhood by advocating appropriate behaviours in men and identifying those who fail to fit the ideal of the involved father."

So Who Is This Ideal "Involved Father"?

In terms of fatherhood scholarship, Lamb and Tamis-LeMonda (2004, 14) point out that "scholars are slowly (and not consistently) recognizing the diverse array of family types and sociocultural expectations and demands that shape paternal roles, family processes, and child development." As noted by the Father Involvement Research Alliance (2006, 1), "we can't talk about father involvement as a monolithic experience ... Fathering occurs under many conditions and many family contexts, depending on factors such as age, ethnicity, marital status and sexual orientation."

Although this caution is often heralded by fatherhood researchers (Allen and Daly 2007; Day and Lamb 2004; Marsiglio et al. 2000; Tamis-LeMonda and Cabrera 2002), there continues to be a lack of studies that explore the heterogeneity of father involvement (Ball 2010; Doucet 2006; Parke 2004). It remains that "most of what we know about father involvement comes from investigations of middle-class men of European descent" (Tamis-LeMonda and Cabrera 2002, 605), with little critique of the assumptions of paternity and heterosexuality that are generally taken for granted in debates about fatherhood (Hearn 2002).

Although some researchers are attempting to listen better to fathers of varying ethnicities (e.g., Ball and George 2006; Marsiglio, Roy, and Fox 2005; Parke et al. 2004; Roopnarine 2004), the lack of understanding of fathers' experiences within diverse ethnic communities impacts how well father initiatives actually include, and thereby support, all fathers. Assumptions about fathering needs and expectations are typically situated within a Eurocentric/Western paradigm. As Parke (2004, 459) explains, "a universalist assumption underlies much of the theorizing in the social sciences. This assumes that the processes noted in studies of Western fathers – or more narrowly, Euro-American and middle-class fathers – will be generalizable both to other cultures and to non-Euro-American groups."

If diverse fathers do get factored in to father initiatives, such as through an active recruitment strategy, the initiatives themselves often remain culturally inappropriate as they are situated within a Western paradigm (Lero et al. 2006; Long 2008). Dominant Western cultural messages about materialism (Stockley and Daly 1999) and individualism (Long

2008) impact how we perceive fathers' "roles," and parenting practices in general, as well as how policies and programs are developed to support families. When the language of inclusion is used, it does not necessarily take into account social, economic, legal, and political injustices that "prevent certain individuals, groups and whole populations from being included" (Long 2008, 13). Long believes that developing and operating father involvement initiatives that are socially inclusive means acknowledging how father involvement policies and programs are informed by normative assumptions and cultural stereotypes that hinder certain groups/populations of fathers and parents from receiving the support they need to be positively involved in the lives of their children (2008, 25).

Aboriginal Fathers in Canada

Compared to other fathers in Canada, Aboriginal fathers face a unique set of circumstances directly related to the legacy of colonialism and assimilation. Segregation of indigenous peoples from colonial society began through a reservation system that removed nations from their traditional territories and often dispersed clans. Attempts to assimilate indigenous peoples into colonial society included the prohibition of tribal governance and cultural practices as well as ongoing efforts to displace clans and separate parents and children through residential schools and later the foster care system (Royal Commission on Aboriginal Peoples 1996).

Extensive neglect and physical and sexual abuse of indigenous children in residential schools and foster homes have been well documented (Fournier and Crey 1997). It is generally acknowledged that most indigenous men and women in Canada either are survivors of residential schools or have suffered "secondary trauma" as a result of being born to parents who lacked parenting role models (Ing, cited by Ball 2010, 32).

Loss of language and culture, intergenerational trauma, the disruption of the intergenerational transmission of parenting practices, and ongoing racism all impact how, when, and why Aboriginal fathers are involved with their children (Ball 2009, 2010). Although there are important differences (as well as similarities) in the experiences of Aboriginal fathers compared with those of non-Aboriginal fathers, among the 1 million people in Canada who identify themselves as Aboriginal (First Nations, Inuit, and Métis) "significant cultural, economic, social, and political differences exist among the hundreds of cultural groups subsumed under the general terms *Indigenous* or *Aboriginal*" (Ball 2009, 31).

Findings from what is known to be the first empirical study exploring fatherhood experiences from the perspectives of eighty Canadian Aboriginal fathers (Ball 2010; Ball and George 2006) highlight "the need for policy reforms and systemic program solutions within a post-colonial, social justice agenda that requires a long-term commitment" (Ball and George 2006, 17). Ball (2009, 36) suggests that a framework for such reforms must include what she terms a "temporal horizon," which "encompasses fathers' understandings of the sociohistorical conditioning of their challenges, recognizing the long shadow cast by colonial government interventions in Indigenous societies, and the desire to 'turn things around." There is also a need for more research based on listening to fathers' stories from different Canadian Aboriginal communities.

Immigrant and Refugee Fathers in Canada

Just as Ball (2010) describes the lack of research that explores Canadian Aboriginal fathers' stories, so too Esté and Tachble (2009, 140) refer to "a dearth of research" on immigrant and refugee men about their experiences as fathers: "In general, migration research has tended to be associated with the experiences of women and the challenges facing them." A major challenge facing many immigrant and refugee fathers in Canada is unemployment or chronic underemployment. Shimoni, Esté, and Clark's (2003) Calgary-based study with twenty-four immigrant and refugee fathers of preschool children from the former Yugoslavia, South America, South East Asia, and China found that unemployment/underemployment was a major theme. Esté and Tachble's (2009) research with twenty Sudanese refugee men and fourteen Russian immigrants raising children in Calgary had similar results. Contributing factors to unemployment/underemployment include the lack of recognition of foreign employment credentials, "inadequate language proficiency and/

or discriminatory hiring practices" (Bhandari, Horvath, and To, cited by Esté and Tachble 2009, 148). Another potential challenge faced by immigrant and refugee fathers is a lack of social support, such as family members and other community support people whom fathers would have had in their previous home countries (Esté and Tachble 2009). Feelings of social isolation are compounded with "the struggles of acculturation, language acquisition, and employment" (Shimoni, Esté, and Clark 2003, 565).

These two studies present unique challenges faced by some immigrant and refugee fathers, but they cannot be generalized to all immigrant and refugee fathers in Canada. Just as Ball and George (2006, 140) caution us against the "over-generalized, 'pan-Aboriginal' interpretation of Aboriginal fathers' experiences," so too a cautious statement can be made in regard to immigrant and refugee fathers. They do not experience or take up acculturation in the same way (Shimoni, Esté, and Clark 2003), nor do they practise fathering in the same way. Even in these few small samples of immigrant and refugee fathers in one urban centre in Canada, there is evidence of the diversity of fathers' experiences. The heterogeneity of fatherhood is not simply between cultural groups but within groups as well. Esté and Tachble (2009, 152) suggest that, "given the increasing diversity of Canada's population, similar research should be conducted not only with other immigrant and refugee populations but also with long-standing racialized communities."

Transforming Social Inclusion
As many father initiatives relate to the perceived "changes in societal expectations for fathers" (McBride and Rane 1997, 191), what does it mean for those fathers who do not see themselves in those terms? Furthermore, in terms of social inclusion, Shakir raises an important question – "included in what?" (cited in Long 2008, 13). She further notes that an assimilationist vision of social inclusion focuses primarily on removing the cultural, legal, and/or economic barriers that prevent certain individuals, groups, and populations from receiving all the privileges of citizenship. Not only does this perspective take for granted that there is something fundamentally right about being in "the centre,"

but it also presupposes that the goal of inclusion is to expand the centre to include those who are willing to pursue some predetermined version of "the good life" (cited in Long 2008, 13).

In his call for inclusive father initiatives that truly respect the diversity and plurality of fathering experiences, Long (2008, 15) suggests a transformative perspective on social inclusion. This means a commitment to challenge assimilationist thinking and to address the range of "social, legal and political as well as economic experiences, circumstances and perspectives of those whom [father initiatives] are intended to serve." Drawing on Richmond and Saloojee, Long states that this also means ensuring that inclusive policy and program initiatives link poverty and economic vulnerability with other sources of exclusion, such as racism, disability, rejection of difference, and historical oppression.

Long's vision of a transformative social inclusion for all fathers fits with Palkovitz's (1997) call to recognize the impact that culture, religion, and economics have on a father's involvement with his children. I would add to Palkovitz's assertion that it is also necessary to recognize an understanding of men and fathers as gendered beings.

Gendering Fatherhood

The post-structuralist notion of the interrelationship between discourse and subjectivity, related contemporary redefinitions of masculinities, and the current focus in the academic literature on the performative dimension of gender have implications for how the concept of "the father" should be understood (and, by corollary, femininity and "the mother") (Lupton and Barclay 1997, 14).

It has been more than ten years since Lupton and Barclay (1997) pointed to post-structuralism and critical studies of gender as promising avenues on which to explore conceptualizations of the father. Their observation was that few scholars had drawn on these theoretical perspectives. Instead, evolutionary and categorical analyses, which do not attend to the complex, dynamic, ongoing, and contradictory shifts found in "doing" fatherhood, had dominated the field. Although a gender construction lens is utilized by some researchers (e.g., Hobson 2002; Lupton and Barclay 1997; Nentwich 2008), I would argue that it is an area deserving of additional attention. Gendering fatherhood, exploring its gendered dimensions, needs to be done at the domestic level (e.g., Lupton and Barclay 1997; Nentwich 2008) as well as within what Morgan (2002) refers to as the institutional triangle: family, state, and market (see Hobson 2002). Examinations of fatherhood within institutional contexts shift the "emphasis from the practices of fathering to the rights, duties and obligations associated with fatherhood" (Morgan 2002, 274). Although exploring the domestic contexts of fathering practices is important, it is imperative that we think beyond the private, domestic, or particular and see fatherhood in terms of its wider structural linkages (Hobson and Morgan 2002).

Parenting Vis-à-Vis the Heterosexual Gender Binary

"The gendering of fathers as men does not suggest any kind of essentialism or inevitability" (Hearn 2002, 245), though the importance of fathers' involvement is often couched in terms of their essential and uniquely male role in parenting. One example is a recent policy document about the social inclusion of all fathers in father initiatives, which begins with the statement "most of us take for granted that fathers play an *essential* role in the lives of their children, families and communities" (Long 2008, 1; emphasis added). Another example is a government briefing note from family service providers that advocates for stronger government funding to support father initiatives due to the essential and unique role fathers play in the lives of their children (Father Involvement Initiative Ontario Network, n.d.).

The notion of fathers' *essentiality* presumes children cannot effectively develop without a participating father, though research studies have demonstrated this is not the case (see Pleck 2007; Silverstein and Auerbach 1999). Furthermore, what form of masculinity is envisioned in this essential, uniquely male parent? Are fathers who are gay, bisexual, or transgendered, or those who do not like sports or rough-and-tumble play, part of this vision (Pleck 2008)? Conceptualizing fathers as important because of their unique maleness in parenting perpetuates the heterosexual gender binary. As Morgan (2002, 275) points out, "most of the discourses around fatherhood have been implicitly or explicitly discourses about the construction ... and privileging of heterosexual identities." Gendering fathers means "naming fathers as men, as socially constructed and not naturally this or that" (Hearn 2002, 271). "Once a discourse becomes 'normal' and 'natural,' it is difficult to think and act outside it" (St. Pierre 2000, 485).

Deconstructing the "essential father" theory (see Pleck 2007; Silverstein and Auerbach 1999) is not necessarily welcomed by those who work with family and father support programs, even if the attempt is made to clearly advocate for the *importance* of fathers, albeit while questioning the notion of *essentiality* and *uniquely male qualities*. As Gergen (2007, 364) has commented, the response to relativist arguments is tepid, "even when it is clear that [they] are not intent on disrupting foundationalist traditions (but rather, on understanding them in a more inclusive context)."

Power and Masculinities

Gendering fatherhood is not "simply about difference, but about power and inequality" (Morgan 2002, 275). Hearn (2002, 245, 271) asserts that "fatherhood needs to be understood as an institution, historically constructed as a form of certain men's power," and further states that "empirical studies and theoretical analyses of fatherhood rarely explicitly attend to the social construction and then deconstruction of the dominant." Critical masculinities studies remind us that, though multiple forms of masculinity exist, they are not all equal in their persuasion or dominance. Morgan (2002, 280) writes that the concept of hegemonic masculinity, as developed by Connell (1987), arguably evolved to counter the sense of complete freedom of choice that the notion of masculinities might conjure up: "The idea of hegemonic masculinity suggests that, despite the apparent range of ways of 'doing masculinity,' there remain deeply embedded and subtly coercive notions of what it means to be a man."

What are the impacts of these subtle (and not so subtle) notions on the social construction of fatherhood in Canada? Do "challenges from new and competing discursive constructions" (Caragata and Miller 2008, 5) of father involvement open up multiple possibilities of doing fatherhood, or have such constructions simply participated in a (re)construction of hegemonic masculinity? Father initiatives might claim to bring fatherhood more centrally into discourses of parenting, but they have been criticized for the extent to which they promote or regulate a narrow model of father involvement that is not necessarily attainable for, or desired by, all fathers. The power of dominant discourse to inscribe is gained "not through the power of agency but through the sedimentation of meaning that occurs through its own citational power and repetition" (Kaufmann 2006, 1142). As Davies (2008, 173) explains, "the ordinary everyday world is sedimented in repeated citations of the way the world is (and it is believed, ought to be). That unreflected ordinariness can, however, deprive some of a reasonable or viable existence."

Transforming Masculinity?

Doucet's research (2004, 2006) with 118 self-identified primary caregiving fathers showed fathers engaged in a process of reconstructing the meaning of both work and family and highlighted the complex intersections among work, home, community, and masculinity. Doucet (2004, 2) views these fathers as engaged in a "slow process of critical resistance" to the dominant discourses of both parenting and masculinity. Her research suggests the need for a wider conception of domestic labour and a move beyond current theorization of masculinity:

> Fathers do not put their masculinity on the line but rather are actively reconstructing masculinities to include aspects of traditional feminine characteristics. Fathers' narratives ... are filled with visible and inchoate contradictions, which tell how fathers are both determined to distance themselves from the feminine but are also, in practice, radically revisioning masculine care and ultimately our understanding of masculinities. (2006, 237)

Nentwich's study with twenty-one parents in Switzerland explored "the discursive doing of gender in the context of parenthood" (2008, 208). Drawing on Butler and her concept of "gender trouble," Nentwich found that it can challenge dominant discourses in some contexts but "raise the danger of reifying it in other [contexts]" (226). She suggests that it is not enough to simply trouble the dominant gendered logic; new discourses and meanings of parenthood are possible only "when at the same time new subject positions are taken up and vice versa" (226).

Lather (2007) describes this active process as "doing it" and "troubling it" simultaneously. Nentwich concludes that "heterosexual [parenting] practices do have the potential of being subversive if alternative ways of positioning within or outside the normative gendered discourse of parenthood are explored" (226).

Conclusion

In recent years in Canada, policy makers, researchers, and family service providers have paid greater attention to fathers and their involvement in parenting. Father involvement initiatives have included social marketing campaigns, family service provision support, and numerous empirical studies. Although calls for fathers' active engagement in parenting continue through avenues such as public marketing, community agencies, and popular media, critiques of father involvement initiatives raise questions about who exactly is constituted as an "active father" and what is sanctioned as "involvement." For service providers, policy makers, and families to truly support father involvement in all its complexity, plurality, and diversity, we must recognize "that fatherhood is a continually changing ontological state, a site of competing discourses and desires that can never be fully and neatly shaped into a single "identity," and that it involves oscillation between various modes of subject positions even within the context of a single day" (Lupton and Barclay 1997, 16).

To open up possibilities for how fathers are conceptualized and how a range of fathering practices might be recognized as positive involvement, I have pointed to Long's (2008) discussion of transformative social inclusion and the gendering of fatherhood as potential avenues to both trouble and take up different fatherhood (parenting) discourses. To look critically at father involvement initiatives is not to question the importance of fathers but to question the assumptions from which father involvement initiatives operate. Ongoing critical reflection is necessary if we are to successfully push for efforts that support father involvement that do not discriminate against women or same-sex couples or privilege a particular type of family. To this end, problematizing fatherhood (parenting) discourses at the private or domestic level and within the context of wider institutional structures must include an exploration of the intersectionality of gender, racialization, socio-economic status, and sexuality and its impacts on inclusion and practices. Through this kind of work, we might get to places where parenting/caring discourses and practices are not segregated along a gender binary but open to the multiple possibilities of what it is to be "involved" in the life of a child and the benefits this involvement brings to individuals, families, communities, and society at large.

References

Allen, S., and K. Daly. 2007. *The Effects of Father Involvement: An Updated Research Summary of the Evidence.* Guelph, ON: Centre for Families, Work, and Well-Being, University of Guelph. http://www.fira.ca/cms/documents/29/Effects_of_Father_Involvement.pdf.

Ball, J. 2009. "Fathering in the Shadows: Indigenous Fathers and Canada's Colonial Legacies." *Annals of the American Academy of Political and Social Science* 624: 29-48.

–. 2010. "Indigenous Fathers' Involvement in Reconstituting Circles of Care." *Men and Masculinities,* special issue of *American Journal of Community Psychology* 45, 1-2: 124-38.

Ball, J., and R. George. 2006. "Policies and Practices Affecting Aboriginal Fathers' Involvement with Their Children." In *Aboriginal Policy Research: Moving Forward, Making a Difference,* ed. J. White, S. Wingert, D. Beavon, and P. Maxim, 123-44. Toronto: Thompson Educational Publishing.

Beck, J. 2005. "Dad: The Next Generation." *Lethbridge Herald,* 3 August, A7.

Bergman, H., and B. Hobson. 2002. "Compulsory Fatherhood: The Coding of Fatherhood in the Swedish Welfare State." In *Making Men into Fathers: Men, Masculinities, and the Social Politics of Fatherhood,* ed. B. Hobson, 92-124. Cambridge, UK: Cambridge University Press.

Bolté, C., A. Devault, M. St. Denis, and J. Gaudet. 2001. *On Father's Ground: A Portrait of Projects to Support and Promote Fathers.* Montreal: Groupe de Recherche et d'Action sur la Victimisation des Enfants. http://www.phac-aspc.gc.ca/dca-dea/publications/pdf/father_e.pdf.

Brott, A. 2006. "The Father-Child Connection." *Canadian Parents,* 12 November. http://www.canadianparents.ca/.

Broughton, T.L., and H. Rogers. 2007. "Introduction: The Empire of the Father." In *Gender and Fatherhood in the Nineteenth Century,* ed. T.L. Broughton and H. Rogers, 1-42. New York: Palgrave Macmillan.

Burman, E. 2008. *Deconstructing Developmental Psychology.* 2nd ed. London: Routledge.

Cabrera, N.J., C.S. Tamis-LeMonda, R.H. Bradley, S. Hofferth, and M.E. Lamb. 2000. "Fatherhood in the Twenty-First Century." *Child Development* 71, 1: 127-36.

Canadian Press. 2003. "More Dads Staying Home with Newborns: StatsCan." *CTV Newsnet,* 21 March. http://www.ctv.ca/.

Caragata, L., and W. Miller. 2008. *What Supports Engaged Fathers? Employment and Family Supports.* Father Involvement Research Alliance, http://www.fira.ca/cms/documents/178/April7_Miller.pdf.

Catlett, B.S., and P.C. McKenry. 2004. "Class-Based Masculinities: Divorce, Fatherhood, and the Hegemonic Ideal." *Fathering* 2, 2: 165-90.

Comacchio, C. 1997. "'A Postscript for Father': Defining a New Fatherhood in Interwar Canada." *Canadian Historical Review* 78, 3: 478-511.

Connell, R.W. 1987. *Gender and Power: Society, the Person, and Sexual Politics.* Cambridge, UK: Polity Press.

Davies, B. 2008. "Re-Thinking 'Behaviour' in Terms of Positioning and the Ethics of Responsibility." In *Provoking Absenses: Critical Readings in Teacher Education,* ed. A.M. Phelan and J. Sumsion, 173-86. Netherlands: Sense Publishers.

Day, R.D., and M.E. Lamb. 2004. "Conceptualizing and Measuring Father Involvement: Pathways, Problems, and Progress." In *Conceptualizing and Measuring Father Involvement,* ed. R.D. Day and M.E. Lamb, 1-15. Mahwah, NJ: Lawrence Erlbaum Associates.

Devault, A., J. Gaudet, C. Bolté, and M. St. Denis. 2005. "A Survey and Description of Projects that Support and Promote Fathering in Canada: Still Work to Do to Reach Fathers in Their Real-Life Settings." *Canadian Journal of Community Mental Health* 24, 1: 5-17.

Dobrowolski, A., and J. Jenson. 2004. "Shifting Representations of Citizenship: Canadian Politics of Women and Children." *Social Politics* 11, 2: 154-80.

Doucet, A. 2004. "'It's Almost like I Have a Job, but I Don't Get Paid': Fathers at Home Reconfiguring Work, Care, and Masculinity." *Fathering* 2, 3: 277-303.

–. 2006. *Do Men Mother? Fathering, Care, and Domestic Responsibility.* Toronto: University of Toronto Press.

Dubeau, D. 2002. *Status of the Research on Fatherhood in Canada.* Toronto: Father Involvement Initiative Ontario Network. http://www.cfii.ca/fiion/.

Esté, D., and A. Tachble. 2009. "The Perceptions and Experiences of Russian Immigrant and Sudanese Refugee Men as Fathers in an Urban Centre in Canada." *Annals of the American Academy of Political and Social Science* 624: 139-55.

Father Involvement Initiative Ontario Network. N.d. *Supporting Father Involvement in Canadian Families: A Practitioner's Proposed Course of Action for Government Leadership.* http://www.cfii.ca/fiion/practitioners_course_of_action.pdf.

Father Involvement Research Alliance. 2006. "Father's Day Should Celebrate Complexity of Dads, Says U of G Prof." Press release. http://www.fira.uoguelph.ca/pdf/FIRA-press-release-2006-FINAL.pdf.

Fleming, L.M., and D.J. Tobin. 2005. "Popular Child-Rearing Books: Where Is Daddy?" *Psychology of Men and Masculinities* 6, 1: 18-24.

Fournier, S., and E. Crey. 1997. *Stolen from Our Embrace: The Abduction of Indigenous Children and the Restoration of Indigenous Communities.* Vancouver: Douglas and McIntyre.

Gavanas, A. 2004. "Domesticating Masculinity and Masculinizing Domesticity in Contemporary U.S. Fatherhood Politics." *Social Politics* 11, 2: 247-66.

Gergen, K. 2007. "Relativism, Religion, and Relational Being." *Common Knowledge* 13, 2-3: 362-78.

Griswold, R.L. 1993. *Fatherhood in America: A History.* New York: Basic Books.

Hawkins, A.J., and D.C. Dollahite. 1997. "Beyond the Role-Inadequacy Perspective of Fathering." In *Generative Fathering: Beyond Deficit Perspectives,* ed. A.J. Hawkins and D.C. Dollahite, 3-16. Thousand Oaks, CA: Sage Publications.

Hearn, J. 2002. "Men, Fathers, and the State: National and Global Relations." In *Making Men into Fathers: Men, Masculinities, and the Social Politics of Fatherhood,* ed. B. Hobson, 245-72. Cambridge, UK: Cambridge University Press.

Hewlett, B.S. 2000. "Culture, History, and Sex: Anthropological Contributions to Conceptualizing Father Involvement." *Marriage and Family Review* 29, 2-3: 59-74.

Hewlett, B.S., and M.E. Lamb. 2005. "Emerging Issues in the Study of Hunter-Gatherer Children." In *Hunter-Gatherer Childhoods*, ed. B.S. Hewlett and M.E. Lamb, 2-18. New Brunswick, NJ: Transaction Publishers.

Hobson, B., ed. 2002. *Making Men into Fathers: Men, Masculinities, and the Social Politics of Fatherhood*. Cambridge, UK: Cambridge University Press.

Hobson, B., and D. Morgan. 2002. "Introduction." In *Making Men into Fathers: Men, Masculinities, and the Social Politics of Fatherhood*, ed. B. Hobson, 1-21. Cambridge, UK: Cambridge University Press.

Hodgins, B.D. 2007. "Father Involvement in Parenting Young Children: A Content Analysis of Parent Education Programs in BC." MEd project, University of Victoria. http://www.ecdip.org/docs/pdf/B.D.%20Hodgins%20Masters%20Project%20Write-up.pdf.

Hoffman, J. 2005. "Involved Dad, Happy Couple." *Today's Parent*, March. http://www.todaysparent.com/.

"Involved Dads Feeling Invisible." 2006. *Toronto Star*, 17 June, A27.

Kaufmann, J. 2006. "Heteronarrative Analysis: A Narrative Analysis for Analyzing the Formation of Gender Identity." *Qualitative Inquiry* 12, 6: 1139-53.

Kruk, E. 2008. *Child Custody, Access, and Parental Responsibility: The Search for a Just and Equitable Standard*. Guelph, ON: Father Involvement Research Alliance. http://www.fira.ca/cms/documents/181/April7_Kruk.pdf.

Lamb, M.E., J.H. Pleck, E.L. Charnov, and J.A. Levine. 1985. "Paternal Behavior in Humans." *American Zoologist* 25: 883-94.

–. 1987. "A Biosocial Perspective on Paternal Behavior and Involvement." In *Parenting across the Lifespan: Biosocial Dimensions*, ed. J. Lancaster, J. Altmann, A. Rossi, and L. Sherrod, 111-42. Hawthorne, NY: Aldine de Gruyter.

Lamb, M.E., and C.S. Tamis-LeMonda. 2004. "The Role of the Father: An Introduction." In *The Role of the Father in Child Development*, 4th ed., ed. M.E. Lamb, 1-31. Hoboken, NJ: John Wiley and Sons.

LaRossa, R. 1988. "Fatherhood and Social Change." *Family Relations* 37, 4: 451-57 http://www.jstor.org/.

–. 1997. *The Modernization of Fatherhood: A Social and Political History*. Chicago: University of Chicago Press.

Lather, P. 2007. *Getting Lost: Feminist Efforts toward a Double(d) Science*. New York: SUNY Press.

Lero, D.S., L.M. Ashbourne, and D.L. Whitehead. 2006. *Inventory of Policies and Policy Areas Affecting Father Involvement*. Guelph, ON: Father Involvement Research Alliance. http://www.fira.ca/cms/documents/22/FIRA-Inventory_of_Policies.pdf.

Long, D. 2008. *All Dads Matter: Towards an Inclusive Vision of Father Involvement Initiatives in Canada*. Guelph, ON: Father Involvement Research Alliance. http://www.fira.ca/cms/documents/176/April7.Long.pdf.

Lorinc, J. 2002. "Men of Class." *Today's Parent*, June. http://www.todaysparent.com/.

Lupton, D., and L. Barclay. 1997. *Constructing Fatherhood: Discourses and Experiences*. London: Sage Publications.

Marsiglio, W., P. Amato, R.D. Day, and M.E. Lamb. 2000. "Scholarship on Fatherhood in the 1990's and Beyond." *Journal of Marriage and the Family* 62, 4: 1173-91.

Marsiglio, W., K. Roy, and G.L. Fox, eds. 2005. *Situated Fathering: A Focus on Physical and Social Spaces*. Lanham, MD: Rowman and Littlefield.

McBride, B.A., and M.M. Lutz. 2004. "Intervention: Changing the Nature and Extent of Father Involvement." In *The Role of the Father in Child Development*, 4th ed., ed. M.E. Lamb, 446-75. Hoboken, NJ: John Wiley and Sons.

McBride, B.A., and T.R. Rane. 1997. "Role Identity, Role Investments, Paternal Involvement: Implications for Parenting Programs for Men." *Early Childhood Research Quarterly* 12, 2: 173-97.

Miller, N. 2006. "Disciplining Fatherhood: An Exercise in Constructing Responsible Fathers." Paper presented at the annual meeting of the American Sociological Association, Montreal. http://www.allacademic.com/.

Morgan, D. 2002. "Epilogue." In *Making Men into Fathers: Men, Masculinities, and the Social Politics of Fatherhood*, ed. B. Hobson, 273-86. Cambridge, UK: Cambridge University Press.

My Daddy Matters Because. 2004. *Fatherhood: It's the Best Job on the Planet.* http://www.mydad.ca/.

–. N.d.a. *Father Tool Kit.* http://www.mydad.ca/.

–. N.d.b. *Research Report on the National Project on Fathering.* http://www.mydad.ca/.

–. N.d.c. *Social Marketing Tools.* http://www.mydad.ca/.

Nentwich, J.C. 2008. "New Fathers and Mothers as Gender Trouble Makers? Exploring Discursive Constructions of Heterosexual Parenthood and Their Subversive Potential." *Feminism and Psychology* 18, 2: 207-30.

Nyhan, P. 2006. "Stay-Home Fathers Figure Out Their New Full-Time Job." *Seattle Post-Intelligencer*, 25 April. http:// www.seattlepi.nwsource.com/.

Owens, A.M. 2006. "Rethinking Anti-Father Bias." *National Post*, 1 June. http://www.canada.com/nationalpost/.

Palkovitz, R. 1997. "Reconstructing 'Involvement': Expanding Conceptualizations of Men's Caring." In *Generative Fathering: Beyond Deficit Perspectives*, ed. A.J. Hawkins and D.C. Dollahite, 201-16. Thousand Oaks, CA: Sage Publications.

Parke, R.D. 2004. "Fathers, Families, and the Future: A Plethora of Plausible Predictions." *Merrill-Palmer Quarterly* 50, 4: 456-70.

Parke, R.D., S. Coltrane, S. Brothwith-Duffy, J. Powers, M. Adams, W. Fabricius, S. Braver, and D. Saenz. 2004. "Assessing Father Involvement in Mexican-American Families." In *Conceptualizing and Measuring Father Involvement*, ed. R.D. Day and M.E. Lamb, 17-38. Mahwah, NJ: Lawrence Erlbaum Associates.

Pleck, E.H. 2004. "Two Dimensions of Fatherhood: A History of the Good Dad-Bad Dad Complex." In *The Role of the Father in Child Development*, 4th ed., ed. M.E. Lamb, 32-57. Hoboken, NJ: John Wiley and Sons.

Pleck, J.H. 1998. "American Fathering in Historical Perspective." In *Families in the U.S.: Kinship and Domestic Politics*, ed. K.V. Hansen and A.I. Garey, 351-62. Philadelphia: Temple University Press.

–. 2007. "Why Could Father Involvement Benefit Children? Theoretical Perspectives." *Applied Developmental Science* 11, 4: 196-202.

–. 2008. "Why Does Father Involvement Promote Child and Adolescent Development? Addressing an Under Theorized Issue." Keynote address (PowerPoint slides) presented at the Father Involvement Research Alliance Conference, Toronto, October. http://www.fira.ca/.

Pleck, J.H., and E.H. Pleck. 1997. "Fatherhood Ideals in the United States: Historical Dimensions." In *The Role of the Father in Child Development*, 3rd ed., ed. M.E. Lamb, 33-48. New York: John Wiley and Sons.

Roopnarine, J.L. 2004. "African American and African Caribbean Fathers: Levels, Quality, and Meaning of Involvement." In *The Role of the Father in Child Development*, 4th ed., ed. M.E. Lamb, 58-97. Hoboken, NJ: John Wiley and Sons.

Royal Commission on Aboriginal Peoples. 1996. *Report of the Royal Commission on Aboriginal Peoples.* Ottawa: Minister of Supply and Services Canada.

Russell, C.C. 2003a. *Parent Education: What Is Required to Build the Skills Parents Need to Raise Healthy Children?* Toronto: Invest in Kids.

–. 2003b. *Parenting in the Beginning Years: Priorities for Investment.* Toronto: Invest in Kids.

Sarkadi, A., R. Kristiansson, F. Oberklaid, and S. Bremberg. 2008. "Fathers' Involvement and Children's Outcomes: A Systematic Review of Longitudinal Studies." *Acta Paediatrica* 97, 2: 153-58.

Shimoni, R., D. Esté, and D. Clark. 2003. "Paternal Engagement in Immigrant and Refugee Families." *Journal of Comparative Family Studies* 34, 4: 555-68.

Silverstein, L., and C. Auerbach. 1999. "Deconstructing the Essential Father." *American Psychologist* 54, 6: 397-407.

St. Pierre, E. 2000. "Poststructural Feminism in Education: An Overview." *International Journal of Qualitative Studies in Education* 13, 5: 477-515.

Stockley, D., and K. Daly. 1999. "Work and Family: Competing Forces in Men's Struggle for Time." *Canadian Journal of Research in Early Childhood Education* 7, 4: 339-47.

Tamis-LeMonda, C.S., and N. Cabrera. 2002. "Cross-Disciplinary Challenges to the Study of Father Involvement." In *Handbook of Father Involvement: Multidisciplinary Perspectives*, ed. C.S. Tamis-LeMonda and N. Cabrera, 599-620. Mahwah, NJ: Lawrence Erlbaum Associates.

Wall, G., and S. Arnold. 2007. "How Involved in Involved Fathering? An Exploration of the Contemporary Culture of Fatherhood." *Gender and Society* 21, 4: 508-27.

PART 3

Expanding Perspectives
in Child and Youth Care Practice

Northern Canadian Practice as a Site for Exploration of Child and Youth Care Identities

Inside and Outside Professionalization

BROOKE ALSBURY

> There is an African saying that "when you are preparing for a journey, you own the journey. Once you've started the journey, the journey owns you."
>
> – CITED IN SHOPE (2006, 165)

There is a need to critically analyze the professionalization of child and youth care. Since the 1970s, there has been debate within the field about the need, rationale, and purpose of professionalization (Beker 2001; Charles and Garfat 2009; Eisikovits and Beker 2001; Krueger 1991; Stuart 2001). Although I understand the intention of professionalization and have fought for acknowledgment of my own professional status, I propose to reconceptualize professionalization through understanding the socially constructed nature of both profession and professional identity. I enter into this exploration of CYC professionalization using the site of northern Canadian practice as a context. This chapter explores the development of professions and the tensions created by their presence. I attempt to move beyond the binary of "profession" and "not profession," but the both/and space is challenging for me to embody.

One of my fundamental concerns with the professionalization movement is the centre from which it radiates and the boundaries and margins that are created. From where do the professional practices, competencies, educational accreditations, and ethics arise? Can professional boundaries be permeable? Can the binary of insider/outsider be abandoned for a middle space? Is there room for professionalization in a socially constructed CYC practice? Can both profession and the professional be considered as local, multiple, and culturally located?

Beginning in Story

> If they want to know
> "What does it mean?"
>   Tell them
>   Read between the Lines.
>
> – GRAVELINE (2000, 369)

My own minority world beliefs about the importance of professional status and post-secondary education were challenged when I moved to a small community in Nunavut in the summer of 2008. My husband was offered the opportunity to become the supervisor of social programs in a small island community. The decision to move to this isolated arctic island was predicated on many things. We had recently returned from travelling and had no money. We had both been accepted into graduate school and needed money. Additionally, we had been considering a move to the Arctic for a few years, and the timing seemed perfect. My friends and family all asked what I would be doing. I assumed that finding social services work would be easy for a master's-level professional with northern work experience. I spent the summer stocking shelves at the local grocery store. I had never stocked shelves, and it had been years since I had punched a time clock. I was the only white person stocking shelves and, with the exception of the manager, the only white employee of the store. I made fourteen dollars an hour, the highest paid clerk, which equalled less than the cost of my rent for one month. I was angry, hurt, and slightly indignant that my "professional skills" were not being put to "good" use.

My first week in town I attended the "Saturday card party." Present were all of the transient, white professionals in the community, including nurses and RCMP. The party highlighted the ongoing segregation and colonial practices in northern communities. The line between insider and outsider is often drawn by the perceived need for expert or professional knowledge from outside the community. As I walked home that night, I reflected on my own desire to complexify my position in the community. I wanted to exist in a middle space and create some rupturing along the boundaries of what was considered "professional" or "expert" knowledge.

I spent the first month at work feeling like an outsider. I did not know the language, the families, the life stories, and the history of the community. Then one day, as I sat in the storeroom with Tracey,[1] one of my co-workers, something shifted. I had been drawn to her from my first day at work, but she took some time to assess whom I would be in her life. As we priced merchandise, she told me part of her story. Tracey was my age and had five children. Her home and family were in another community, but her husband's family was in our community. She loved her children and her husband passionately. She missed her community desperately. She had attempted to become a teacher, but this education had meant leaving her family and attending school in a larger community. Tracey had finished one semester but had not considered returning. Her story contained both joy and pain. I was honoured by the telling. One of her dreams was to become a counsellor. There was no college campus in our community or distance training program offered in the territory. I realized, in that moment, that my presumption of working as a professional in the community helped to perpetuate the idea of expert or professional knowledge. Our conversations continued, our friendship grew, and my attitudes shifted. I began to negotiate both inside and outside within the community.

During that summer, my own deep-rooted sense of privilege was exposed for me to deconstruct. I am thankful for my summer in Nunavut because this window onto my own assumptions and biases is critical. I use this story to explore and unpack my role as researcher and CYC practitioner in northern communities.

This story of my summer in Nunavut is honest – hard but honest. The arrogance and privilege I read in my thoughts and actions are embarrassing. Shope (2006, 169) identifies her need for constant reflexivity in researching in a cultural context that is not her own. She states, after recognizing inherent power dynamics in her relationships with research participants, "the breach signalled the need for me to constantly interrogate my own assumptions about knowledge and about the complex alchemy of gender, class, and race and/or ethnicity in specific historical and sociocultural contexts." I recognize that when I moved to Nunavut I expected to be accepted as an insider, but I wanted the privileges provided to "professional" outsiders. As my story implies, the relationship between insider and outsider, professional and not professional, must be more complex than the binary suggests.

Professionalization in a Minority World Context

Since that summer in Nunavut, I have spent a great deal of time reflecting on how professional CYC roles are taken up in northern communities and what the implications for education and professional development are. I have begun to ask a variety of questions. How does a northern community envision a youth worker? How might this vision be different from the construction of youth worker within government services or educational institutions? How are youth workers positioned through discourses within communities, curricula, and the media? How do youth workers position themselves? How does professionalizing care essentialize and create boundaries around who can care for children and youth? What knowledge, and which experiences and people, does this leave out?

My own unease with professionalization builds on discourses that began in the 1970s. In 2001, Beker and Maier stated that "teachers, practitioners and researchers concerned with child and youth care and development have talked for a long time about professionalization – what it means, why we need it or why we don't, in what relationship to other professions and the like" (377). These discussions linger in the hallways of professional schools of child and youth care and arise regularly in undergraduate CYC classes. Recently, a young student told me that she had entered the school of social work because it is a better-known profession than child and youth care. As she walked away, I considered whether a collective identity as a CYC professional might be needed to understand one's individual identity as a youth worker. Cerulo (1997, 387) explores more recent changes to the understanding of collective identity: "A collective's members were believed to internalize these qualities, suggesting a unified, singular social experience, a singular canvas against which social actors constructed a sense of self. Recent treatments of collective identity question the essentialism of collective attributes and experiences."

How does the traditional idea of a profession that attempts to create a universal identity influence the identity of the professionals? How might understanding the process as localized and mutually constituting usefully complexify this process? How might this rupture boundaries of "expert" knowledge?

Freidson (1986, 20) defines a profession as "a method of gaining a living while serving as an agent of formal knowledge and implies as well the fact that bodies of formal knowledge, or disciplines, are differentiated into specialized occupations." The rise of professions and of professionalization movements can be connected to the Enlightenment era. This period supported scientific knowledge and the development of universal, rational truths. Furthermore, the rise of Western bureaucratic governments, during the Industrial Revolution and the modern period, supported the separation of knowledge and skills into professions.

The link between Enlightenment ideals and modern bureaucracy is apparent in the criteria used to define professions. Turner and Hodge (1970) identify four areas important to the identification of a profession: (1) the degree of substantive theory and technique, (2) the degree of monopoly claimed over professional activities, (3) the degree of external recognition, and (4) the degree of organization. Furthermore, Greenwood (cited in Vollmer 1966, 9) describes five elements that distinguish a profession: (1) basis of systematic theory, (2) authority recognized by the clientele of the professional group, (3) broader community sanction and approval of this authority, (4) code of ethics regulating relations of professional persons with clients and colleagues, and (5) professional culture sustained by formal professional associations. These sets of criteria identify that the development of a profession is tightly connected to both a recognition and a privileging of the professionals and their knowledge by the community. Professions, therefore, are constructed and maintained within specific social systems. This connection between community sanction and professional status has been an ongoing concern and a challenge for CYC practitioners involved in the professionalization movement. Although groups such as CYC practitioners have been working to advance their professional position, postmodern scholars and practitioners have begun to trouble the nature of professions, professional elitism, and tensions created by professionalization movements within communities.

For example, Bradford (2007, 22), in a recent UK-based critique, notes that the purpose of a profession is to "achieve closure by producing a commodity whose acquisition and distribution [are] assiduously monopolised by professionals themselves." In his description, the link between power and professional practice is clear. Professions draw boundaries around knowledge to create a stable and self-sustaining place from which to justify their existence and advocate for increased wages and improved working conditions. Chambers (1994, 3-4), working in international development, supports these ideas, stating that professions are "sustained by the core periphery structure of knowledge and knowledge generation, by education and training, by organizational hierarchy, and by rewards and career patterns." Through the establishment of a unique body of knowledge, a profession can claim "expertise" in its field. This process creates an inside and an outside. Insider knowledge thus justifies the existence of the profession. Moloney (1992, 24) states that "the theoretical aspects of professional knowledge, knowledge gained through practice and long periods of training, are what create the air of mystery surrounding established professions. An occupation aspiring to full professionalism has to be able to control a more substantial body of knowledge than that controlled by other occupations."

This desire to control both knowledge and education through professional boundaries is apparent in northern bureaucratic structures. This control has led to the construction and perpetuation of the northern "expert." I believe that such an expert is an individual who moves to the territories to take on a professional role and holds the belief that his or her knowledge and expertise are essential to support systems in northern communities. The 1992 Nunavik Educational Task Force report high-lighted the impacts of expert and bureaucratic structures on northern communities: "When these institutions came into our lives we had no way to deal with their poisonous side effects, their tendency to under-mine wisdom, our spirits slowly began to die. In our weakened condition we attracted even more services and more rescuers, and the cycle got worse" (cited in Rasmussen 2001, 105).

This idea of expert became more relevant to me when I became friends with the community child protection worker. Sara had no formal hu-man services training and worked under the supervision of a "profes-sionally" trained social worker. Sara was not allowed to have keys to the health centre or the agency vehicle even when she was required to be on call beyond agency hours. Furthermore, her former supervisor neither encouraged nor permitted her to seek training or education in the social work field. According to Sara, the supervisor believed that with formal education Sara would begin to request more professional and practice opportunities and spend less time focusing on her current job. This is not a unique story within the bureaucratic structures of northern com-munities. Alternatively, my understanding is that resonant practices in small, rural, and northern communities harness the diversity of know-ledge, wisdom, and experience to seek approaches relevant to the com-munity context. The shift away from the northern expert is occurring in some communities; however, as McKnight (1995, 12) indicates, "our modern experience with service technologies tells us that it is difficult to recapture professionally occupied space. We have also learned that it is more difficult to construct a new social order that will not be quickly co-opted again." Communities are seeking to recapture these occupied spaces, and this is where one of my research questions burgeons. How can child and youth care position itself beyond a binary of "expert" and "other" in northern communities? What are the implications for educa-tion and training in such a sought-after positioning?

Development of the Problem and the Profession
In presenting a critique of the idea of professions, postmodern scholars have suggested that both social problems and the professions necessary

to "fix" them have been co-constructed within a rational bureaucratic government and society. Freidson (1986, 4) notes that professions are "intimately associated with the accounting and management methods that developed with capitalism and the administrative methods of developing predictable social order that rose along with the modern state in the form of 'rational-legal bureaucracy.'" Bradford (2007, 22) supports these connections by acknowledging that professions are a central project of government: "Expertise institutionalized in professional form has increased the reach of the state in its capacity to represent social problems in such a way as to make them amenable to governmental helping practices." Specific to the CYC field, Bradford also suggests that the interest of the state in developing youth work training is directly tied to concerns about "young people's capacity for social disruption" (24). Other writers argue that professions seek to define a client's problems for the best interest of the profession rather than that of the client (Kermode 1993).

In social and human services, this co-construction of the social problem and the professional fix has been further co-opted by positivist and rational scientific methods that include tools such as the fourth edition of the *Diagnostic and Statistical Manual* (DSM-IV) (American Psychiatric Association 1994). Freidson (1986, 4) notes that professions are "intimately associated with the rise of modern science and the application of the scientific method to technical and social problems." This link between rational knowledge and modernity is manifested in the government support for evidence-based practice within social service professions. Staller (2006, 515) suggests that the evidence-based research is already predicated on the bias of dominant discourses around societal problems: "Because best evidence is expensive to produce, research projects are frequently supported with government funding, which presupposes that a public problem has been socially constructed and politically embraced." This connection between social policy and professional practice is particularly important in the context of child and youth care, where "best practice" is tied directly to "best interest" of the child. Colton (2002, 129) notes that "the professional ability to make decisions in the 'best interests of the child' is a central power of child welfare professionals." The question of who decides what constitutes best interest has been raised in the consideration of cross-cultural practices (Hammarberg and Homberg 2000). Rossides (1998, 268) argues that the ability of human services professions to address the best interests of the clients they serve is highly questionable: "The professions and disciplines are essentially value-laden, political and biased, with a highly deficient record of solving social problems." The work of these scholars highlights that the critique of evidence-based practice is tightly intertwined with the tensions of ongoing professional development.

The shift to using and advocating for best practices and evidence-based knowledge in social services professions is particularly relevant to my interest in troubling professionalization in a northern context. Pence and Hix-Small (2007, 89) suggest that, "in the name of scientific rigor, much evidence that speaks to the complex particulars of what it is to be human is culled from consideration. This shaping and processing of 'approved information' does not strengthen science, but weakens it." If best practices and evidence-based knowledge are established outside the northern territories, then knowledge and practices related to child and youth work from the North might be ignored, devalued, or misunderstood. For example, in many northern communities those working in the social services field will be related to some of their clients. Based on mainstream professional codes of ethics, in southern Canada this would be considered a "dual relationship" and regarded as unethical, but in small, rural, and remote northern communities it is a reality. Multiple, overlapping relationships and the boundaries of professional relationships are constantly needing to be negotiated within a northern CYC practice. In the North, advocating for "best" practices might be another vehicle for perpetuating colonial relations and practices.

I suggest that practice-based evidence could help to reframe how CYC practice and knowledge are understood within the local context. Staller (2006, 513) provides the following explanation and rationale for practice-based evidence:

> In this way, emphasis is placed on real practice so that social context and social situations can be reintroduced. It gives agency to the

practitioner in considering evidence, thus reintroducing the notion of process. Finally, it acknowledges that role of multiple and competing sources of evidence. In short, it embraces the process of evaluating a wide variety of sources of evidence in a practice context.

A re-visioning of how the profession of child and youth care develops practice knowledge locally has implications for the professionalization movement within the field.

The Process of CYC Professionalization

The field of child and youth care has been seeking acknowledgment and understanding of its "unique" skills and knowledge for at least forty years. In that time, CYC practitioners and scholars have been making steps toward professionalization for the purpose of gaining acceptance and equity within the human services field. The justification for professionalization has most often been framed in terms of the need for improved working conditions and increased salaries. In the 1970s, Jerome Beker published a series of articles discussing the development of a professional identity for CYC practice. He stated that "the impetus toward professionalization has emerged from a variety of circumstances, among them the low current status of the field and the associated working conditions, low pay, limited opportunities and the like" (2001, 346). Despite the models presented and other efforts toward professionalization, the editors of *Professionalization and Participation in Child and Youth Care* (Knorth, Van Den Bergh, and Verheij 2002) note that "salary ... and appropriate working condition form the tangible expression of a society's recognition of a profession – a recognition which, however, is quite limited, especially when viewed from the point of financial reward." These two commentaries written thirty years apart highlight that, despite multiple efforts toward professionalization, the field of child and youth care continues to be marginalized and misunderstood.

In North America, child and youth care has followed the traditional process of professionalization. Rose-Sladde (1990) identified the milestones reached in the efforts toward CYC professionalization in North America. These efforts included establishment of formal post-secondary training and education, development of professional journals, establishment of national and provincial associations, development of a code of ethics, and ongoing professional conferences at provincial, national, and international levels. In reflecting on the criteria provided by Freidson (1986) and Greenwood (1966), this analysis of the field provides child and youth care with a solid foundation on which to identify itself as a profession. Since the publication of Rose-Sladde's thesis, further work has moved the field of CYC toward other professionalization outcomes. In 2001, the North American Certification Project Competencies for Professional Child and Youth Work Practitioners was produced. In the introduction to the competencies document, the editors stated that "more colleagues than can be named responded with expert opinions and additional information when called on. We believe that this document articulates the competencies necessary for first level professional practice across the various settings in which Child and Youth Care Professionals practice" (Mattingly, Stuart, and VanderVen 2001, 3). The 2001 CYC competencies include educational requirements, foundational attitudes, and five core professional competencies: (1) professionalism, (2) cultural and human diversity, (3) applied human development, (4) relationship and communication, and (5) developmental practice methods. Additionally, the field has an established code of ethics and a process for educational accreditation under way in Canadian postsecondary institutions.

Although professionalization has followed a step-wise progression in North America, CYC has not undertaken a universalist approach to professional standing in every country where it is practised. Noticeable differences across practice settings and international contexts exist. Bradford (2007, 23) identifies that the challenge to CYC professionalization is due to "its informality and permeable boundaries [that] seem, until very recently at least, to have undermined its capacity to attract recognition as an expert practice with its own distinctive territory."

Although CYC professionalization advocates lament the fracturing across practice contexts and permeable boundaries of youth work, a tension exists in the field about the overall process and the philosophy of professionalization in child and youth care. Stuart (2001, 264) describes this tension: "The professionalization of child and youth care has been viewed as the means by which we can achieve autonomy, recognition, and respect for our work. We have continued to strive to achieve the hallmarks of a profession in spite of questions by leaders in the field regarding whether it is appropriate to hold these professional hallmarks as our goal." The nexus of this tension can be described as the difference between CYC values, including inclusion, collaborative practice, a focus on strengths, and self-awareness, and the Western bureaucratic model that essentializes the idea of the universal professional identity. I echo these concerns as I consider the northern Canadian context. I wonder whether CYC needs to follow the same path toward professional identity that fields such as social work and nursing have undertaken. Does child and youth care need to be part of what Kermode (1993, 103) called "the glamour occupations of our time"? Do we need to create boundaries around our knowledge? Could the perpetual struggle to be "understood" allow CYC the space to continue to define and redefine, construct, deconstruct, and reconstruct our knowledge and practice?

Rose-Sladde (1990) concluded her own analysis with caution, indicating that the field needs to proceed slowly toward other aspects of professionalization. Stuart (2001, 268) articulated that our struggle might be between considering ourselves as a value-based field versus a knowledge-based profession: "By examining the value conflicts in the struggle to professionalize a model emerges that is consistent with our core professional values." I believe that entertaining the possibility that traditional professionalization might not fit with the core values of CYC is important and opens spaces to consider more permeable options.

Professionalization as Co-Construction

Books and articles written about professionalization begin with an essential framework that articulates the steps toward professional status. Codes of ethics, university education programs, and professional associations are a few of the milestones described. All of these documents and processes follow the functionalist approach to professionalization described by Stuart (2001). However, postmodern scholars have begun to complexify, trouble, and deconstruct the essential frameworks of professionalization. In this writing, the discussion shifts from outcome to process of professionalization. Freidson (1986, 31) states that "to speak about the process of professionalization requires one to define the direction of the process, to define the end state of professionalism toward which an occupation is moving." In critically reflecting on the process of professionalization, I began to understand the socially constructed, contextually laden idea of professionalization. The tension seems to occur when this socially constructed process attempts to align with the functionalist outcomes of professional standards. This is not a new tension. In 1966, Greenwood wrote that

> In the construction of an ideal type some exaggeration of reality is unavoidable, since the intent is to achieve an internally coherent picture. One function of the ideal type is to structure reality in such a manner that discrete, disparate, and dissimilar phenomena become organized thereby bringing order out of apparent disorder. We now possess a model of a profession that is much sharper and clearer than the actuality that confronts us when we see the occupational scene. (18)

In support of this perspective, Freidson (1986, 32) notes that "the problem ... is created by attempting to treat *profession* as if it were a generic concept rather than a changing historic concept with particular roots in those industrial nations that are strongly influenced by Anglo-American institutions." To consider professions as social constructions embedded in a historical and cultural context complexifies the notion of professionalization. This epistemological lens necessitates that each profession and possibly each professional make room for shifting identities and redefinition across context and time.

To address this idea of shifting identity, an exploration of the co-constructed nature of profession and professional is needed. Is identity as a professional constructed by the profession or by the work, or are they mutually constituted? Casey (2008, 762) summarizes this tension between individual and collective identity in constructing profession and professional while exploring the work of social housing managers in England:

"Much of the literature on occupations assumes that professionals develop distinctive shared identities as a consequence of their occupation and working practices carried out over many years" (Freidson 1994). In contrast to this approach, other studies start from the premise that people take with them well-formed identities into their chosen professions and consequently demonstrate important distinctions in attitudes, performances and strategies (Goodson 1981, 69).

Casey (2008) argues that focusing on the role and duty of housing manager has failed to enhance understanding of how the individual influences the process and shapes the identity of the profession. In an article that explores the challenge that professionalization has placed on professional counsellors' collective identity, Gale and Austin (2003, 3) state that,

> Paradoxically, achieving professional status has done little to promote professional counsellors' sense of collective identity or to distinguish counsellors from other mental health professionals. In fact, the criteria for professionalism have been attained through multiple avenues, some of which conflict with one another. Achieving professional status has led to the creation of greater diversity and less unity among persons who identify as professional counsellors.

Referencing research in teacher identities, Day et al. (2006, 603) might provide an explanation for the diversity within a professional identity by exploring the multiple factors that influence the development of that identity:

> Several researchers ... have noted that teacher identities are not only constructed from technical and emotional aspects of teaching (i.e., classroom management, subject knowledge and pupil test results) and their personal lives, but also "as the result of an interaction between the personal experiences of teachers and the social, cultural, and institutional environment in which they function on a daily basis" (Sleegers and Kelchtermans 1999, 579).

I consider that my own professional identity has been constructed through the intersections of my history, values, and beliefs with my education; the agéncies I have worked for; other professionals, colleagues, and supervisors; political structures of the towns, territories, and countries in which I have worked; and shifting global and societal values.

This constructed and ecological lens presènts the possibility of mutually constituting identities of a profession and professional. Understanding that each professional is socially constructed challenges the traditional definition and process of creating a universal understanding of a profession. This challenge can support a reconceptualization of CYC identity and assist in understanding the difficulties CYC has faced in gaining professional status. Additionally, this challenge can allow the field to reconsider the impacts professionalization has had on the identity constructions of children, youth, and families.

The editors of *Professionalization and Participation in Child and Youth Care* (Knorth, Van Den Bergh, and Verheij 2002) advanced the concept of including children, youth, and families in the construction of the profession of child and youth care, inextricably linking professionalization of practitioners to participation of clients and families. I believe this connection creates space for practitioners and academics to imagine ways to maintain the CYC values of collaborative practice, social justice, and knowledge construction through the professionalization movement. This re-visioning creates opportunities for CYC to be constructed as a value-based rather than knowledge-based profession (Stuart 2001). Including youth and families in a mutually negotiated relational process changes the role of the professional: "The wish for youth participation puts the whole traditional idea of the professional under strong pressure. When a youth is (seen as) a co-expert, how does the professional, with his professional knowledge and experience[,] position himself? At that moment the professional is no longer the expert who tells the youth what is good for the youth" (Kroneman, cited in Knorth, Van Den Bergh, and Verheij 2002, 10). That a youth or family could be considered a co-expert necessitates that the boundaries of professional knowledge be expanded and implies a re-visioning of the march toward functionalist professionalization. This reconceptualization of professions would include not only practice-based evidence but also client-based evidence (Sargeant and Casey 2008). The question that lingers for me is this: How would governments and organizations embedded in essentialist professional discourses understand a socially co-constructed CYC model of professional practice?

Another Story ... Deconstructing ... Reconstructing

A few months ago Sara called from Nunavut to tell me she was going to be a granny. She is thirty-seven with four children of her own and has been longing to be a grandmother since her eighteen-year-old daughter began trying to become pregnant two years ago. One of the benefits of working at a grocery store in Nunavut was the opportunity I had to watch the "whole community" parent and raise their children. Many people had babies well before they were twenty, and many more were raising children of family members. The store was a playground, and parenting styles might have been labelled "permissive" by those from the South. Children were "dirty" from always playing outside. I would often awake to a group of nine year olds playing outside under the midnight sun. The actual time would be two o'clock in the morning.

Most of what I witnessed pressed me to deconstruct and shatter the "nutshell" that was my belief system about CYC practice. Caputo (1997, 31) states that "nutshells enclose and encapsulate, shelter and protect, reduce and simplify, while everything in deconstruction is turned toward opening, exposure, expansion, and complexification, toward releasing unheard-of, undreamt-of possibilities to come, toward cracking nutshells wherever they appear." I have attempted in this chapter to rupture the nutshell of professional CYC discourses. I see promise in considering co-constructed and culturally located CYC identities and practices. Charles and Garfat (2009, 27) suggest the CYC "profession has at its core the responsibility to promote change in young people" and thus should itself be "inextricably involved in the process of change." Maybe this is indeed an opportunity to reconceptualize understanding of the CYC profession and professionals.

Note

1 The name of Tracey and all other names used in the stories have been changed to maintain confidentiality.

References

American Psychiatric Association. 1994. *Diagnostic and Statistical Manual of Mental Disorders.* 4th ed. Washington, DC: American Psychiatric Association.

Beker, J. 2001. "Development of a Professional Identity for the Child Care Worker." *Child and Youth Care Forum* 30, 6: 345-54.

Beker, J., and H. Maier. 2001. "Emerging Issues in Child and Youth Care Education: A Program for Planning." *Child and Youth Care Forum* 30, 6: 377-86.

Bradford, S. 2007. "Practices, Policies, and Professionals: Emerging Discourses of Expertise in English Youth Work." *Youth and Policy* 97-98: 13-28.

Caputo, J.D. 1997. *Deconstruction in a Nutshell: A Conversation with Jacques Derrida.* New York: Fordham University Press.

Casey, R. 2008. "On Becoming a Social Housing Manager: Work Identities in an Invisible Occupation." *Housing Studies* 23, 5: 761-80.

Cerulo, K.A. 1997. "Identity Construction: New Issues, New Directions." *Annual Review of Sociology* 23: 385-409.

Chambers, C.M. 1994. "Worlds Apart: Educational Inquiry North of 60." *Northern Review: A Multidisciplinary Journal of Arts and Social Sciences of the North* 12, 13: 47-69.

Charles, G., and T. Garfat. 2009. "Child and Youth Care Practice in North America: Historical Roots and Current Challenges." *Relational Child and Youth Care Practice* 22, 2: 17-28.

Colton, M.J. 2002. "Professionalization and Institutional Abuse in the United Kingdom." In *Professionalization and Participation in Child and Youth Care,* ed. E.J. Knorth, P.M. Van Den Bergh, and F. Verheij, 121-34. Surrey, UK: Ashgate.

Day, C., A. Kington, G. Stobart, and P. Sammons. 2006. "The Personal and Professional Selves of Teachers: Stable and Unstable Identities." *British Educational Research Journal* 32, 4: 601-16.

Eisikovits, Z., and J. Beker. 2001. "Beyond Professionalism: The Child and Youth Care Worker as Craftsman." *Child and Youth Care* 30, 6: 415-34.

Freidson, E. 1986. *Professional Powers: A Study of the Institutionalization of Formal Knowledge.* Chicago: University of Chicago Press.

Gale, A.G., and B.D. Austin. 2003. "Professionalism's Challenges to Professional Counsellors' Collective Identity." *Journal of Counselling and Development* 81: 3-10.

Graveline, F.J. 2000. "Circle as Methodology: Enacting an Aboriginal Paradigm." *Qualitative Studies in Education* 13, 4: 361-70.

Greenwood, E. 1966. "Attributes of a Profession." In *Professionalization,* ed. H.M. Vollmer and D.L. Mills, 10-19. Englewood, NJ: Prentice-Hall.

Hammarberg, T., and B. Homberg. 2000. "Best Interests of the Child: The Principle and the Process." In *Children's Rights: Turning Principles into Practice,* ed. T. Hammarberg, A. Belembao, and A. Petren, 31-41. Stockholm: Save the Children Sweden.

Kermode, S. 1993. "The Power to Be Different: Is Professionalization the Answer?" *Contemporary Nurse* 2, 3: 102-9.

Knorth, E.J., P.M. Van Den Bergh, and F. Verheij. 2002. "Professionalization and Participation in Child and Youth Care: Two Sides of One Coin." In *Professionalization and Participation in Child and Youth Care*, ed. E.J. Knorth, P.M. Van Den Bergh, and F. Verheij, 1-23. Surrey, UK: Ashgate.

Krueger, M. 1991. "A Review and Analysis of the Development of Professional Child and Youth Care Work." *Child and Youth Care Forum* 20, 6: 379-88.

Mattingly, M., C. Stuart, and K. VanderVen. 2001. "North American Certification Project: Competencies for Professional Child and Youth Care Practitioners." *Journal of Child and Youth Care* 17: 16-49.

McKnight, J. 1995. *Careless Society: Community and Its Counterfeits*. New York: Perseus Books Group.

Moloney, M.M. 1992. *Professionalization of Nursing: Current Issues and Trends*. Philadelphia: J.B. Lippincott.

Pence, A., and H. Hix-Small. 2007. "Global Children in the Shadow of the Global Child." *International Journal of Educational Policy, Research, and Practice: Reconceptualizing Childhood Studies* 8, 1: 83-110.

Rasmussen, D. 2001. "Qallunology: A Pedagogy for the Oppressor." *Canadian Journal of Native Research* 25, 2: 105-16.

Rose-Sladde, L. 1990. "Professionalization of Child and Youth Care in British Columbia: A Case Study." MA thesis, University of Victoria.

Rossides, D.W. 1998. *Professions and Disciplines: Functional and Conflict Perspectives*. Upper Saddle River, NJ: Prentice-Hall.

Sargeant, T., and A. Casey. 2008. "The Silent Voices of Research: What Can We Do to Help Them Speak?" *Counselling and Psychotherapy Research* 8, 3: 193-96.

Shope, J.H. 2006. "You Can't Cross a River without Getting Wet: A Feminist Standpoint on the Dilemmas of Cross-Cultural Research." *Qualitative Inquiry* 12, 1: 163-84.

Staller, K. 2006. "Railroads, Runaways, and Researchers Returning Evidence Rhetoric to Its Practice Base." *Qualitative Inquiry* 12, 3: 503-22.

Stuart, C. 2001. "Professionalizing Child and Youth Care: Continuing the Canadian Journey." *Journal of Child and Youth Care Work* 15-16: 264-82.

Turner, C., and M.N. Hodge. 1970. "Occupations and Professions." In *Professions and Professionalization*, ed. J.A. Jackson, 19-41. London: Cambridge University Press.

Vollmer, H.M., ed. 1966. *Professionalization*. Upper Saddle River, NJ: Prentice-Hall.

Considering Street Outreach to Youth   **8**
Politics, Policies, and Practice

MARK L. KELLY

This chapter is an attempt to reconceptualize the practice of youth outreach and is intended to benefit practitioners, policy makers, politicians, and researchers. I present a way of thinking about outreach in honour and support of those youth who are on the street. The chapter includes a message to be passed on by those closely connected to the street. There is fledgling acceptance of what street-involved youth have been suggesting all along: *bigger issues are at play beyond the common perception that street involvement is simply a choice.* Street-involved youth are affected by a complex interplay of societal construction, our investment in that structure, and a certain paralysis to change. That is, street-involved youth are caught in the social, economic, and political factors that sustain the status quo. My aim here is to revisit and revise my career-long considerations of street-involved youth and to examine more fully the systems that perpetuate their marginalization. Through revisiting client photography, I present my current thoughts, practice experiences, and understandings of political interplay in the lives of street-involved youth. I further attempt to trouble the notion of a "poverty industry" with a key question: *how do we as outreach professionals contribute to street involvement, and how do we benefit from our work at the margins?*

I have approached the practice of outreach from many angles. I have walked the streets, exchanged needles and pipes, provided food, and

Figure 8.1   *Untitled (Red Shoes)* by Daze

helped to find shelter and housing. I often work with clients to explore issues of street involvement through the creation of photographic images. My clients explore the narratives of these images and re-story the meanings held within them. By revisiting and reworking these photographs, thoughts, and writings, I seek to better understand a new trajectory of thought. Remaining in the uncertainty of my role in the politics, policies, and practice of street outreach offers a freedom of sorts. In previous considerations of street outreach to youth, I had yet to discover the discourse on neoliberal values, politics, and governance (Harvey 2005). I believed, and perhaps continue to believe, that youth need to be off the street. I believed that at the heart of our society was a kind of caring and nurturance. I believed in the individual's ability to chart his or her own course, but that course was affected by the individual's beliefs, choices, and experiences. My work is immersed in my faith in people's ability to overcome adversity. I have invested time and effort toward making a more just and right society. Yet the very presence of street-involved youth exposes a crack in the foundation of our society. I have only begun to surface from my immersion in minority world living. I have yet to fully step outside my neoliberal ethics, thoughts, and practices – I am unsure doing so totally is ever possible. I continue the struggle to step back and critically examine what the structures of Canadian society mean to those who live on the street and engage with street life.

A Curb-Side View

I often come on scenes of marginalization, although witnessed through the eyes of an advocate rather than a client. A young woman named Daze created the image in Figure 8.1. She and I worked together for a time while I was doing my master's degree in counselling. I was completing an internship at an addictions agency, and my work included young people who were in between the youth treatment system and the adult treatment system. Daze was referred to me by a street-outreach agency where I was providing some addictions support services. When we met, she was eighteen years old and had been on the street for three years. She shot this image while on an impromptu walk we took around the streets where she lived. Daze wanted to show me places where she had slept, and this was one. She had left home because, as is the case for many youth, those in the environment from where she came could not adapt to her nor her to them. So she felt forced to make it on her own and adapt to a life on the street. She did not choose the street; simply, the conflict and rejection she experienced at home forced a decision to leave, the consequences of leaving were an existence of exploitation, poverty, and societal marginalization (Kidd 2003; Koeller 2006), and as a person under the age of majority she had little access to a social safety net outside charity or government care. Daze saw the street as a better option than her previous situation (Karabanow 2004). She had bounced from shelter to shelter and group home to group home, always meeting a rule, a regulation, or a policy that mostly served to encourage her conformity and perpetuate what Gergen, McNamee, and Barrett (2001) refer to as othering. This othering created a power imbalance that forced a sort of "alienation, marginalization, ... internalized oppression, and exclusion" (Canales 2000, 19). That is, as Daze did not conform to the rules, regulations, or norms of a given structure, say a youth shelter, she was labelled as defiant (or deviant) and pressed once more to the street.

Daze gifted the photograph to me under the condition that I use it when I discuss issues facing street-involved youth. This image connects me to her view. It reminds me this is the scene that outreach practitioners share with those with whom they work. Since that impromptu walk, her picture has come to represent much of my academic work and therapeutic practice. I return to it often as it reminds me of a common view for youth who live on the street. Through my outreach work, I navigate a web of tensions between my varying roles, identities, and ideologies. This web is affixed to the labyrinth of bureaucracy created to bring youth from the margins to the mainstream. It is not difficult to develop negative perceptions of the systems these youth encounter when involved in this work. I walk the same streets, hang out in the same places, talk to the same people, feel similar frustrations, and see similar horrors. I am charged with this advocacy work leading me into *the system:* the child protection system, the white welfare system, the First Nations welfare system, the group home system, the food bank system, the soup kitchen system, the shelter system – the system of endless systems. Verbalization of stories and emotions is often difficult or out of reach for these young people, yet they reach out for help. For these youth, finding their way through a bureaucratic maze of systems only serves to further marginalize them, and the accompaniment of an outreach practitioner is often key in their navigation of these social service systems. For those who live on the street, a relationship with someone who provides support, caring, and nurturance is essential to moving into a healthier environment.

What Does It Mean to Be Young and Marginalized?

Daze's image, though providing one account of street life, does not fully represent all street-involved youth. Yet it is not difficult to create a mental image of what a street-involved youth looks like. Perhaps one thinks of the squeegee kids cleaning windshields at the traffic lights on the way to work. Or an image of the young busker or panhandler outside the liquor store asking for spare change comes to mind. Conceivably, it is the kid with a spiked Mohawk, chains, and a dog, bumming a smoke in the park. All of these images perpetuate a stereotype of a young population marginalized and undefined, a group of individuals as diverse as the communities to which they travel and in which they live. It is the tensions between the commonalities that link street-involved youth, the stereotypical descriptions and the unnoticed diversity that create a blurry understanding of these young people. Yet Karabanow's (2004, 3) description of street-involved youth offers a place to begin to consider the complexity of street involvement and its intersection with marginalization. Karabanow suggests the following description of a street-involved youth:

> Any young person (generally between the ages of eleven and twenty-one) who does not have a permanent place to call home, and who instead spends a significant amount of time on the street, which is to say, in alleyways, parks, storefronts, and dumpsters, among many other places; in squats (located usually in abandoned buildings); at youth shelters and centres; and/or with friends (typically referred to as "couch surfers").

There is a kaleidoscope of research on street-involved youth, yet there is no agreement on an appropriate description of street involvement. Peressini and MacDonald (2000) agree that "there is no universally accepted definition of the term street youth. A common umbrella definition for this population is persons between twelve and twenty-four years of age without shelter or with inadequate or insecure shelter" (cited in Higgett et al. 2003, 14). Although this provides an initial framework for thinking about who is included under the term "street-involved youth," it does not encompass the diversity of these individuals. Caputo, Weiler, and Anderson (1997, 4) clarify this diversity:

> So-called street youth are not a homogeneous group. Instead they come from a variety of backgrounds with a range of personal qualities, needs and experiences. These high-risk youth are exposed to different risk factors predisposing them to becoming involved in the various hazards associated with street life. The young people on the street

have varying skills and resources. Some are more resilient than others and are better able to deal with the challenges they meet.

Undeniably, street-involved youth live at the margins of our culture. They are often seen as society's discards – trash to be swept to the curb. Thus, it is difficult, if not inappropriate, to provide a sweeping definition of this eclectic group of individuals.

There are myriad terms relating to the severity of street involvement, but it is "absolute" and "relative" homelessness that surface most regularly. Higgett et al. (2003, 14) suggest that

> People who experience relative homelessness have shelter, but it is poor quality, inadequate, or unstable. Absolute homelessness refers to the complete lack of long-term shelter. Homelessness can also be described in terms of its duration and recurrence. For some youth, homelessness is a one time, short-term experience. For others, it is a recurring or chronic condition from which they cannot escape.

In addition, Caputo, Weiler, and Anderson (1997, 4) suggest there is a continuum of street involvement from "curbsiders to entrenched." Higgett et al. (2003, 14) describe curbsiders as those who engage in selected street involvement; they move between home and street living but mainly take on "socially acceptable behaviour." Entrenched street youth are those who spend most, if not all, of their time on the street and are engaged in "extremely marginal situations" (Caputo, Weiler, and Anderson 1997, 4). Blending the descriptions of curbsiders/entrenched and relatively/absolutely homeless provides an initial understanding of what it means to be street involved but does not provide a picture of the complexity. Although significant effort has been directed toward *defining* street-involved youth, for example by attending to where they live, and the duration of their street involvement, does it not also behoove us to ask whose interests this type of categorization serves? To this point, all my questions about the thinking and practice of outreach required a definition, or so I assumed. Hacking (1999, 5) encourages me to see beyond, fitting with my concern over personal ideological flight: "With so many inflamed passions going the rounds, you might think that we first want a definition to clear the air. On the contrary, we first need to confront the point of social construction analyses. Don't ask for the meaning, ask what's the point?"

With all that we know about street involvement, what is the purpose of creating such precise definitions? Is the creation of an agreed-on definition of street-involved youth a simplified way of creating the *other* – the unworthy? If individuals do not meet the criteria for street involvement, are they then *not* street involved? Are they less worthy of a professional helping relationship – victims of their own choices, undeserving of help? These questions are a return to the notion that street involvement is more complex than choosing the street. Loseke (2008) suggests the creation of definitions objectifies the social problems that street-involved youth face – that, once these issues are identified, they can be measured and addressed. However, as Loseke also suggests, to assign sole credence to objective definitions of social problems, in this case street involvement by youth, is to miss the subjective and assign the power for change to one side of the concern. This, I contend, continues the push of street-involved youth to the margins by insisting on a movement to the mainstream; any deviation from this mainstream further justifies the stigmatization of street-involved youth by the establishment.

Similar to Canales's (2000) notion of the other, Weiser (1983, 178) links stigma to marginalization by suggesting that "those with a stigma depart from usual expectations and are often seen to be not quite human, and thus subject to discrimination, deliberate or unintended." Street-involved individuals, specifically youth, experience life at the margins of society and as a result are often stigmatized. This is compounded by the typical feelings of alienation that youth in general often experience. "If stigmatized people cannot avoid or find alternatives to situations in which stigma may create stress, they may withdraw socially. One form of social avoidance is avoiding comparisons with non-stigmatized people" (Miller 2001, 80). This avoidance of *non-stigmatized* people can be seen as evading those who conform to societal norms, governance, and neoliberal values. This stigmatization further exacerbates any existing personal issues experienced by youth. In his now classic work, Erving Goffman (1963, 5) suggests that "we believe the person with a stigma is not quite human. On this assumption we exercise varieties of discrimination, through which we effectively, if often unthinkingly, reduce his [or her] life chances."

If it is stigmatization and systemic factors that limit street-involved individuals, then common, entrenched, mainstream stereotypes further marginalize those who are street involved. Their struggles are compounded by homelessness. Peressini and MacDonald (2000, 529) suggest that "the overriding stereotype is that the homeless are deviants who, for a variety of reasons, have rejected mainstream values in favour of an alternative lifestyle. This model represents drug and alcohol abuse, mental illness and disability, criminality, juvenile delinquency, unemployment and even poverty as a matter of free will and individual choice."

It is essential, for those of us working with street-involved youth, to bring a holistic understanding to the issues they face. It is equally essential to resist defining them by these issues: that is, not to have the term "street-involved youth" become a totalized identity. Helping professionals must see these issues from the perspectives of the young people with whom they work and to accept their emotional and physical places – to work where they are. It is necessary to be immersed in the environment, culture, and experience of the clients. It is difficult to work with street-involved youth from the comforts of one's office. This approach to the problems faced by street-involved youth offers opportunities to aid them in the transition from the instability of street life to stable, healthy living but not necessarily to bring them into the mainstream.

Outreach?

Before I continue, it is important to note that I use the terms "outreach worker" and "outreach practitioner" interchangeably. I do so because the former term is dominant in the literature. However, as Ngai (2007, 313) suggests, "giving credence to the voices of these workers will help focus on their potential as a force for change ... Identity enables theorization of an active agency, which in turn might point to hopeful possibilities of social change." As such, I wish for the practice of outreach to be seen as a valuable, professional, and critically conscious approach to working with street-involved youth. I wish for the practitioners of outreach to develop an identity as professionals and as a result use the term "outreach practitioner."

The understanding of outreach as an approach to the helping professions and as an extension of identity is common among outreach practitioners (Peck and Norman 1999). Many have made the move to the margins of professional helping as a calling. Outreach work affords a way of being in the helping professions that no other setting does. There is a freedom in the work, but that freedom can come at a price. Rowe (1999, 158) provides a strong comparison of outreach work as professional identity at the margins:

> Workers undergo an identity crisis ... Their exposure to extreme poverty at the margins arouses in them conflicting emotions of outrage and pity, revulsion and the wish to flee. In becoming something like homeless persons in order to get close to them, they experience a psychological homelessness that can sharpen their skills or drive them into the back rooms of soup kitchens.

It is essential in the development of a professional identity that outreach practitioners acknowledge this occupational hazard. It is a vulnerability not likely to be experienced in any other professional setting, for we are often witnesses to the horrors of our clients' experiences. When the outreach practitioner engages in work on the street, just like clients he or she steps outside the norm. A career of street outreach comes with certain invisibility and, at present, professional marginalization.

As a result, the work of outreach practitioners is largely seen as a paraprofessional aid to the more mainstream professions of psychologists, social workers, and clinical therapists. Outreach has been seen as a method of bringing individuals from the margins to the mainstream in order to receive services (Ford et al. 2007; Susser, Goldfinger, and White 1990) and not necessarily as a service in itself. Tsemberis, Gulcur, and Nakae (2004, 651) suggest that, in the specific case of outreach to individuals facing homelessness, "the purpose of outreach and transitional

residential programs is to enhance clients' 'housing readiness' by encouraging the sobriety and compliance with psychiatric treatment
considered essential for successful transition to permanent housing."
This supports the common understanding that outreach provides transitional services, yet in practice outreach practitioners often deliver
services directly on the street (Newbery 1993).

Many outreach practitioners hold the skills, abilities, and training of
other helping professions (Ford et al. 2007) but have chosen to work at
the margins with the clients there. As Rowe (1999, 1) describes it, "homeless encounters ... involve face-to-face meetings between people who are
homeless and the rescuers, called outreach workers, whom society dis-
patches to its margins." Furthermore, much of the discussion of outreach
practice is contained in the realm of mental health (Burns and Firn
2002; Ng and McQuistion 2004; Rowe 1999; Ryan and Morgan 2004)
and as a result gains its credence in the mainstream health-care system
only. What I am referring to here, what is but a whisper in the literature,
are the therapeutic encounters between professional helpers from an
interdisciplinary perspective (Ford et al. 2007). That is, outreach practice
must include the professions stated above along with child and youth
care practitioners, counsellors, and peer helpers. The provision of professional help to those on the street must be equitably rooted in a multidisciplinary approach. Professional outreach practitioners bring a
therapeutic intentionality rooted in theory and practice. Furthermore,
I posit that, given the relative emptiness of understanding of outreach
practices, professional outreach practitioners are in a place to develop
new theories and approaches in the manner that Reed (2008, 318) refers
to as "guerrilla-based strategies": "unconventional, culturally sensitive,
embedded or integrated in the local context, and dedicated to a human
cause or mission." Reed further provides a parallel to the creative nature
of outreach work by suggesting that "guerrilla art involves making
something that is innovative, flexible, and impermanent and which
derives from the practitioner's inspiration and knowledge, as well as
out of ethical consideration with one's immediate world." Thus, the
individuals who are best suited to outreach practice have strong connections to issues of street-involved youth, are committed to change,
and understand the complexities beyond the work directly on the street.

Reach Out

Providing effective outreach services to street-involved youth is a challenging endeavour and has become one of the foundations of community-based CYC work. Gabor and Kuehne (1993, 193) support the need for outreach and suggest that "some of the most innovative community child and youth care work takes place in street programs." Outreach is firmly planted in the work of relational practice, and, as Gergen (n.d., para. 24) suggests, "meaningful communication in any given interchange ultimately depends on a protracted array of relationships, not only 'right here, right now,' but how it is that you and I are related to a variety of other persons, and they to still others – and ultimately, one may say, to the relational conditions of society as a whole."

The struggles faced by those who are street involved often overwhelm outreach practitioners. Concerns of those who do not live on the street are similarly faced by those who do, such as the risk of assault when walking alone late at night. However, the means to deal with these concerns can be limited. Many young people living on the street have come from troubled backgrounds. The research literature on street-involved youth focuses on naming and describing issues and concerns, including abuse, alcohol/drugs, assault, crime, family conflict, HIV, homelessness, mental health, poverty, pregnancy, racism, sexuality, and violence (Caputo, Weiler, and Anderson 1997; Cohen and Sullivan 1990; CS/RESORS Consulting 2001; Higgett et al. 2003; Kidd 2003; Kidd and Scrimenti 2004; Koller and Raffaelli 2001; Kurtz, Kurtz, and Jarvis 1991; Mayers 2001; Robertson and Toro 1998).

It is precisely because of the complex issues facing street-involved youth that I have great empathy for, respect for, and belief in the stories of homelessness, marginalization, and stigmatization entrusted to me. I do not often have detailed backgrounds on the young people with whom I work, and as a result I take them at face value. Doing so enables me to build relationships with these young people quickly but can put me at odds with the system. Simply, I have experienced what the systems do for and against street-involved youth. I am slanted in favour of the rights of the youth, not the rights of the system. My connection to Daze and her photograph has, over the time since our encounter, provided me with pause to consider what we were doing in those interactions. I am interested in how practitioners *do* street outreach: that is, I seek to understand the interactions at play in client-outreach practitioner relationships.

Although there is some suggestion of value in outreach programs and work (Barry, Ensign, and Lippek 2002; Gottheil, Sterling, and Weinstein 1997; Ng and McQuistion 2004), the discussion generally revolves around what practitioners *do as* an activity to move street-involved youth to mainstream services (European Monitoring Centre for Drugs and Drug Addiction 1999; Karabanow and Clement 2004). What remains elusive is a complete picture of what outreach practitioners *do when* engaging street-involved youth in the process of change. Valentine and Wright-DeAgüero (1996, 69) bring this to life by recognizing the difference between "contact" and "encounter," where contact provides the opportunity to begin interaction with the client but encounter "provides more significant opportunity for helping the client initiate and sustain behaviour change." Valentine and Wright-DeAgüero's research supports a reconceptualization of outreach to include an understanding of outreach as a therapeutic method for change in its own right.

It is tempting to move toward the problematizing of street-involved youth themselves, but this is a rug over a trap door. This is what much of the literature together with mainstream helping services has done – to place the blame for street involvement directly on the shoulders of those on the street. What is the nature of this blame, and what is it for? Is it to draw attention to the effect of the other on the perception of the rights of the mainstream individual? In our neoliberal approaches to societal development and governance, we are convinced that the individual is ultimately responsible for him- or herself. *If only they would work harder, gain skills, conform, then their lives would improve.* Would we as housed, mainstream, middle-class, or wealthy individuals actually care about poverty and street involvement if they did not directly affect us – that is, if we were not asked for spare change or if we were not the victims of theft or violence? The troubling piece is that these are children. Are we not responsible, as care-giving adults, to aid youth in development, not simply blame them for their lot because it is easier to do so – to discard them at the first sign of non-conformity and independent thought? This, I contend, is exactly what we have done with our youth

Figure 8.2   *Have Not Too* by Daze

who live on the street. The politics, policies, and practices of the adult world have put our kids out in the cold.

Spare change for a revolution? Does something need to change? I often contemplate this photograph (see Figure 8.2), from the same walkabout with Daze. Her cardboard sign reminds me that it is more than money that is required to shift life for those on the street. We, those of us housed and warm, supported, loved, and accepted, must be willing to spare a change, to make it a priority to shift from what we have now to something better for all. But what would this revolution look like, and what would the outcome be?

What remains clear is that I have a deep desire to balance practice and considerations of politics, policy, and work with street-involved youth; to simultaneously plunge into and retreat from practice and thinking of practice; to translate my thoughts into practice and my practice into thoughts. I have gained clarity that the system in which these youth live does not work, but I remain at a loss as to what the system should look like. I am under the weight of my own neoliberal perspective. I acknowledge that I am as much a part of the problem as I am a part of the solution. As Funiciello (1993, 162) reminds me, it is "under the rubric of helping homeless people ... [that] little empires were built, expanded, and strengthened, careers were boosted, and media stars created overnight."

The notion of a poverty industry is not new. The critique of helping the poor began with welfare reforms in the United States in the 1960s but has recently all but disappeared from the discussions of academics, practitioners, and politicians. It is from this place that I now begin. I accept the notion of an industry dedicated to helping those at the margins, but to trouble the poverty industry as a whole I must start with my place in it. I have spent the past fifteen plus years understanding issues facing street-involved youth from the perspective of a helper – my goal always to help youth *off* the street. Recently, I have begun to wonder how I have contributed to keeping youth *on* the street. I am a professional helper. My career has been made on the provision of outreach services to street-involved youth and by teaching the clinical interventions required to do so. As a result, I must begin to trouble the industry and my place in it. *Does our society need street-involved youth? Am I an active agent in the perpetuation of the need for street-involved youth simply by maintaining an interest in working with them? How dedicated am I to the alleviation of issues leading to the existence of street-involved youth?* I suspect the answers to these questions can be found in the long process of deconstructing their complexity – a task that will take me well into the future. As I attempt to provide answers, I only generate more questions, and that is simply overwhelming. Reflecting on my practice as an outreach practitioner is also overwhelming, and the work often feels impossible. "It is so difficult to find the piece you can lift up and look under [for the answer]. It is like a manhole cover that is too heavy, you cannot lift it up to see what is underneath it" (A. Pence, personal communication, 26 March 2009). Pence's simile speaks directly to the difficulty I face in understanding the complexity, difficulty, and hopelessness of the systemic change I seek.

There is an army of helpers out there, all with an unacknowledged stake in the maintenance of their work. Although many outreach practitioners have experienced poverty and street involvement, it is often accepted that we as outreach practitioners have a right to a life free from poverty. However, if our work is intricately connected to poverty, is our goal truly to eliminate the very thing that sustains us? What implications does this question hold for those of us in practice at the margins? What would happen if we woke up one morning to a society devoid of poverty and street involvement? Where would those professional helpers go to work? Although I realize these are unrealistic questions, to which answers likely will never materialize, I am troubled by how the simple act of my going to work maintains the status quo of poverty and street involvement. Ironically, I might find some peace while sitting in the midst of this problem.

Arguably, street-involved youth have provided much to our society, particularly in the areas of art, culture, and politics. Street-involved youth have pushed the envelope of acceptable street-based music (many mainstream musicians began as street corner buskers), sport (skateboarding), visual art (graffiti and photography), and political discourse (APEC, Afghanistan, homelessness, Iraq, Vietnam, WTO, etc.). If street-involved youth no longer existed, where would these contributions come from? This is partly the difficulty I have with my questioning. There is much to gain from street life for our culture in general. Society has in many ways embraced the culture of the street, but are the pain and suffering of the underworld of the street worth the valuable contributions?

One side of me is feeling disturbed and horrified by the abandonment of children and youth to the street; the other side of me values the contributions of street-involved youth culture to our society. But do I, by attempting to provide relief, inadvertently discourage youth from engaging in a culture that is necessary for the diversity of our society? This speaks directly to my curiosity regarding the need for street-involved youth. If I value the contributions of a culture at the margins, are my actions to alleviate the pain of being at the margins a commission of a sort of cultural genocide? What is to be gained and what is to be lost in the transformation of street life from a social problem to an accepted culture? This is a difficult reflection, and I consider this less as a binary and more as what Lather (2007) describes as the middle space.

A Return to Practicality ... for Now

I have a sense of urgency. I have a sense of injustice. I am incredulous that the issues causing youth to be street involved exist in our wealthy society – that there are kids who sleep under a bridge every night. I am outraged every time I see the news, every time I write about this, every time I read a paper about this – I cannot believe I am even having this conversation. It makes no sense to me. This issue is like a bus wreck, so difficult to look away from. Why am I intrigued with this topic? Why do I keep looking?

So I must consider for now the notion that furthering understanding of how outreach is conducted for street-involved youth might be un-wanted by the systems to which I have referred in this chapter. I might be at the margins of academic inquiry and professional practice. I am forced to acknowledge parallels between the poverty of individuals and the poverty of organizations and institutions. Multiple organizations struggle to keep themselves alive. Agencies and workers are constantly justifying themselves to the funder (as an agency) and to the organiza-tion (as an outreach practitioner). It is the same for young people on the street; they are constantly trying to find resources to survive. In the face of shrinking funds, why should we keep doing this? Who benefits from this work? Who is interested? What is the point of considering those who work with youth at the margins of society?

I feel a certain indulgence in the work and learning in which I engage, and this is different from my previous incarnations. This time my sep-aration from practice while writing is an estrangement from what grounds me, a connection to community, yet I have a nascent awareness of an implanted neoliberal lens, an individualistic approach to the bet-tering of society by the bettering of self. As a result, I find myself im-mersed in what Caputo (1996, 29) refers to as a "community without identity." Although I acknowledge this existential floating, I remain committed to the understanding of the complex realities and disciplines of outreach practice. When I take these ideas back to my work with street-involved youth, what will they look like? It is this practical question that cues me to consider my own place in Daze's (2003b) request for *revolution*. I am compelled to return to her cardboard sign, to translate her *spare change for a revolution* into a challenge for our society. I internalize it and challenge my self and my outreach contemporaries to consider *sparing change* within our own discipline for the betterment of the lives of street-involved youth, whether on or off the street.

References

Barry, P.J., J. Ensign, and S.H. Lippek. 2002. "Embracing Street Culture: Fitting Health Care into the Lives of Street Youth." *Journal of Transcultural Nursing* 13, 2: 145-52.

Burns, T., and M. Firn. 2002. *Assertive Outreach in Mental Health: A Manual for Practitioners.* London: Oxford University Press.

Canales, M.K. 2000. "Othering: Toward an Understanding of Difference." *Advances of Nursing Science* 22, 4: 16-31.

Caputo, J.D. 1996. "A Community without Truth: Derrida and the Impossible Community." *Research in Phenomenology* 26, 1: 25-37.

Caputo, T., R. Weiler, and J. Anderson. 1997. *The Street Lifestyle Study.* Ottawa: Health Canada.

Cohen, N.L., and A.M. Sullivan. 1990. "Strategies of Intervention and Service Coordination by Mobile Outreach Teams." In *Psychiatry Takes to the Streets*, ed. N.L. Cohen, 63-79. New York: Guilford.

CS/RESORS Consulting. 2001. *Gap Analysis of Research Literature on Issues Related to Street-Involved Youth.* Ottawa: Department of Justice Canada.

Daze. 2003a. Untitled photograph. In "Phototherapy with Street-Involved Youth," presentation by M. Kelly, 7th International Child and Youth Care Conference, University of Victoria.

–. 2003b. *Have Not Too: Self Portrait.* In "Phototherapy with Street-Involved Youth," presentation by M. Kelly, 7th International Child and Youth Care Conference, University of Victoria.

European Monitoring Centre for Drugs and Drug Addiction. 1999. *Outreach Work among Drug Users in Europe: Concepts, Practice, and Terminology.* Geneva: European Monitoring Centre for Drugs and Drug Addiction.

Ford, C.L., W.C. Miller, M. Smurzynski, and P.A. Leone. 2007. "Key Components of a Theory-Guided HIV Prevention Outreach Model: Pre-Outreach Preparation, Community Assessment, and a Network of Key Informants." *AIDS Education and Prevention* 19, 2: 173-86.

Funiciello, T. 1993. *The Tyranny of Kindness.* New York: Atlantic Monthly Press.

Gabor, P., and V. Kuehne. 1993. "Child and Youth Care Work in the Community." In *Professional Child and Youth Care*, 2nd ed., ed. R. Ferguson, A. Pence, and C. Denholm, 188-211. Vancouver: UBC Press.

Gergen, K.J. N.d. "When Relationships Generate Realities: Therapeutic Communication Reconsidered." Unpublished manuscript. http://www.swarthmore.edu/SocSci/kgergen1.

Gergen, K.J., S. McNamee, and F.J. Barrett. 2001. "Toward a Transformative Dialogue." *International Journal of Public Administration* 24, 7-8: 679-707.

Goffman, E. 1963. *Stigma: Notes on the Management of Spoiled Identity.* Englewood Cliffs, NJ: Prentice-Hall.

Gottheil, E., R. Sterling, and S. Weinstein. 1997. "Outreach Engagement Efforts: Are They Worth the Effort?" *American Journal of Drug and Alcohol Abuse* 23, 1: 61-66.

Hacking, I. 1999. *The Social Construction of What?* Cambridge, MA: Harvard University Press.

Harvey, D. 2005. *A Brief History of Neoliberalism.* Oxford: Oxford University Press.

Higgett, N., S. Wingert, J. Ristock, M. Brown, M. Ballantyne, S. Caett, et al. 2003. *Voices from the Margins: Experiences of Street-Involved Youth in Winnipeg.* Winnipeg: Winnipeg Inner-City Research Alliance.

Karabanow, J. 2004. *Being Young and Homeless: Understanding How Youth Enter and Exit Street Life.* New York: Peter Lang.

Karabanow, J., and P. Clement. 2004. "Interventions with Street Youth: A Commentary on the Practice-Based Research Literature." *Brief Treatment and Crisis Intervention* 4, 1: 93-108.

Kidd, S.A. 2003. "Street Youth: Coping and Interventions." *Child and Adolescent Social Work* 20, 4: 235-61.

Kidd, S.A., and K. Scrimenti. 2004. "Evaluating Child and Youth Homelessness: The Example of New Haven, Connecticut." *Evaluation Review* 28: 325-41.

Koeller, R. 2006. "Background Report: Homelessness and Street-Involved Youth in HRM [Halifax Regional Municipality]: Summary of Local Research Findings." http://www.halifax.ca/qol/documents/Backgrounder-YouthhomelessnessinHRM.pdf.

Koller, S.H., and M. Raffaelli. 2001. "Street Children's Rights and Well-Being: Psychological, Behavioral, and Policy Concerns." *International Society for the Study of Behavioural Development Newsletter* 38, 2: 3-5.

Kurtz, P.D., G.L. Kurtz, and S.J. Jarvis. 1991. "Problems of Maltreated Runaway Youth." *Adolescence* 26, 103: 543-55.

Lather, P. 2007. *Getting Lost: Feminist Efforts toward a Double(d) Science.* New York: State University of New York Press.

Loseke, D.R. 2008. *Thinking about Social Problems.* 2nd ed. New Brunswick, NJ: Adeline Transaction.

Mayers, M. 2001. *Street Kids and Streetscapes: Panhandling, Politics, and Prophecies.* New York: Peter Lang.

Miller, C.T. 2001. "A Theoretical Perspective on Coping with Stigma." *Journal of Social Issues* 57, 1: 73-92.

Newbery, P. 1993. "'Youth Outreach': Crisis Intervention with Marginal Adolescents." *Asian Journal of Counselling* 2, 2: 97-105.

Ng, A.T., and H.L. McQuistion. 2004. "Outreach to the Homeless: Craft, Science, and Future Implications." *Journal of Psychiatric Practice* 10, 2: 95-105.

Ngai, S.S. 2007. "Analyzing Hong Kong Outreach Work Identity: Associated Discourses and Power Mechanisms." *International Journal of Adolescence and Youth* 13, 4: 311-26.

Peck, E., and I.J. Norman. 1999. "Working Together in Adult Community Mental Health Services: Exploring Inter-Professional Role Relations." *Journal of Mental Health* 8, 3: 231-42.

Peressini, T., and L. MacDonald. 2000. "Urban Homeless in Canada." In *Canadian Cities in Transition: The Twenty First Century,* 2nd ed., ed. T. Bunting and P. Filion, 525-43. Don Mills, ON: Oxford University Press.

Reed, P.G. 2008. "Practitioner as Theorist." *Nursing Science Quarterly* 21, 4: 315-21.

Robertson, M.J., and P.A. Toro. 1998. "Homeless Youth: Research, Intervention, and Policy." In *Practical Lessons: The 1998 National Symposium on Homelessness Research,* ed. L.B. Fosburg and D.L. Dennis. Washington, DC: US Department of Housing and Urban Development and US Department of Health and Human Services.

Rowe, M. 1999. *Crossing the Border: Encounters between Homeless People and Outreach Workers.* Berkeley: University of California Press.

Ryan, P., and S. Morgan. 2004. *Assertive Outreach: A Strengths Approach to Policy and Practice.* Edinburgh: Churchill Livingstone.

Susser, E., S.M. Goldfinger, and A. White. 1990. "Some Clinical Approaches to the Homeless Mentally Ill." *Community Mental Health Journal* 26, 5: 463-79.

Tsemberis, S., L. Gulcur, and M. Nakae. 2004. "Housing First, Consumer Choice, and Harm Reduction for Homeless Individuals with a Dual Diagnosis." *American Journal of Public Health* 94, 4: 651-56.

Valentine, J., and L. Wright-DeAgüero. 1996. "Defining the Components of Street-Outreach for HIV Prevention: The Contact and the Encounter." *Public Health Reports* 3 (Supplement 1): 69-74.

Weiser, J. 1983. "Using Photographs in Therapy with People Who Are 'Different.'" In *PhotoTherapy in Mental Health,* ed. D.A. Krauss and J.L. Fryrear, 174-99. Springfield, IL: Charles Thomas.

Contextualizing Care

9

Generating Alternatives to the Individualization of Struggles and Support by Considering Loss

JANET NEWBURY

This chapter is an effort to "strain against the constraints of the fore-seeable and possible, to *open* the horizon of possibility to what it cannot foresee or foretell" (Caputo 1997, 133-34). By so doing, I wish to work toward the creation of a space in which alternatives in how human services are currently conceived and practised might become possible. Hopefully, one paragraph of critique will suffice as a starting place.

I fear that intervening as though the "individual" is the unit through which change needs to occur might be less than helpful. This is not to say that individuals should not be offered support; rather, current conceptualizations of "support" feel dangerously close to blame (Gergen 1994). As stated by Butler (2004, 5), "isolating the individuals involved absolves us of the necessity of coming up with a broader explanation for events." It also perpetuates conditions in which help seekers and professionals continue to play the respective roles of "afflicted and de-liverer" (Szasz 2002, 169). Moreover, reducing "interventions" down to what is understood as essential (for the sake of legibility and practical ease) strips away the "particular, situated, and contextual attributes" of a given situation (Scott 1998, 346). I worry that, regardless of my good intentions, if I continue to participate in roles that take the (generic) individual as their starting place while refusing to honour the singularity of *each* individual, I run the risk of perpetuating conditions that are not only inequitable but also oppressive.

I wish to add my voice to the chorus of people who are both suggesting and working toward alternatives (e.g., Aldarondo 2007; Gergen 1994, 2009; Lakoff and Johnson 1999; McKnight 1995; Scott 1998) and to stand in solidarity with those who recognize the potential of that which is not yet on us but *can* be (Caputo 1997). Butler (2004, 7) suggests that, to understand ourselves as "acting within a historically established field, and one that has other actions in play, we will need to ... consider the ways in which our lives are profoundly implicated in the lives of others."

Although the routes by which this can be done are endless, I am interested in finding an opening in our *current* conditions through which we can begin to understand the significance of collective responsibility and connectedness. In a recent presentation, Jeremy Berland (26 February 2009) suggested that policy makers' tendency to misunderstand the child welfare system (as opposed to health or education, for example) is due in part to their lack of personal experience with it. Thus, rather than relying purely on imagination to bring these possibilities into consideration, it might be helpful to reflect on current experiences to make possible a future in which the potential of such connectedness can be maximized. I intend to follow Butler's (2004, 19) lead and consider the role of grief[1] and loss[2] in "finding a basis for community."

How Can Loss Illuminate Potential?

My choice to consider loss is in part a political choice. I see the current exploration as a step toward a deeper understanding of human connectedness and thus potential for a new way of considering our roles as helpers.

Regardless of gender, class, and ethnicity, the experience of loss "has made a tenuous 'we' of us all" (Butler 2004, 20). It does so in part because we all experience it (albeit differently) and in part because it instills a profound "reverence for life" (see Scott 1998, 345). Perhaps more importantly, it highlights the relational nature of human experience in that loss seems "to follow from our being socially constituted bodies, attached to others, at risk of losing those attachments, exposed to others" (Butler 2004, 20). Indeed, it serves as a real reminder of the vulnerability of all human beings. In these ways, loss makes space for the possibilities that the future is highly contingent and that we are interdependent. Starting from there, space can be made for less individualized approaches as we move forward in practice.

Even in the social sciences, whose object of study is inherently complex, diverse, and animated, fixed and static truth claims continue to prevail (Scott 1998). Following the lead of many post-structuralist and social constructionist scholars (e.g., Butler 2004), I wish to direct my focus not on the "essence" of loss but on the function of it. That is, I am interested in experiences (individual, social, and political) rather than truths. Considering how loss *has* functioned, how it *does* function, and how it *might* function can contribute to valuable learning when it comes to dynamic social engagement (instead of studying what loss *is*, which is more likely to result in a static claim to truth). The very act of shifting from truth claims to concerns about how to get on together "in the meantime" (Caputo 1997, 70) is an intentional move beyond polarizing debate over what is toward concerted action regarding what might be.

On a more theoretical note, and to avoid epistemological confusion, I wish to make explicit my social constructionist orientation (see Gergen 1994). Although my perspective is informed in many ways by postmodern notions of multiplicity and anti-foundationalism (St. Pierre 2000), I am concerned with the practical implications of knowledge as well. For instance, if the world is indeed constantly constituting us *and* being constituted by us as actors within it, how might we make decisions and engage in action in the midst of it all? Social constructionism does not assert (or necessarily deny) a particular reality, but such a perspective does acknowledge that we move about *as if* there is one, at the least (Gergen 2009; Hacking 1999). Admittedly, the discussion might at times appear to reflect a positivist understanding of this "reality." This is difficult to avoid, for I am attempting to critically engage with current social realities (in which I, too, am embedded), which are themselves largely informed by a modernist paradigm (Taylor 2007). I simply acknowledge that such is the (socially constructed?) reality in which this exploration occurs.

The remainder of this chapter, then, explores *some* of the various functions of loss over time, concluding with a discussion of implications for practice in the helping professions.

How Loss Has Functioned

A literature review of grief and loss inevitably leads to theories about its essence and universality (see Bonanno 2001; Kubler-Ross 1983; Murray 2001; Worden 2001). Challenges to these formulations are often made through cross-cultural comparisons, making the point that grief responses are culturally constituted (e.g., Bonanno et al. 2005; Yasien-Esmael and Shimshon Rubin 2005). Some scholars have made the shift further still by considering grief's purpose, highlighting how differences in ideological constructions across time and place inform understandings of the purpose of grief differently (Stroebe et al. 1992).

Literature about the *function* of loss as a valuable site for learning is more difficult to access. Eberle (2005, 541) edges closer to the type of inquiry I am seeking. He observes that, prior to the medical and economic developments that currently afford most North Americans fewer brushes with death, the experience of loss was common throughout life, not primarily in old age. Although few of us would wish for such conditions now, the function of this "acquaintance with the trappings of death" can still be acknowledged. Eberle suggests that, in times when and places where bereavement was (and is) more common, an "appreciation of the human condition," "a dignified acceptance of individual mortality," and "a bravery of spirit" were stimulated. He warns against nostalgia for a past in which life was both shorter and less predictable, but he also draws attention to the value of loss under such conditions in that humility was cultivated in life when death was both more familiar and more expected.

The function of loss is contingent on the circumstances that surround it. This point is made clear by Hunter (2007), who explores the collective mourning in Invercargill, New Zealand, during and following World War I. Loss as a result of war functioned to create an extensive "circle of mourning," which reached beyond the family, while it also "accelerated some changes in attitudes towards death and dying" (41). Some of these changes in attitude (due to the scale, manner, and proximal distance of these deaths) included a shift to "a comprehensive medical model of death" (43); a pragmatic interest in "keeping emotions in check" (48); increased ritualization of mourning practices; and a heightened understanding of one's own mortality. In addition, the search for meanings made of such hardships varied, including belief that it was God's will, solace in the legacy of a good human being, and patriotic heroism and duty.

This idea of duty warrants further discussion. Although memorial days and the erection of war memorials are often understood as instances of public mourning, Hunter (2007, 55) differentiates between community values and the "imperial rhetoric of valiant death and glorious sacrifice." Loss can and does function as a powerful tool for state propaganda and can be observed to rally support for nationalistic initiatives (often war). Hunter notes that loss was manipulated to silence dissidence, although the same losses also fuelled dissidence for some who refused to remain silent.

Damousi (2002, 102) notes that attending to loss historically can call to attention the ways in which it has functioned politically, along the lines of gender, race, and class. She is concerned that historical and cultural life is often explored at the exclusion of emotional life. The exploration of loss is one way of acknowledging the three are, in fact, inseparable. "For many marginalized groups," Damousi says, "grief and injury have become the 'very condition' of their politics." She elaborates this important point as follows: "Collective group memory of historical loss and continued suffering mobilized [people] to not only claim remuneration for their losses, but also to demand a cultural and political recognition of their grief." This can be observed through breast cancer survival, residential school survival, apartheid, the Holocaust, and the Hiroshima bomb. The notion that throughout history loss has served as an impetus for social change is evident in each of these – and limitless other – cases. Perhaps at this point it is also worth stating that my interest in this chapter is to examine how loss functions politically and collectively. Of course, there are personal dimensions to experiences of loss that I will not take up in this exploration, but I certainly recognize their significance.

How Loss Does Function

Increasingly and globally, a wide variety of groups have organized in efforts to combat the inequitable conditions that precipitated and perpetuate their traumas and losses. If treated as individual cases, there is nothing to say they will not be repeated. However, if the collective nature of such losses is identified, then their political nature can also be acknowledged. For example, in recognizing the Montreal Massacre as an indication of underlying societal misogyny, the politicization of grief can serve to provoke shifts toward gender equity.

Indeed, public grief has also become an avenue through which a spirit of solidarity can be expressed. The creation of impromptu memorials, such as those erected after the Columbine school shooting, is one clear example (Doss 2002). However, Klein (2000, cited in Doss 2002, 69) urges that "memory can come to the fore in an age of historiographic crisis precisely because it figures as a therapeutic alternative to historical discourse." In other words, reactively engaging in public mourning rituals is not – in and of itself – political practice. It can in fact serve to satiate the public rather than engage them/us, having the opposite of a politicizing effect.

There are many who agree that it is not just engagement but also *critical* engagement with collective loss that is required to move us toward effectively addressing conditions. The absence of certain losses from the realm of public grief can illustrate this point. Foote (cited in Doss 2002, 64) suggests that certain tragedies are publicly grieved whereas others are not because experiences that "produce reactions of shame and revulsion are often obliterated or silenced." Damousi (2002) goes further and argues that, by omitting certain realities of loss from political and historical discourse, not only are those experiences of oppression silenced but also the very people who experience(d) them are rendered invisible, thus perpetuating ongoing states of injustice.

Butler (2004, 15) suggests that, by way of media representations, partisan news coverage, war memorials, and obituaries, citizens are actively encouraged to publicly grieve certain losses but not others, and this "is tantamount to the suppression of dissent." This function of loss, though not addressed specifically by Rose (1998, 63), can serve as an example of how "the conduct of conduct ... [can] accumulate a kind of ethical basis." In this way, the protracted and ritualized mourning of certain losses (e.g., images of flags on the caskets of fallen soldiers) can "justify a more or less permanent war" (Butler 2004, xix).

Thus, on the one hand, loss serves social justice in that it ties our emotional experiences to a political one, highlighting the political nature of personal life. In so doing, loss can stir us into action and inspire us to incite social change. On the other hand, it can also freeze us into inaction; our desire to stand in solidarity with those we grieve can silence our questions about why and how they died, thus restricting the possibilities for critical social engagement.

How Loss Might Function

My concern, as stated earlier, is with the tendency of human services to situate the onus for change within individuals who seek support. Why do we treat *social* issues individually? Taylor (2007, 49) identifies the "progress of disenchantment" as largely responsible for this tendency. Disenchantment refers to the emphasis on empirical evidence over magic and spirituality. It was believed that disenchantment could make equality among individuals attainable by removing the privilege from those considered closer to God or gifted.

Disenchantment did not entirely succeed, but it continues to have an impact. Along with a matrix of contextual factors, it shifted modern worldviews to such an extent that citizens have come to view society as comprising coexisting and cooperating *individuals* – that which is emotional, spiritual, and beyond the immediately visible realm has been dismissed as unscientific or irrational. This emphasis on individual agency contributed to what Taylor (2007, 49) calls the "great disembedding" as we began prioritizing ourselves over the collective in an unprecedented way.

Derrida (1995, 9) cautions, however, not to take such genealogies too literally. That is, even though these shifts can certainly be observed, we must remember that, though the earlier state of affairs might have been subordinated, "it is never eliminated." In other words, our previous (more collective) ways of getting on together still exist as possibilities. I do not intend to romanticize the past here, as it has already been stated that unquestionably oppressive systems have always existed. However, I do wish to acknowledge the value that might lie in drawing from both the past and the present when considering how to move forward.

And this is where I see the potential in how loss *might* function. Although in many ways loss is a uniquely individual and personal experience, in many other ways it is also (not instead) a relational and political experience. Given my central concern with human service practice, it is this aspect of loss I am addressing here. Additionally, exploring loss enables consideration of those emotional, non-material aspects of political and social life that have been largely dismissed as a result of the modern emphasis on rationality. I will separate the remainder of this discussion into three sections: connectedness, hope, and social responsibility.

Connectedness

Current liberal notions of individual agency are often considered prerequisites to social equality. However, some scholars have suggested that by recognizing how behaviour is in large part socially conditioned we can work toward responsibly engaging with one another and striving toward the creation of equitable conditions (Butler 2004; Derrida 1995; Reder, Duncan, and Gray 1993). Perhaps the individualism of modernity has distracted us from entertaining this possibility, but loss can serve as a current and constant reminder that citizens remain relational beings (Gergen 1994). Through the experience of loss, our undeniable connectedness can be made legible in that grief "displays the thrall in which our relations with others hold us ... in ways that challenge the very notion of ourselves as autonomous and in control" (Butler 2004, 23).

Such embodied awareness of human interdependence can signal us to some real possibilities when it comes to how we might move forward together. For example, after the national loss experienced by the United States on 11 September 2001, the fallacy of inherent "first world privilege" was made apparent, as was the inevitability of global interdependence

(Butler 2004, xii). Although the American government responded with retribution, Butler sees this tragedy as a missed opportunity for the United States to "redefine itself as part of a global community" (xi). To do this, Butler insists, it is necessary to address conditions, not causes, for the latter are simplified, personified, and decontextualized. This is not to say that conditions are at fault instead of individuals; rather, people only act within their conditions.

Acknowledging connectedness among individuals, communities, and even nations is not simply an attempt to soften the harsh realities of life. In fact, it is often through those harsh realities – such as loss – that such connectedness is made most apparent, even when commonly embraced ideologies do not make room for this possibility. The argument here is that, if this connectedness is acknowledged, then our responses would fundamentally change to become more relational.

Hope

While listening to an interview with Emmanuel Jal (CBC Radio 2009), former Sudanese child soldier, I was struck by the profound commitment to positive change that has sprung from his multiple losses. Jal said, "I've lost my childhood. There's no way I can ever gain anything I've lost ... The only thing I can change now is the future." His experiences of loss have ignited his determination to work toward a just future. In hearing those words, I felt ashamed at the cynicism I sometimes entertain when it comes to possibilities for positive social change. How can loss provoke hope?

Derrida (1995, 15) pronounces that "conscience that looks death in the face is another name for freedom." In other words, it is only when the desire for control, immortality, and absolute power over ourselves and others is relinquished that we can live and give with genuine and complete freedom. According to Derrida, it is death that gives us no choice but to embrace our vulnerability to such an extent that this openness is not only possible but also inevitable.

In the case of Jal, now that preserving himself and seeking retribution have ceased to be his primary goals, he can engage in the goal of social justice more completely. He is both optimistic and hopeful that alternatives are possible; indeed, his optimism and hope are in themselves contributions to such alternatives since they partially determine how he engages on a social and political level (Gergen 1994). It is through the experience of vulnerability in the face of immense loss that this can clearly be felt and by which alternative goals are given the space to be pursued (Derrida 1995).

Connectedness + Hope = Social Responsibility
Although the individual experience of loss is often described as extreme separation rather than connectedness (Stroebe et al. 1992), and as a sense of hopelessness as opposed to hope (Murray 2001), the collective response is often quite the opposite. "There is losing, as we know," Butler (2004, 21) says, "but there is also the transformative effect of loss, and this latter cannot be charted or planned." When loss is understood contextually and collectively, how it *might* function becomes apparent.

Of course, in times of loss, the tendency to blame can feel cathartic or even be perceived as a movement toward justice, as in the case of well-publicized child death inquiries. However, Hallett (cited in Reder, Duncan, and Gray 1993, 18) suggests that, "in criticizing the actions of individuals, the basic social order remains unchallenged." Thus, by observing the realities of human interconnectedness, acknowledging the vulnerability that lies in this, and foregrounding hope rather than retribution, perhaps responsible social action can become a more central component of human service practice. In the context of this exploration, responsibility is understood from a Derridean (1995) perspective in that it is openness, responsiveness, and humbling of oneself to the always unknown "other." There are no presumed objective or a priori criteria for "responsible action."

Implications for Practice
In February 2009, I attended a full-day workshop with Gerry Oleman, representing the Reservation School Survivor Society. Despite the lifelong experiences of personal, community, and spiritual loss he shared with us, an abundance of hope – even joy – poured out of him. His account was grounded historically, but his commitment to connectedness as a tool for constructing a more equitable future was centred. At least as powerful as his words was the potential I experienced through

the coming together of many different human service professionals in my community to hear Oleman.

Among the group that day were doctors, nurses, police officers, social workers, youth justice workers, and family preservation workers. The practices these professionals engage in daily are often centred on the individual. Indeed, most are mandated as such. For example, Gove's 1995 recommendations after the review of five-year-old Matthew Vaudreuil's death insisted that "the safety of the individual child [be] the paramount concern of child welfare" (Callahan and Swift 2007, 163). Although a child's safety is of paramount concern, it led to individualized interventions (e.g., risk assessments) that overlooked important systemic inequities and the role of poverty in conditions of abuse and neglect. Moreover, limited resources were drawn from other community and family supports to uphold these interventions of child protection (Callahan and Swift 2007).

So, though child and youth care practice identifies itself as "relational," this relational engagement can often occur only on interpersonal levels (if at all); the theoretical assumptions that drive practice and interventions are still largely informed by individual theories of change (Reder, Duncan, and Gray 1993). It is frequently argued that the systems within which practitioners work perpetuate existing power hierarchies, leaving limited room for the role of authentic relationships (Fewster 2002).

What I found promising about the workshop with Oleman, on the other hand, was the shift that occurred when the relational and contextualized nature of the hardships clients experience was acknowledged by helping professionals. Somehow the same human service practitioners who so often "intervene" as the knowing experts in the lives of families (McKnight 1995) were brainstorming together about how changes in our own practices, social systems, and ways of being in community can actually contribute positively to the experiences of those whom we aim to support. In this alternative view, relationships are not a choice or an intervention but an inherent part of social life. Acknowledging them as such disperses the onus for change into the hands of all players rather than simply those "problematic" individuals and families who seek professional support (Reder, Duncan, and Gray 1993).

To suggest that consideration of loss has implications for human service practice is not novel: indeed, the inquiries into the deaths of children involved in the child welfare system demonstrate that loss already has immense implications for service delivery. Thus, I am not suggesting *that* we should consider loss in human service delivery; rather, we should consider an alternative perspective on *how* we might do so. Armitage and Murray (2007, 154) argue, for example, that "death reviews ... [lead] to a reassertion of the traditional 'child saving' role at the expense of other broader and more structural family and child service objectives."

So what learning can take place for helping professionals by shifting the focus from the "truths" about loss to how it functions? I believe that, in shifting our vantage point, CYC practitioners and other helpers might move closer to the socially responsible role we hope to play. Some possibilities are listed below.

Making Space for Unique Individuals, Not the "Generic Individual"

Even though Gove and other decision makers wish to protect individual children from harm, current policies are not succeeding (Foster and Wharf 2007). In my quest for reasons why this is the case, I encountered Derrida's (1995, 36) differentiation between a generic individual and a unique (actual) individual: "The individualism of technological civilization ... is an individualism relating to a role and not a person." Loss can serve as a readily accessible metaphor by which this distinction can be grasped. The unique, personal, and emotional nature of loss brings into consideration the very dimensions so often the first to be dismissed within "rational" inquiries in child welfare, which are more likely to take on a universalistic and legalistic tone (Reder, Duncan, and Gray 1993). These dimensions are often central to the experiences of the people whom we aim to support (Damousi 2002). If means and norms continue to guide human service practice, then we will certainly continue to "get it wrong" for many of our clients. However, perhaps engaging in or with conditions with an open and humble posture can make space for those unique individuals' experiences to rise to the surface. That way practitioners can respond to *their* clients rather than "the" (impersonal) client. Although this speaks to practice relationships, what can be made of this discussion of loss on a policy level?

Releasing the Desire for Predictability and Control

The move toward evidence-based practice (EBP) has had a profound effect on human service practices in a variety of fields. For example, addressing social work in particular, Thyer (2008) promotes EBP based on its ability to measure phenomena, evaluate efficacy, save time, attain grants and credibility, and contribute to professionalization. He takes pride in positivist philosophy's ability to give further credit to social work practice by asserting that the field "deals with an objective world, not simply a socially constructed one" (341). In so doing, practitioners can learn to "ask answerable questions" (344), making success – and the evaluation of it – possible.

In her exploration of the American response to the losses of 9/11, however, Butler comes to a different conclusion about the usefulness of striving toward predictability. As stated earlier, she says that loss must remind us that "no final control can be secured, and that final control is not, cannot be, an ultimate value" (2004, xiii). From such a perspective, developing methods by which we can strive toward more precise control means missing an opportunity to change our course. If interpreted in this way, loss can lead to the "humbling insight that there is a lot that we don't understand" (Taylor 2007, 196) rather than stricter mandates reactively implemented in professional practice (as evidenced in Foster and Wharf 2007).

Acknowledging that our understanding will always be partial can lead to more socially responsible practice (i.e., responsive, not reactive) in that as workers we will look more closely, listen more actively, ask more questions, and presume less. Polkinghorne (2005, 138) reminds us that "methods designed to study the physical world are not a good fit for the study of experience." Thus, with the humility and vulnerability provoked by consideration of the complexities of loss, perhaps more professional energy can be invested in designing interventions and developing policies that embrace the unpredictability of human experience rather than sifting it out of consideration. Flexibility in procedures and practices can then allow us to be effectively responsive to more diverse situations and clients rather than serving (well) only those who fit neatly within our models (Scott 1998). By contextualizing experience in this way, policy makers, practitioners, and help seekers are more likely to experience success.

Challenging the Market Economy Model of "Care"

Returning to EBP, there has been considerable debate over its implications. In the field of nursing, for instance, Walker (2003, 146) critiques this "seduction by superlatives" and its flawed assumption that EBP will result in "best" practice. On the contrary, she joins Foucault in his skepticism of movements based on a desire for certainty. Walker fears that positivism is not a route to the truth but a "regime of truth" (146; see also Foucault 1972; Rose 1998) that is more closely linked to economic rationalism due to limited resources than it is to a commitment to "best" practice. Indeed, Walker fears that EBP might limit patient choice, create biases that misrepresent evidence, oversimplify the complexities of care, wrongly interpret averages as norms, and compromise clinical freedom. Recognizing that EBP is one (not *the*) "approach to what constitutes knowledge" (152), she urges a commitment to developing alternatives in order to remain critical and informed, thus contributing to the provision of quality care.

I wish to draw particular attention to the role of economic rationalism in service design and delivery and how consideration of loss can strengthen the perspectives of those pursuing an alternative. Economic rationalism is one of the key considerations in human service implementation and bureaucratic organization (Foster and Wharf 2007). In other words, the interventions considered to be economically feasible in terms of delivery, measurement, and supervision are often favoured, and these are most often interventions that centre the individual. Callahan and Swift (2007, 158) note that this business model of services has sought "little input from its customers." Moreover, when conditions are not taken into consideration, the fact that the families most in need of support are not randomly dispersed can easily be overlooked. For instance, Aboriginal children, families, and communities are far more likely to be deemed "at risk" than non-Aboriginal Canadians (Armitage and Murray 2007). Thus, an individual-centred business model can give both practitioners and policy makers tunnel vision when it comes to the broader forces at play and places feasibility higher on the list of priorities than efficacy for the groups most often marginalized.

Loss can serve to widen this tunnel vision if we allow ourselves to take notice of the commonalities among the populations in need of "intervention." Indeed, simply reading the international news with this as our lens can draw attention to the fact that the current state of affairs marginalizes some groups, who then experience perpetual and multiple losses as a result first of certain social conditions and second of the global refusal to acknowledge those conditions. Violence, displacement, poverty, and further marginalization can then follow (see, e.g., Marwaha 2008 on the Democratic Republic of Congo). Centring interventions only at an individual level does little to alter such unjust conditions. By widening our perspective, we can perhaps begin to see our own complicity in sustaining the hardships we then busy ourselves trying to remedy (Klein 2000; McKnight 1995).

Sharing the Responsibility for Change

The previous section indicated how a discussion of economy easily slips into power dynamics. Once such inequities are acknowledged, "intervening" on an individual level without addressing those conditions feels irresponsible. By considering loss as a reminder of human connectedness, an alternative becomes apparent.

When Gerry Oleman brought together the group of human service practitioners to discuss the plight of Aboriginal communities in British Columbia, entirely different solutions were elicited than likely would have been the case if the same group of professionals were discussing a particular individual's case. Without said individual, we had nowhere to look but at ourselves and the relationships among us and within our community. It is not a coincidence, I believe, that the subject through which we related was one of profound loss. As Butler (2004, 22) suggests, "many people think that grief is privatizing ... But I think it furnishes a sense of political community of a complex order, and it does this first of all by bringing to the fore the relational ties that have implications for theorizing fundamental dependency and ethical responsibility."

By contextualizing loss and hardship, we can perhaps begin to contextualize life. And this, in turn, would profoundly shape the way in which we imagine positive change, with each of us bearing some responsibility.

Concluding Thoughts

I have outlined how consideration of loss might contribute to the engagement in human service practices with an emphasis on social responsibility by contextualizing (rather than individualizing) our work. Particularly, I have suggested that, by (1) making space for unique individuals, not "the generic individual," (2) releasing the desire for predictability and control, (3) challenging the market economy model of "care," and (4) sharing the responsibility for change, practitioners and policy makers can move toward not only reacting to instances of injustice but also contributing to the creation of more just conditions. I have suggested that the example of loss might provide us with access to these possibilities.

I suspect there might still be a niggling concern about the fact that sometimes individuals do need support. To that I say "absolutely." My argument is in no way meant to suggest that by attending to conditions a utopia can then be established in which no individuals need help. Rather, I am suggesting that our current approach is rendering those individuals invisible by obscuring the effects of conditions. By stepping back and contextualizing practice, we might see individuals for the first time or at least more clearly. Perhaps in so doing our *interventions* will morph into the *support* we wish to provide.

Considering loss is offered not as the secret gateway to this shift but as one available avenue by which we might begin to espouse a "reverence for life" (Scott 1998, 345) that could serve to strengthen practice and communities and thus contribute to social justice. Particularly since loss itself is often pervasive but unacknowledged in the experiences of the children and youth we serve, it is a relevant place to begin for human service professionals.

Notes

1 Murray (2001, 219) defines "grief" as "the emotional response to loss." This idea is reflected in much of the literature I read (see Cohen and Mannarino 2004; James, Friedman, and Landon Matthews 2002) as well as among my research participants (Newbury 2007), who all indicated that grief encompasses the feelings they have been left with as a result of their losses.

2 I have used the word *loss* as opposed to *bereavement* so as not to limit my exploration to the experience of loss due to death or to loss at an individual level. The lines between loss, bereavement, and grief are often murky as the experiences frequently occur together. My dictionary's definition of "lose" is to "be deprived of or cease to have" (Bisset 2002, 594), but the word is highly nuanced and frequently used in many contexts. It is this intangible nature of the word I appreciate.

References

Aldarondo, E., ed. 2007. *Advancing Social Justice through Clinical Practice*. Mahwah, NJ: Lawrence Erlbaum Associates.

Armitage, A., and E. Murray. 2007. "Thomas Gove: A Commission of Inquiry Puts Children First and Proposes Community Governance and Integration of Services." In *People, Politics, and Child Welfare in British Columbia*, ed. L. Forster and B. Wharf, 139-57. Vancouver: UBC Press.

Bisset, A. 2002. *The Canadian Oxford Compact Dictionary*. Don Mills, ON: Oxford University Press.

Bonanno, G. 2001. "The Crucial Importance of Empirical Evidence in the Development of Bereavement Theory." *Psychological Bulletin* 127, 4: 561-64.

Bonanno, G., A. Papa, K. Lalande, N. Zhang, and J. Noll. 2005. "Grief Processing and Deliberate Grief Avoidance: A Prospective Comparison of Bereaved Spouses and Parents in the United States and the People's Republic of China." *Journal of Counselling and Clinical Psychology* 73, 1: 86-98.

Butler, J. 2004. *Precarious Life: The Powers of Mourning and Violence*. New York: Verso.

Callahan, M., and K. Swift. 2007. "Great Expectations and Unintended Consequences: Risk Assessment in Child Welfare in British Columbia." In *People, Politics, and Child Welfare in British Columbia*, ed. L. Foster and B. Wharf, 158-83. Vancouver: UBC Press.

Caputo, J. 1997. *Deconstruction in a Nutshell: A Conversation with Jacques Derrida*. New York: Fordham University Press.

CBC Radio. 2009. "Q: Jion Ghomeshi Talks to Hip Hop Singer Emmanuel Jal about His Memoir, *War Child*." http://www.cbc.ca/.

Cohen, J., and A. Mannarino. 2004. "Treatment of Childhood Traumatic Grief." *Journal of Clinical and Adolescent Psychology* 33, 4: 819-31.

Damousi, J. 2002. "History Matters: The Politics of Grief and Injury in Australian History." *Australian Historical Studies* 118: 100-12.

Derrida, J. 1995. *The Gift of Death*. Translated by D. Wills. Chicago: University of Chicago Press.

Doss, E. 2002. "Death, Art, and Memory in the Public Sphere: The Visual and Material Culture of Grief in Contemporary America." *Mortality* 7, 1: 63-82.

Eberle, S.G. 2005. "Memory and Mourning: An Exhibition History." *Death Studies* 29: 535-57.

Fewster, G. 2002. "Growing Together: The Personal Relationship in Child and Youth Care." *Journal of Child and Youth Care* 15, 4: 5-16.

Foster, L., and B. Wharf, eds. 2007. *People, Politics, and Child Welfare in British Columbia.* Vancouver: UBC Press.

Foucault, M. (1972) 1984. "Truth and Power." In *The Foucault Reader,* ed. P. Rabinow. New York: Pantheon Books.

Gergen, K. 1994. *Realities and Relationships: Soundings in Social Construction.* Cambridge, MA: Harvard University Press.

–. 2009. *Relational Being: Beyond Self and Community.* New York: Oxford University Press.

Hacking, I. 1999. *The Social Construction of What?* Cambridge, MA: Harvard University Press.

Hunter, K. 2007. "'Sleep on Dear Ernie, Your Battles Are O'er': A Glimpse of a Mourning Community, Invercargill, New Zealand 1914-1925." *War in History* 14, 1: 36-62.

James, J., R. Friedman, and L. Landon Matthews. 2002. *When Children Grieve: For Adults to Help Children Deal with Death, Divorce, Pet Loss, Moving, and Other Losses.* New York: HarperCollins Publishers.

Klein, N. 2000. *No Logo.* Toronto: Random House.

Kubler-Ross, E. 1983. *On Children and Death: How Children and Their Parents Can and Do Cope with Death.* New York: Simon and Schuster.

Lakoff, G., and M. Johnson. 1999. *Philosophy in the Flesh: The Embodied Mind and Its Challenge to Western Thought.* New York: Basic Books.

Marwaha, A. 2008. "Battle for Congo's Mineral Assets." http://news.bbc.co.uk/.

McKnight, J. 1995. *The Careless Society: Community and Its Counterfeits.* New York: Basic Books.

Murray, J. 2001. "Loss as a Universal Concept: A Review of the Literature to Identify Common Aspects of Loss in Diverse Situations." *Journal of Loss and Trauma* 6: 219-41.

Newbury, J. 2007. "'Even Now': Ongoing and Experiential Interpretations of Childhood Loss." Master's thesis, University of Victoria.

Polkinghorne, D.E. 2005. "Language and Meaning: Data Collection in Qualitative Research." *Journal of Counselling Psychology* 52, 2: 137-45.

Reder, P., S. Duncan, and M. Gray. 1993. *Beyond Blame: Child Abuse Tragedies Revisited.* New York: Routledge.

Rose, N. 1998. *Inventing Our Selves: Psychology, Power, and Personhood.* New York: Cambridge University Press.

Scott, J. 1998. *Seeing Like a State: How Certain Schemes to Improve the Human Condition Have Failed.* New Haven: Yale University Press.

St. Pierre, E.A. 2000. "Poststructural Feminism in Education: An Overview." *International Journal of Qualitative Studies in Education* 13, 5: 477-515.

Stroebe, M., M. Gergen, K. Gergen, and W. Stroebe. 1992. "Broken Hearts or Broken Bonds: Love and Death in Historical Perspective." *American Psychologist* 47, 10: 1205-12.

Szasz, T. 2002. "'Diagnosing' Behaviour: Cui Bono?" In *Studies in Meaning: Exploring Constructivist Psychology,* ed. J.D. Raskin and S.K. Bridges, 169-79. New York: Pace University Press.

Taylor, C. 2007. *Modern Social Imaginaries.* Durham: Duke University Press.

Thyer, B. 2008. "The Quest for Evidence-Based Practice? We Are All Positivists!" *Research on Social Work Practice* 18, 4: 339-45.

Walker, K. 2003. "Why Evidence-Based Practice Now? A Polemic." *Nursing Inquiry* 10, 3: 145-55.

Worden, W. 2001. *Grief Counselling and Grief Therapy: A Handbook for the Mental Health Practitioner.* New York: Springer Publishing Company.

Yasien-Esmael, H., and S. Shimshon Rubin. 2005. "The Meaning Structures of Muslim Bereavements in Israel: Religious Traditions, Mourning Practices, and Human Experience." *Death Studies* 29: 495-518.

PART 4

Policy Discourses in Child and Youth Care

Constructing and Regulating the Young Offender
Trends in Punishment from Colonial to Contemporary Canada

10

LORINDA STONEMAN

On 19 November 2007, Robert Nicholson, then minister of justice and attorney general of Canada, introduced Bill C-25, An Act to Amend the Youth Criminal Justice Act, on behalf of the Harper government.[1] The bill proposed two key changes to the youth justice system: increasing the availability of remand (pre-trial detention before a youth has been found guilty) and adding specific mention of deterrence and denunciation to the principles of sentencing for youth crime (Bill-C-25 2008). Bill C-25, only one example designed to give "teeth" to the Conservative government's political direction of "toughening" youth justice policy, reflects a punitive philosophy toward crime control and prevention (Bala, Carrington, and Roberts 2009). It also represents the latest in a long-standing engagement with various ways of understanding youth, crime, and individualism in Canadian society.

This chapter is about how we choose to address and respond to the "young offender" in Canada. By illustrating the historical and contemporary notions of youth justice in Canada, I argue that our current constructions of youth are not new but have been embedded in a long history of social policy favouring microsystem explanations over complex multilevel understandings. Like the history of "the child" more generally, the specific history of youth justice has been surrounded – if not *characterized* – by ideological debates. The current Conservative federal government has created a suitable environment in which to host punitive "crime control" policies that support a shift in the criminal justice system *away* from recognizing "children" as a category, distinct from adults (e.g., Blanchfield 2008; *National Post* 2008). The move toward (or, more precisely, *back to*) a harsh denunciatory system of youth punishment does not seem to be based on either existing crime prevention evidence or what is known about the effects on youth of incarceration. Instead, it sets up a false dichotomy in which the individual rights of offenders are posited as conflicting with those of victims, creating an artificial battle not necessary to the acquisition of justice. Although the Canadian imperative expressed in current legislation, the Youth Criminal Justice Act (2002), is to avoid custodial terms for youth where possible, political sentiments tend to favour it (e.g., Canadian Press 2006, 2008; Clark, Alphonso, and Perreaux 2008). Many scholars and activists have protested institutionalized violence meted out to Canadian youth, decried inaccurate portrayals of youth in the media, and challenged the corresponding adoption of managerial and actuarial approaches to justice issues (e.g., Hannah-Moffat and Maurutto 2003; Kelly 2003; Pate 2006; Silver and Miller 2002; Wotherspoon and Schissel 2001).

This chapter is divided into sections to explore two core questions: (1) how have the ideas of "youth justice" and "the child offender" been framed over time through key professional, political, and public discourses, and (2) how has this history *created* the contemporary "punishable offender" as "individual" and in contrast to the "ideal" by employing a managerial mentality fixed on constructions of public safety and surveillance? The chapter illustrates the politicization and managerial process currently employed in obtaining "justice" as key factors in maintaining a social structure implicated in the marginalization of young people. Although I will suggest more respectful and less exploitive justice practices, my aim here is to contribute to the critical discussion surrounding youth justice policy. Policy makers, academics, and the public alike would benefit from attention to "young offenders" as a social construct. In other words, conceptualizations and descriptions of the seemingly objective category of young offenders should instead be perceived as products of subjective, cooperative social interactions.

Knowledge, truth, and understanding, from a constructionist perspective, are necessarily entangled with the dominant discourse disseminated by those who exercise power and control (Foucault 1977), contingent on social and political movements (Gergen 2003).

Youth Justice and the Child Offender since Colonial Canada

To conceptualize how the Euro-Western world, specifically Canada, constructs and treats the "child offender," it is telling to revisit some historical understandings of delinquency. As with the history of child education and child psychology, the history of youth justice in Canada is profoundly influenced by immigration, private charity, modernization, and industrialization (Carrigan 1998). The European settlement period in Canada provides an effective comparison with the more contemporary recognition in Canada of children as individuals within the specific developmental phase of "childhood."

Youth Justice in Colonial Canada: 1600 to Industrialization

Shared characteristics of the histories of delinquent children in colonial Canada, as well as in the United Kingdom and continental Europe, are the harsh corporal treatments and disproportionate abuses faced by children of the under classes relative to those of the propertied classes. Carrigan (1998, 5) describes "delinquency" (e.g., specific deviant behaviour committed by young people) during 1600 colonial Canada as concerning mostly immigrant children and "girls of indifferent virtue" arriving on the shores of New France (Saint Lawrence River Valley, Acadia – Nova Scotia, Mississippi River Valley). The tens of thousands of "unruly" children who had immigrated to Canada over a period of about 200 years suffered extraordinary poverty exacerbated by continued and growing European immigration that taxed the limited resources of the new colony. In fact, in the early part of the 1800s, the population of New France (Lower Canada) more than doubled. Statistics Canada (2008) reports that, from 1806 to 1825, Lower Canada's population increased from 250,000 to 479,000. This increase eventually led to urban slums as well as rural areas filled with "dishonest vagabonds," as they were characterized by the new upper class (Carrigan 1998, 7). Street-level delinquency was readily attributed to negative social circumstances (including delinquent group formation and a lack of daily activities) thought to offer perfect training grounds for youth crime. Particularly in a context in which many youth tended to avoid the early school system, immigrant children were thought to be involved in few acceptable expenditures of their time (Houston 1972).

When settlement spread from New France to English Canada, concerns about delinquency spread. Unease was partly due to heightened anxieties regarding moral degeneracy associated with previously unknown populations with different cultural norms inhabiting new, unfamiliar territories, posing possible or perceived threats to the economic progress of the new colonies (Houston 1972). This pattern of lower-class juvenile delinquency, comprising predominantly property crimes such as vandalism and morality crimes such as vagrancy, begged for a remedy for the "idle hands" of youth (Carrigan 2004). Houston (1972, 257) suggests that it was not the condition of lower-class children that caused reformers concern but the habits they displayed, such as "ignorance and idleness." These behaviours threatened social order and morality and were identified as precursors of criminality. Rather than attributing delinquency to community and social disorder, as some had done during early settlement, disorder began to be blamed on what were regarded as young social misfits themselves, representing the beginning of the individualization process. The practice of child immigration agencies sending unaccompanied children from the United Kingdom to the colonies since the seventeenth century continued: from 1869 to 1919, at least 73,000 to 95,000 unaccompanied children immigrated to Canada from the United Kingdom (Carrigan 2004; Sutherland 2000). Besides the high rate of immigration of these unaccompanied children, long voyages on crowded and unsafe ships meant that many families immigrating to Canada suffered high mortality rates, further increasing the number of orphans (Carrigan 2004). The result was a large pool of at-risk children in the new colony of Canada.

In his review of first-hand historical accounts, Sutherland (2000) highlights the difficulty in discerning the attitudes early Canadians had toward children. He suggests with certainty, however, that toward the end of the 1800s, for the purpose of removing street children from

London, the United Kingdom sent more than 1,000 orphaned and street children to Canada annually. Those in support of organized child emigration were comforted by favourable publicity regarding the distribution of children arriving on Canadian shores (6). Although publicity had been encouraging, a review of the system by British officials eventually found systemic concerns, including a failure by Canadian officials to carry out inspections on children placed in residential settings and families as well as careless attitudes toward the care and well-being of the children.

Sutherland (2000) presents the scathing Doyle report of 1874 as offering valuable insight into the treatment of immigrant children in early Canada and of their Canadian-born counterparts. He speculates that children in this period were not recognized as individual, emotional beings with opportunities for growth; rather, they were vital components of the economy, particularly in agricultural settings. Because children were so integral to the rural society that characterized pre-industrial Canada, significantly more families volunteered to foster immigrant children than could possibly be placed with them. Sutherland argues that, though some consideration of children was due to humanitarian or moral underpinnings, the benefit children provided by labouring developed the dominant view of children in Canada as underformed adults to whom virtue could be taught through hard work. Carrigan (2004, 6) characterizes this time as one of severe punitive measures "tempered with mercy" in which English and French Canada established that children under seven could not grasp the nature of their offences, and thus could not be punished, and saw state intervention in some cases of children between seven and fourteen to withhold penalties. Mercy, however (like punishment), was generally not uniform in early Canada.

The popular explanatory models to account for youth criminality in pre-Confederation Canada are uncannily similar to some of the proposed contemporary explanations in that they shaped public policy from a modernist stance and, more importantly, highlighted the *individual* as the key holder of responsibility for crime. Anti-social behaviour, one's failure to live up to the standard of the ideal youth, was seen to be a result of an inadequate upbringing, leading to delinquency being blamed on the individual youth and/or the family unit as the key agent of juvenile socialization (Carrigan 1998).

New ideas from philosophers and penal reformers, including classical criminologists Cesare Beccaria from Italy and Jeremy Bentham from Great Britain, prevailed during nineteenth-century Canada. Although thought in the reformist era was diverse, thinkers were united in identifying individual rationality and the "hedonistic" or pleasure-seeking criminal as keys to understanding criminality and, accordingly, recognized deterrence as the key to crime reduction. In 1835, Dr. Charles Duncombe, a key penal reformer in Upper Canada, authored a report on prisons, paying close attention to the social causes of delinquency (Davis-Barron 2009). His view was that delinquents should be treated in an environment separate from that of adult offenders and, under the care of the state, removed from poor parental care. In the midst of the humanitarian approach taken by reformers, Alvi (2008) recognizes that blame for inappropriate child rearing was often placed on the family or the mother. The idea of humanity surrounded reformist thinking and was somewhat well received in Canada. Later the government response to the second volume of the report on prisons, the Brown Commission of 1849 (Davis-Barron 2009), led to changes in the treatment of juveniles after George Brown's caustic review of the penitentiary system, in which particular emphasis was placed on the needlessly strict treatment of juveniles (Carrigan 2004). At this point in history, controversy was a constant companion of the question of what could be done with delinquents – and views that youth should be punished severely persisted and pushed back against penal reform of the day.

The Delinquent Youth: Industrialization to 1847

Several competing explanations have been generated about the dramatic shift in understanding childhood as a separate, distinct developmental phase, first introduced in Europe, and later in Canada, during the nineteenth and early twentieth centuries. Some authors point to the attitudes of the state shifting in favour of healthy, positive development in children – a "new childhood" – marked by the introduction of legislation regulating the activities of children (e.g., compulsory education). Others prefer a less altruistic explanation, identifying the important role of economic

changes. For instance, the absence of labour in an increasingly indus-
trialized and mechanized economy sparked concerns about what to do
with many unemployed children in urban areas (Cruickshank 1981). A
mixture of the two explanations suggests that it was the already formed,
culturally embedded ideas of "childhood" during the Enlightenment
that coincided with massive economic modifications, producing social
changes. Nevertheless, the changes in thought, concurrent with shifting
market forces and revised constructions of mother, father, and child,
resulted in child protective sentiments – in practical terms, a drop in
the need or desire for child labour and the accompanying question of
what to do with unoccupied children (Carrigan 1998; Rahikanen 2004).

To occupy young people, what were once Sunday schools for working
children were transformed into conventional schools (those operating
on a daily basis). The concept of regulated, mandatory education became
widely accepted and expected as notions of childhood began to change
once again. The labour reform and child welfare acts of the mid- to late
nineteenth century legalized new notions of childhood and became part
of the regular understanding of an extended childhood. Schools marked
the first institutionalization of children to ensure social regulation
(Cruickshank 1981). Judge Hagarty reveals the vital need for schooling
as a mechanism of social control from the perspective of nineteenth-
century criminal justice reformers: "An ulcer is eating into the vitals of
our social system in the shape of crowds of people growing up in neglect
and ignorance, rapidly ripening into crime, too many of them destined
to form the chief population hereafter of our gaols and Penitentiaries"
(cited in Houston 1972, 261). Additionally, Rose (1991) identifies legislation capping workday hours and introducing minimum wage standards
as devoid of altruism. These policy advances provided by the British
Factory Act (1847) emerged as yet another method of social control
responding to the technological shift and resulting decreased need for
workers and the corresponding decrease in formal and accepted activities
to keep children busy.

Regulating Youth in Canada: 1857 to Post-World War II

In 1857, Parliament passed the first piece of Canadian federal legislation
concerning delinquents, An Act for the More Speedy Trial and

Punishment of Juvenile Offenders (Alvi 2008), followed in 1894 by the Act Respecting Arrest, Trial, and Imprisonment of Youthful Offenders (Carrigan 2004; Davis-Barron 2009). Passed within the context of several other legislative items restricting punishment for youth, the acts mandated that youth under sixteen years of age have special trials in private and be incarcerated separately from adults. Carrigan (2004) interprets these changes as state acknowledgment of the systemic victimization and adult criminal mentorship of youth in custody. The 1894 act also provided a role for charitable organizations to house some youth by maintaining homes for neglected children and foster care in lieu of incarceration. Eventually, the voices of reformers lobbying to provide leniency for many delinquents who suffered from neglect and family breakdown found a place alongside those favouring harsh punitive responses (Carrigan 2004). Houston (1972, 265) identifies the individual-level perspective on delinquency adopted by reformers: "While these mid-Victorian reformers did indeed anchor their analysis of social problems firmly in personal character ... character before adulthood was [seen as] pliable."

The Juvenile Delinquents Act (JDA) was passed in 1908, during the child savers movement – a time when children were regarded as vulnerable beings in need of state protection (Denov 2004). The period also saw the introduction of positive criminology, a school of thought – later adopted by the child savers (Davis-Barron 2009) – describing the causes of crime as beyond the control of the criminal (Alvi 2008). The JDA emphasized social welfarism and the newfound ideals of protection and support. The youth justice system, based on the guiding principle of *parens patriae*, was required to view and treat juvenile delinquents as misdirected children of the state rather than as criminals (Denov 2004). This idea, once heralded for its innovation, was later criticized for its inherent coercive, paternalistic, and interventionist philosophy. Some suggest that the JDA was not a response to *actual* incidents of deviance but yet another motion controlling the delinquents of the lower class to maintain the capitalist structure of power and wealth (Alvi 2008; Platt 1969, cited in Tanner 1996). As Platt (1977) notes, even the ideals of the child-saving movement itself have been interpreted with skepticism. A social movement in the progressive era (the last quarter of the nineteenth century), the child savers might not have been "successful in humanizing the criminal justice system, rescuing children from jails and prisons, and developing dignified judicial and penal institutions for juveniles" (xvii). In fact, Platt argues, middle- and upper-class child savers attempted to impose bureaucracy and organize social and criminal justice reform into a reasoned system as a new form of social control guaranteed to uphold their power. The changes in dealing with delinquents were made not in isolation but in cooperation with similar liberal "enlightened" changes across the social and economic spheres toward increased state regulation and control.

Although the JDA was in many ways a positive improvement on its legislative predecessors, representing a shift toward viewing youth as separate from adults, Alvi (2008) notes that the provisions tended to widen the net of social control over children on a path to ensuring conformity among lower-class children with middle-class norms. Because social causes were increasingly being reconceptualized as individual pathologies during this era, Alvi finds that delinquency was understood as an individual ill predominantly afflicting lower-class children. Delinquency was implicitly devoid of social context; it was a problem that could be remedied by treating the individual.

Lafferty (2002) observes that, during the first half of the twentieth century, state control over delinquents was seen as one part of a complex interplay of practices concerned with the success of Canada's social and economic future. For instance, on Canada's east coast, one's potential to be the "ideal" child, embodying moral and sexual purity and freedom from racial or religious differences, was seen as a right. This right was paired with the burgeoning country's need for hard-working, morally concerned citizens. In this view, children were not the property of their parents but potential producers and workers for their country. Thus, the state should, at all costs, protect the innocence and purity of all of its children. When state and agency institutions (e.g., the Halifax Child Aid Society – designed to oversee the protection of the "ideal" child) institutionalized children, it was the child welfare system that was seen as an important upholder of social morals.

Post-World War II Canada can also be understood as a time of change in understanding "the young offender," to some extent abandoning the paternalistic view of the early 1900s. Prochner (2000, 37) identifies World War II as a key event *increasing* awareness of "the welfare of young children that was brought on by wartime conditions, combined with an increase in the number of mothers working for pay." Others, however, see post-World War II Canada as a place where children deserved self-determination, signifying a more complex view of children (Denov 2004). Libel (2004) characterizes the introduction of child self-determination as a positive step in terms of a subject-oriented theory of children in postmodern and post-industrial times. This meant that, in some cases, children were no longer "objects of education" or "recipients of care" but active individuals in society – not seen to be under the complete influence and control of adults but understood as beings with agency (Landsdown 2001). Like the other major paradigm shifts identified above, the reasons for this change are debated and signify a diversifying and complicating of the ways in which children were viewed rather than a complete philosophical change (these discourses are still present and competing). Libel (2004), for example, gives credit to the view that, as soon as children were seen as consumers, their status within society adapted in response. Thus, the fact that children are constructed as being independent serves to illuminate their participation in the market, indicating broader thematic changes within society, and demonstrates an "accelerated childhood" (Landsdown 2001, 280). Others, including Alvi (2008), suggest that viewing youth as being independent allows for the expansion of social control agents designed to treat and reform those considered wayward.

By the 1960s, severe criticisms were being lodged at the youth justice system in light of the emerging rights-based climate, a climate concerned with emancipation and equality (Alvi 2008). Canada's first Bill of Rights (1960) and subsequent discussions throughout the 1980s laying the groundwork for the United Nations Convention on the Rights of the Child (1989)[2] caused concern about whether the JDA provided appropriate rights protection for delinquents and whether a paternalistic, welfare approach to youth justice remained favourable (Denov 2004). Others concerned with public protection from delinquents also found fault with the welfare approach of the JDA and lobbied for a new policy that would protect victims of youth crime. Furthermore, after passing the Canadian Charter of Rights and Freedoms in 1982, it became clearer that the JDA was not congruent with Canada's new rights-based approach to justice (Alvi 2008; Denov 2004).

Youth Justice in Canada: 1985 to 2007

The idea of the self-determining child pressed forward in the late twentieth century, marked by a drive to recognize children as existing with their own rights, as separate entities, and accordingly as sites of culpability and responsibility in the event of punishment (Denov 2004). With values, beliefs, and views separate from those of his or her parents, the *individual* child of Canada became identifiable as distinct from his or her family unit. Within the Canadian criminal justice system, the idea of children having their own rights was enshrined in law with the passing of the Young Offenders Act (YOA) in 1985; youth involved in crime were owed the same due process rights as adults, marking the dissolution of the JDA's principle of *parens patriae* (Corrado and Markwart 1994). Fundamentally, "the principles of the YOA were declared ... to protect the civil liberties of young people and specifically to provide them with non-judicial options" (Schissel 2006, 10). Denov (2004) highlights the apparent philosophical and practical contradictions of the YOA. Although the legislation considered the legal rights and freedoms and the unique conditions of children in conflict with the law, it simultaneously emphasized public protection and youth accountability. The JDA had emphasized the role of the state in providing assistance to delinquent and misguided youth; the YOA complicated this view of delinquents, adding that they are *criminals* in need of discipline and control (Alvi 2008; Denov 2004). Although there was a strong movement toward alternative measures to divert first-time or minor young offenders from the formal justice system, Alvi (2008, 248) suggests that the YOA "paid lip service to the possibilities inherent in alternative measures, overemphasized individual responsibilities, ... and ... witnessed the steady entrenchment of punishment and incarceration."

After nearly two decades with the YOA, widespread criticism caused Canada to make another change (Denov 2004). Public safety and security are considered the main principles of the Youth Criminal Justice Act (YCJA), which came into force in 2003. A far cry from the child rights perspective of the YOA, the YCJA responded to public and political outcry regarding the YOA's alleged lenience toward criminal behaviour of youth (Alvi 2008; Giles and Jackson 2003). The formalized debate within the federal government began in 1996 with *A Review of the Young Offenders Act and the Youth Justice System in Canada*, a report authored by the Federal-Provincial-Territorial Task Force on Youth Justice in Canada, and was closely followed in 1997 by a report from the House of Commons Standing Committee on Justice and Legal Affairs, *Renewing Youth Justice*. Finally, the Department of Justice published *A Strategy for the Renewal of Youth Justice* in 1998 that dealt with three broad criticisms of the YOA and called for remedies with new legislation: a lack of provisions to prevent youth involved in the criminal justice system from entering a "life of crime"; a need for more attention to serious offenders; and a need to respond to the excessive incarceration of Canadian youth relative to countries such as the United Kingdom and Australia. Before it was passed, Giles and Jackson (2003) critiqued the approach offered by the YCJA as suffering from numerous inadequacies, including limits to due process rights and being overly punitive in various ways.

Several new ideas were introduced in the act, including allowing provisions for older youth accused of violent crimes to automatically be tried as adults, to be held in custody in adult prisons, and to have access to extrajudicial measures (Davis-Barron 2009; YCJA 2002). On first glance, the changes brought about by the YCJA seem to be diverse – some encouraging harsher penalties, others expressing more concern with treatment. A critical analysis, however, indicates that the approach is straightforward: youth convicted of minor offences (likely not eligible for incarceration in any case) are grouped in the diversion-appropriate category, whereas those "riskier youth" convicted of more serious offences are likely to receive much harsher carceral treatment. The resulting bifurcation of the system more clearly delineates "diversion-eligible youth" from "punishable youth" and justifies more severe (non-integrative and non-restorative) responses toward the latter, who, some would argue, have the greatest need for help and care (Hogeveen 2005). Also, though the policies of the YCJA surrounding diversion appear attractive, their practical effectiveness has been undermined by systematically receiving only limited funding and consistently facing extreme funding shortfalls merely to meet operating expenses (Wotherspoon and Schissel 2001). Finally, the phenomenon of "net widening" must also be assessed when, for example, justice professionals who might otherwise offer an informal warning to a youth place a formal charge so that the youth might be eligible for an enforcement-based restorative justice program. Although there might be benefits to the program, in some cases the decision might cause unnecessary numbers of youth to become involved formally in the justice system (Hudson and Galaway 1996).

The move toward a more punitive youth justice system has been attributed in part to a political reaction to public demands (Denov 2004). Although crime data indicate that property and violent crimes by youth have decreased since the 1990s, the public and media discourses inaccurately portray youth crime as rising and react by demanding more punitive measures. "Youth who have 'failed' to integrate into society have to some extent always been demonized in Canada" (Alvi 2008, 253). The contemporary "punishable youth," those unable to obtain "ideal" status, are repeat offenders who are eligible to receive adult sentences, who have their names published by the media, and whose parents are now eligible for periods of incarceration when a child in their care commits an offence (Hogeveen 2005). The new policies of the YCJA are a far cry from the child welfare approach used in Canada for the two decades prior and are a return to increased punitiveness, increased reliance on individual and family responsibility, a "retributive" approach to justice, and a "return to the narrow individualism and decontextualized framework of classical criminology" (Alvi 2008, 253). Although the history of youth justice demonstrates a shift away from youth as small versions of adults and toward youth as being in need of protection and having rights, a more recent shift views youth as villains of society from whom we must be protected.

Dangerousness: Constructing and Regulating the Young Offender
Given the creation of the individual and ideal child, the following section considers the tools of managerial/actuarial justice and their marked stance opposing individuals as situated in context and unlike the archetype of the ideal child. "The panic that vilifies children is a coordinated, calculated attempt to nourish the ideology that supports a society

stratified on the bases of race, class and gender and that the war on kids is part of the state-business mechanisms that continually reproduces an oppressive social order and consumer exploitation" (Schissel 2006, 14). The "panic" discourse surrounding the child offender since early Canada continues to resurface, instructing us that, to become a "proper" citizen, an "ideal" youth, the individual "wayward youth" requires punishment and correction for his or her own good. This contemporary panic mentality of the late twentieth and early twenty-first centuries that disregards social context (Pate 2006) is now widely regarded as a symptom of media, political, and expert discourses that serve to blame marginalized groups of society for systemic social ills.

How is the delinquent youth constructed in our daily practice? Callahan and Swift (2007, 159) suggest that "neo-liberal governments concern themselves with facilitating the global movement of capital, and producing wealth," instead of promoting social capital and supporting populations in need. Actuarial methods used in criminal justice and social service sectors, often described as objective and non-biased, play important parts in subjective case analyses (Hannah-Moffat and Maurutto 2003). Kempf-Leonard and Peterson (2007, 444), writing in the contemporary American context, suggest that, though the recent rehabilitative strides (where youth justice is concerned) have been instrumental in protecting youth against the full reign of actuarial justice, the more recent drive toward "early intervention and prevention coupled with the current push for just deserts-oriented dispositions and corresponding emphasis on cost-savings" tends to re-emphasize the actuarial movement. When assessments implicitly and explicitly place importance on departures from middle-class norms (e.g., low education, no bank account), socially disadvantaged youth are reconceptualized as dangerous and risky (Pate 2006).

In this sense, the calculability of individuals is framed as the newest technology of power and domination: "We have entered, it appears, the age of the calculable person whose individuality is no longer ineffable, unique, and beyond knowledge, but can be known, mapped, calibrated, evaluated, quantified, predicted, and managed" (Rose 1998, 88). Thus, what Colin Gordon (cited in Rose 1998, 89) has called "institutional epistemology" refers to the production of knowledge from these organized and administrative managerial systems – managerialism and control using tools, standards, and statistics presented as "objective" but ripe with subjective, power-laden conceptualizations. A Foucauldian account holds that social control is generally exerted through non-invasive, routinized mechanisms of surveillance and discipline (Foucault 1977). Tied firmly to notions of rationality, "knowledge, here, needs to be understood as itself, in a crucial sense, a matter of technique, rooted in attempts to organize experience according to certain values" (Rose 1998, 89). Actuarial methods normalize to the extent that they are unable to recognize differences between the individual youth and the ideal archetype as anything other than negative risk. Pate (2006) identifies regular characteristics of adolescent development, such as risk taking, disobedience in the face of authority, and pushing against limits, as behaviours seen by actuarial assessments as predictors of future risk. Thus, it is the most disagreeable youth, furthest from the "ideal," who tend to be classified as posing the greatest risk to reoffend.

Risk or need assessments have not been thoroughly researched with youth populations, and Hannah-Moffat and Maurutto (2003) state that several youth-screening tools have been developed on adults and then adopted or adapted and applied to youth populations without intensive study. Tools that have been tested were likely to have been administered to youth in Ontario, prompting the question of generalizability across diverse Canadian populations. Hannah-Moffat and Maurutto found "some concerns about gendered and racialized interpretations of risk and need criteria and the importance of the age of the youth (and developmental stage) in making determinations about the appropriateness of particular behaviours ... These tools inappropriately label youth and ... these labels are punitive and stick with the youth their entire time in the system" (17). The aggregate population from which the tools are created might be a poor representation of the individual to whom they are directed (Pate 2006); some instruments, including the Statistical Inventory on Recidivism (SIR), were designed to calculate recidivism among incarcerated adult males, not adolescents specifically. The ecological fallacy (the error occurring where aggregates are used to explain individuals) has long been a concern for social scientists but seems to have been forgotten in the managerial world of systematization, efficiency (not effectiveness), and rationality. Furthermore, though risk has been used to identify degrees of dangerousness in the community and by the courts, risk tools "DO NOT measure dangerousness, nor can they identify the severity of an offence" (Hannah-Moffat and Maurutto 2003, 12). Suggesting that a youth is highly likely to reoffend does not differentiate between violent offences, non-violent offences, and technical violations of community supervision.

Amid these concerns, it is interesting that risk or need tools have been used to make correctional decisions more transparent. By identifying the decision process as emanating from an empirically grounded and uniformly applied standard, one could more easily justify the case plan for the youth (Hannah-Moffat and Maurutto 2003). Unfortunately, actuarial justice bears little comparison with "justice" in that it takes as its focus *management* of the individual, who is unable to obtain ideal status, and crime as a given. Actuarial justice thus identifies and contains problems instead of responding to them or working toward change (Silver and Miller 2002). "This emphasis on individual responsibility and participation allows the focus to shift away from social issues like poverty, violence, systemic racism, and unemployment that I argue are, in fact, the greatest impediments to social success for the individual, especially marginalized youth. The result is a society controlled by dominatory techniques cloaked under the mask of 'liberalism' and 'correctionalism'" (Eisler 2007, 115-16).

Furthermore, "when regulation shifts from individual offenders to the *probability* that some offense might occur, traditional presumptions of innocence are transformed into assumptions of guilt ... Guilt is inferred from how closely your behavior matches some profile of likely offenses – a form of statistical justice" (Reichman 1986, cited in Silver and Miller 2002, 165). We are no longer as concerned with explaining crime, transferring our focus instead to predicting which individuals might commit future crimes.

Must What Is Old Be New Again?

The contemporary Canadian discourse of youth justice instructs us to calculate risk to determine where interventions are needed, how they should be implemented, and where our costs are best allocated. None of these questions can be answered with certainty since the equation asks us to look into the future and make a well-informed gamble. Managerial science, however, asks us to forget that our predictive capabilities are fallible and that the "objective" tools upon which they are based cannot be separated from the subjectivity, values, and orientations that create them.

One innovative response (Norrie 2000) argues for a replacement of the discourses of individualism and determinism in the criminal justice system, favouring instead a relational theory in which individual action is situated in relation to structural context, each act involving a dialectic relationship between corresponding factors. This approach would focus on individual responsibilities to one another within a community and apportion responsibility for deviance to both the individual and the community. Benhabib (2002) reconstructs universalism (the ideal youth) as a concrete other, an embodied person rather than an abstraction. Both reconceptions reject justice as a normalizing, generalizing structure embedded with sameness and highlight the "situated, embodied and relational self" as involved in each interaction (Hudson 2005, 70). Likewise, Barron (2000) asks that criminal justice organizations stop blindly focusing on individual explanations of youth violence and start contextualizing behaviour by addressing social and cultural factors such as race and socio-economic status. For practice with young offenders, this means that we need to work beyond the constructed binaries generalizing, essentializing, and describing subjects and move toward relational understandings. The somewhat ironic similarity between the tensions of today and post-Enlightenment thinking are not lost; we are still grappling with how to entrench an approach to liberal individualism identifying parents as key in raising children (Platt 2005) while simultaneously seeking an approach that will guarantee state intervention and responsibility when macro-social intervention is required.

Notes

1 Bill C-25 proposed amendments to Canada's current youth justice legislation, the Youth Criminal Justice Act, enacted in 2003. Although the bill was not passed in 2008 due to the federal election, the proposal was a strong part of the Conservative platform and was slated to be reintroduced when the Conservative Party was re-elected (Bala, Carrington, and Roberts 2009). In November 2008, the Speech from the Throne largely omitted

mention of a complete reform of youth justice policy, instead mentioning only briefly that youth justice would be strengthened (Davis-Barron 2009). The bill was in fact reintroduced in 2010 as bill C-4, Sebastian's Law (Protecting the Public from Young Offenders) and was featured in the 2011 Federal Conservative policy platform as one of several crime bills to be passed in the first 100 days of the 41st Parliament should the Conservatives gain majority status. The May 2011 election resulted in a majority Conservative government.

2   Although the United Nations Convention on the Rights of the Child came into force in 1990, Canada did not sign until 1991.

References

Act Respecting Arrest, Trial, and Imprisonment of Youthful Offenders, S.C. 1894, c. 58.

Alvi, S. 2008. "A Criminal Justice History of Children and Youth in Canada: Taking Stock in the YCJA Era." In *Marginality and Condemnation: An Introduction to Criminology*, ed. C. Brookes and B. Schissel, 238-57. Halifax: Fernwood.

Bala, N., P.J. Carrington, and J.V. Roberts. 2009. "Evaluating the Youth Criminal Justice Act after Five Years: A Qualified Success." *Canadian Journal of Criminology and Criminal Justice* 51, 2: 131-67.

Barron, C.L. 2000. *Giving Youth a Voice: A Basis for Rethinking Adolescent Violence*. Halifax: Fernwood.

Benhabib, S. 2002. *The Claims of Culture: Equality and Diversity in the Global Era*. Princeton: Princeton University Press.

Bill C-7, *An Act to Amend the Youth Criminal Justice Act*, 2nd Session, 39th Parliament, 2008.

Blanchfield, M. 2008, 22 September. "Stakeholders Speak Out on Harper's Promise to Toughen Youth Crime Law." Canwest News Service. http://www.canada.com/vancouversun/.

Callahan, M., and K. Swift. 2007. "Great Expectations and Unintended Consequences: Risk Assessment and Managerial Practices in Child Welfare in British Columbia." In *People, Politics, and Child Welfare*, ed. L. Foster and B. Wharf, 158-83. Vancouver: UBC Press.

Canada. Department of Justice. 1998. *Strategy for the Renewal of Youth Justice*. http://www.justice.gc.ca/.

–. Federal-Provincial-Territorial Task Force on Youth Justice. 1996. *A Review of the Young Offenders Act and the Youth Justice System in Canada*. http://www.justice.gc.ca/.

–. Standing Committee on Justice and Legal Affairs. 1997. *Renewing Youth Justice*. http://www.justice.gc.ca/.

Canadian Bill of Rights, R.S.C. 1960, c. 44.

Canadian Press. 2006. "Harper Sees Crime Issue as Political Winner." *CTV News*, 28 October. http://www.ctv.ca/.

–. 2008. "Conservatives Vow to Toughen Youth Justice Act: Youth 14 and Over Would Be Named when Convicted of Serious Crimes." *CBC News*, 22 September. http://www.cbc.ca/.

Carrigan, D.O. 1998. *Juvenile Delinquency in Canada*. Toronto: Irwin.

–. 2004. *The Evolution of Juvenile Justice in Canada*. Report prepared for the International Cooperation Group, Department of Justice Canada. http://www.justice.gc.ca/eng/pi/icg-gci/jj2-jm2/jj2-jm2.pdf.

Clark, C., C. Alphonso, and L. Perreaux. 2008. "Harper Pitches Two-Tier Youth Justice Plan." *Globe and Mail*, 22 September. http://www.theglobeandmail.com/.

Convention on the Rights of the Child, 20 November 1989, 1577 U.N.T.S. 3.

Corrado, R., and A. Markwart. 1994. "The Need to Reform the YOA in Response to Violent Young Offenders: Confusion, Reality, or Myth?" *Canadian Journal of Criminology* 36, 3: 343-78.

Cruickshank, M. 1981. *Children and Industry: Child Health and Welfare in North-West Textile Towns during the Nineteenth Century*. Manchester: Manchester University Press.

Davis-Barron, S. 2009. *Canadian Youth and the Criminal Law: One Hundred Years of Youth Justice Legislation in Canada*. Markham, ON: LexisNexis.

Denov, M. 2004. "Children's Rights or Rhetoric? Assessing Canada's Youth Criminal Justice Act and Its Compliance with the UN Convention on the Rights of the Child." *International Journal of Children's Rights* 12, 1: 1-20.

Eisler, L.D. 2007. "An Application of Foucauldian Concepts to the Youth Criminal Justice System: A Case Study." *Critical Criminology* 15, 1: 101-22.

Factory Act, 1847 (U.K.), 3 & 4 Will. IV, c. 103.

Foucault, M. 1977. *Discipline and Punish: The Birth of the Prison*. New York: Pantheon.

Gergen, K.J. 2003. "Knowledge as Socially Constructed." In *Social Construction: A Reader*, ed. K.J. Gergen and M.M. Gergen, 15-17. Thousand Oaks, CA: Sage.

Giles, C., and M. Jackson. 2003. "Bill C-7: The New Youth Criminal Justice Act: A Darker Young Offenders Act." *International Journal of Comparative and Applied Criminal Justice* 27, 1: 19-38.

Hannah-Moffat, K., and P. Maurutto. 2003. *Youth Risk/Need Assessment: An Overview of Issues and Practices*. Submitted to the Research and Statistics Division, Department of Justice Canada. http://www.justice.gc.ca/.

Hogeveen, B.R. 2005. "'If We Are Tough on Crime, if We Punish Crime, Then People Get the Message: Constructing and Governing the Punishable Young Offender in Canada during the Late 1990s." *Punishment and Society* 7, 1: 73-89.

Houston, S.E. 1972. "Victorian Origins of Juvenile Delinquency: A Canadian Experience." *History of Education Quarterly* 12, 3: 254-80.

Hudson, B. 2005. "The Culture of Control: Choosing the Future." In *Managing Modernity: Politics and the Culture of Control*, ed. M. Matravers, 49-75. New York: Routledge.

Hudson, B., and S. Galaway. 1996. *Net Widening*. Restorative Justice Organization. http://www.restorativejustice.org/.

Juvenile Delinquents Act, S.C. 1908, c. 40.

Kelly, P. 2003. "Growing Up as Risky Business? Risks, Surveillance, and the Institutionalized Mistrust of Youth." *Journal of Youth Studies* 6, 2: 165-80.

Kempf-Leonard, K., and E. Peterson. 2007. "Expanding the Realms of the New Penology: The Advent of Actuarial Justice for Juveniles." *Punishment and Corrections* 2, 1: 66-97.

Lafferty, R. 2002. "Modernity and the Denominational Imperative: The Children's Aid Society of Halifax 1905-1925." *Journal of the Canadian Historical Association* 13, 1: 95-118. http://id.erudit.org/.

Landsdown, G. 2001. *Children's Rights: A Second Chance*. International Save the Children Alliance Communications Working Group. http://www.savethechildren.net.

Libel, M. 2004. *A Will of Their Own: Cross-Cultural Perspectives on Working Children*. New York: St. Martin's Press.

National Post. 2008, 6 June. "Harper Vows Changes to 'Failed' Youth Justice Act." Canwest News Service. http://www.canada.com/.

Norrie, A.W. 2000. *Punishment, Responsibility, and Justice: A Relational Critique.* Oxford: Oxford University Press.

Pate, K. 2006. *The Risky Business of Risk Assessment.* Ottawa: Canadian Association of Elizabeth Fry Societies. http://www.elizabethfry.ca/.

Platt, A. 1969. *The Child Savers.* Chicago: University of Chicago Press.

–. 1977. *The Child Savers: The Invention of Delinquency.* 2nd ed. Chicago: University of Chicago Press.

Platt, L. 2005. *Discovering Child Poverty: The Creation of a Policy Agenda from 1800 to the Present.* Bristol: Polity Press.

Prochner, L. 2000. "A History of Early Education and Child Care in Canada, 1820-1966." In *Early Childhood Care and Education in Canada,* ed. L. Prochner and N. Howe, 11-65. Vancouver: UBC Press.

Rahikanen, M. 2004. *Centuries of Child Labor: European Experiences for the Seventeenth to the Twentieth Century.* Hampshire: Ashgate.

Reichman, N. 1986. "Managing Crime Risks: Towards an Insurance Based Model of Social Control." *Research in Law, Deviance, and Social Control* 8: 151-72.

Rose, L. 1991. *The Erosion of Childhood.* New York: Routledge.

Rose, N. 1998. *Inventing Ourselves: Psychology, Power, and Personhood.* Cambridge, UK: Cambridge University Press.

Schissel, B. 2006. *Still Blaming Children: Youth Conduct and the Politics of Child Hating.* 2nd ed. Halifax: Fernwood.

Silver, E., and L.L. Miller. 2002. "A Cautionary Note on the Use of Actuarial Risk Assessment Tools for Social Control." *Crime and Delinquency* 48, 1: 138-61.

Statistics Canada. 2008. *Censuses of Canada: 1665 to 1871: The 1800s.* http://www.statcan. gc.ca/.

Sutherland, N. 2000. *Children in English-Canadian Society: Framing the Twentieth-Century Consensus.* Waterloo: Wilfrid Laurier University Press.

Tanner, J. 1996. *Teenage Troubles: Youth and Deviance in Canada.* Toronto: Nelson.

Wotherspoon, T., and B. Schissel. 2001. "The Business of Placing Canadian Children and Youth 'at-Risk.'" *Canadian Journal of Education* 26, 3: 321-39.

Young Offenders Act, S.C. 1985, c. Y-1.

Youth Criminal Justice Act, S.C. 2002, c. 1.

Once upon a Time There Was a Ready Child
Challenging Readiness as a Single Story

11

KATHLEEN KUMMEN

> The single story creates stereotypes. And the problem with stereo-
> types is not that they are untrue, but they are incomplete. They
> make one story the only story.
>
> – ADICHIE (2009, PARA. 24)

Carlton and Winsler (1999, 338) write that "how a child becomes ready
and exactly what readiness means are still a mystery." Within the field
of education, researchers, scholars, and educators have ardently contested
the notion of readiness for over a century (Dockett and Perry 2009;
Graue 2006; Scott-Little, Kagan, and Frelow 2006; Winter and Kelley
2008). Scott-Little, Kagan, and Frelow (2006, 1) explain that "the concept
of readiness has been influenced by varying (and often competing) views
of readiness." Although a universal definition of readiness has not been
determined, readiness has become a central feature of policy development in early year services in an attempt to provide young children with
a smooth transition to school and future academic success (Wesley and
Buysse 2003).

The sentiments of this discussion are captured by Dockett and Perry
(2009, 20) in the statement that "parents and educators anguish over

whether or not a child is *ready* for school as they try to make decisions they believe will best support children." In their time of anguish over the issue of readiness, parents and educators might be relieved (if not surprised) that the current School Act (1996, c. 28) defines eligibility for entrance into school as the following: being of school age;[1] being a resident of the province; and having adequate classroom space and facilities as determined by the school board. Although "readiness" is not legislated, its relevance within the general public is illustrated by the fact that Graue's (2006) Google search of "readiness for kindergarten" obtained 117,000 hits.

In this chapter, I explore and problematize readiness to make visible the controversies and challenges inherent in this concept. I begin by presenting different concepts of readiness to understand how the concept is positioned within the child (Dockett and Perry 2009; Graue 2006). Drawing on the ideas of Foucault, I then critically examine how readiness can privilege specific ways of knowing young children that position children as ready and not ready and in doing so can reinforce social inequities that are barriers to the well-being of some groups of young children in British Columbia. In the third section, I explore how the discourses of readiness are enacted into practice and made into truths within the province. My aim is to provide a critique of readiness as a single story – a concept that assumes a definable and known child with a predictable future. I suggest that other possibilities for understanding young children invite multiple images of early learning and definitions of successful developmental outcomes. My intent is to encourage educators, researchers, and policy makers to seek "critically informed knowledge about children" in order "to live more justly with children" (MacNaughton 2005, 50).

Readiness

Defining readiness depends on the theoretical framework being used. Within each definition of readiness are embedded assumptions and beliefs about children, development, and learning. This section provides a brief overview of different ways of understanding readiness.

An Issue of Nature versus Nurture

Historically, readiness has been understood through two contrasting views of development and learning (Graue and DiPerna 2000). In the first view, children are considered ready when they are mature enough to learn the skills and concepts necessary to be successful in school. This view can be described as a maturationist view of child development. From this standpoint, genetics drive the child toward adulthood in an orderly and universal fashion. Central to this perspective is the belief that development precedes learning, that there are necessary developmental requirements that must be achieved by the child to be able to meet the academic requirements of the classroom.

Social policy responded to the maturationist concept of readiness by testing to see if individual children were mature enough to be ready for school. Children deemed not ready were subsequently held back a year or put in a transitional program, thereby giving them additional time to mature before they moved into the formal school system. Graue and DiPerna (2000) describe this process of retention as the gift of time, but their review of the literature suggests that this practice did not enhance the likelihood of academic success.

In the second view of readiness, children are ready for school when they have already acquired a specific set of skills that will make them ready to meet the requirements of school (Meisels 1998; Scott-Little, Kagan, and Frelow 2006). This is considered the behaviourist perspective, which focuses on the acquisition of predetermined skills that allow children to meet the demands of the classroom setting (Carlton and Winsler 1999). Readiness is "commensurate with knowing colours, shapes, one's address ... and concentrates on what the child can do and how the child behaves" (Meisels 1998, 47).

The response to the behaviourist perspective is to promote early identification of and intervention with children not demonstrating the appropriate skill set (Dockett and Perry 2002). Scott-Little, Kagan, and Frelow (2006) suggest that this understanding of readiness promotes the notion of early learning standards that provide guidelines to promote the acquisition of skills necessary for formal schooling.

An Issue of Interaction between Child and Environment

Readiness has also been presented from an ecological perspective, drawing on the work of Urie Bronfenbrenner. Development is understood as occurring in bidirectional relationships between individual and environment (Dockett and Perry 2009). A child's development is influenced not only by the environment but also by how the environment responds to the child. For example, Barbarin et al. (2008) found that parents' beliefs about readiness were mirrored in their expectations for their children and that problems arose when there was a lack of congruency between school and home. Successful readiness relies on the characteristics of the child, the family, the community, and the school. A child might be ready for one school in a particular community but not for another school in a different community (Dockett and Perry 2002, 2009; Graue 2006; Graue, Kroeger, and Brown 2002).

In responding to this understanding of readiness, both the environment and the adults within that environment are required to provide children with the necessary experiences to acquire the skills and knowledge to be successful within that setting (Dockett and Perry 2002, 2009; Graue 2006). For example, when a mismatch is discovered between parental expectations and school expectations around readiness, parenting programs are constructed to teach parents the necessary techniques and knowledge to ready their child (Millei and Lee 2007). Readiness from this perspective is measured and regulated within the context of a community.

An Issue of Population Health

A more recent perspective on readiness extends the concept from being an individual concern and positions it as a population health issue. Hertzman and Williams (2009, 68) argue that "the importance of developing measures of early child development at a population level should be self evident if we believe that 'what gets counted, counts.'" The Early Development Instrument (EDI) is an example of a measure based on individual child scores as assessed by kindergarten teachers but designed to provide the average level of readiness of a specific population (Janus and Offord 2007). The EDI assesses readiness across developmental domains and reports readiness in terms of the percentage of children deemed vulnerable in a community, as compared with those children who are found to be developing well across developmental domains (Janus and Offord 2007). The EDI measures five domains of development: (a) physical health and well-being; (b) social competence; (c) emotional maturity; (d) language and cognition; and (e) communication skills and general knowledge. Information obtained from the EDI has been used by policy makers to plan interventions and designate funding to communities to promote readiness at the community level (Goelman and Hertzman, n.d.).

A Single Story of Children Who Are Either Ready or Not?
What is troubling for me is that each of these understandings of readiness can reduce the complexities of early childhood to a single story of preparation for the future. A future that Moss and Petrie (2002, 102) assert "is unpredictable ... will furnish future adults with social, economic, political, environmental and cultural contexts which we cannot foresee." The discourse of readiness must consider the question asked by Graue (1993), "ready for what?" Do we want children to be, to quote Ralph Waldo Emerson (cited in Weiss 2002, 88), "always getting ready to live but never living"?

Disrupting the Discourses of Readiness
Social constructionist theory holds that knowledge is not a static truth but constructed in a community shaped by culture, history, gender, language, beliefs, and practices (Hacking 1999). Since knowledge is always in a state of construction, it is never seen as whole, only partial, and understood as an interpretation rather than an objective fact or truth. Facts, writes Hacking, are the "consequences of ways in which we represent the world" (33).

From a social constructionist perspective, readiness is not a definable or measurable characteristic of either an individual or a community. Readiness "is lived *through* others' perceptions and interpretations" (Graue, Kroeger, and Brown 2002, 350). In this way, readiness is understood within a particular time and social context so that "the beliefs, expectations, understandings, and experiences of those in the school, and in the community in which the school exists, largely determine definitions of readiness for that context" (Dockett and Perry 2002, 71). As with any discourse, readiness reflects the politics and knowledge of the time and the culture and place in which it is created. Readiness must then be conceptualized from the perspective in which it is being positioned at any given time.

In trying to understand readiness, professionals working with young children have been enchanted by the methods of positivist science, in particular the science of psychology (Cannella 1997; Dahlberg, Moss, and Pence 1999, 2007; MacDonald 2007). The child becomes definable, quantifiable, and classifiable (Rose 1998). Science has provided measurable variables to determine the difference between a child who is developing according to universal norms and one who is developing outside or below those norms. This ability to assess a child's developmental level through chronological age or a skill assessment allows professionals working with young children to determine a child's readiness for school. Child development has created a discourse of children from which social policy regarding readiness can be constructed. The child is seen as a universal concept that can be "known objectively" (Rose 1998, 118).

Readiness as a Universal Concept

In recent years, the assumptions of universality and generalizability, embedded within the concept of a normal child, have been challenged (Burman 2008a, 2008b; Cannella 1997; Dahlberg, Moss, and Pence 1999, 2007). For Walkerdine (1988), child development constitutes a universal set of "fantasies" about a typical child. From her perspective, there are no universal truths from which standards or norms can be generated to measure readiness. Burman (2008b, 27) suggests that child development, as a field of developmental psychology, has created "narratives of development [that] have tended to presume a spurious universality and generality that [are] increasingly recognized as untenable." The definition of normal has become so narrow that fewer children are meeting that definition. This idea provokes a sense of unease when an agency such as the Canadian Council on Learning (2007) reported that the National Longitudinal Survey of Children found that, from 2004 to 2005, 25 percent of Canadian children entering kindergarten did not have the foundational skills required for successful acquisition of literacy and numeracy skills.

The concept of readiness relies on the assumptions of child development to be true and universal for all children. Foucault (cited in MacNaughton 2005) writes that officially sanctioned truths (e.g., the knowledge generated by child development) govern what is held to be both normal and desirable. He refers to these truths as a regime of truths since they allow for the domination of one discourse over another. In the case of readiness, the discourse of child development is the dominant discourse in governing the understanding of the ready or not ready child. Other ways of seeing or understanding children that contradict child development are silenced by the dominant discourse of child development in a conversation of readiness. "Such a hegemony makes inevitable the further segmentation of knowledge (i.e., disallowing multiple epistemologies), and further marginalizes many forms of knowing/knowledge" (Holmes et al. 2006, 181).

Particularly troubling is that the universal understanding of development is based on research conducted primarily on children living in the western regions of the world, thus disregarding the experiences of more than 90 percent of the world's children (Arnett 2008; Pence and Hix-Small 2007). This finding contests the ability of science to generalize child development findings to a world population on the basis of its own criteria for scientific validity. It appears that readiness is not a neutral or objective concept based on a natural developmental progression but an assessment that privileges one way of understanding childhood over another.

A number of challenges have been raised against the notion of readiness as a universal set of indicators that demonstrates a child's readiness to enter school. As this perspective positions readiness as inherent within the child or children, it pathologizes individual children or communities of children who do not conform to the universal standards (Phoenix, cited in Burman 2008b). Cultural and economic inequities are evident in a number of studies (cited by Wright, Diener, and Kay 2000), suggesting that children from particular ethnic groups and lower socioeconomic groups are over-identified as not ready to enter kindergarten. In a critique of the EDI measurement, for example, Li, D'Angiulli, and

Kendall (2007) assert that the tool favours children who speak English as their first language since administration of the test is in English in communities where classroom instruction is in English.

A further point of contention over the concept of school readiness being a universal set of indicators is that the act of naming specific indictors can result in those indicators becoming the very skills and knowledge deemed important for later school achievement (Scott-Little, Kagan, and Frelow 2006). In other words, the factors identified as readiness indicators can direct the curriculum in later school years and narrow the criteria of success. Ailwood (2008) contends that the practice of identifying developmental markers creates early years' programs that operate as factories to produce "school-ready" children.

Readiness discourses reflect the notion that we can determine if a child is, or is not, ready for school. Additionally, readiness discourses assume that, if we can discern the unready child from the ready child, we can also create the conditions that will promote readiness within the general population of children.

Bringing the Discourses of Readiness to Life

Drawing on Foucault, Gore (1998) identified eight "micropractices of power" that bring a regime of truth into being: surveillance, normalization, exclusion, classification, distribution, individualization, totalization, and regulation. She asserted that the practices that conform to a truth act to inscribe that truth as a normal part of everyday life. In acting out a truth, the power of the truth is strengthened, thus creating a "regime of truth."

The discourses of readiness are problematic in that they isolate readiness as something within a child (Dockett and Perry 2009). There is the added assumption that children, as future citizens, are homogeneous in their needs and can be prepared for a known future (Scott 1998). In the preceding discussion, I explored how child development has privileged the concept of a normal child and marginalized a child who deviates from the norm. By examining the micropractices of power, I attempt to make visible how the practices associated with readiness bring into being the child development regime of truth. In so doing, I demonstrate that readiness acts as a means of preparing the future citizen, from a place that values a particular notion of what an ideal citizen is and what skills and behaviours he or she will possess. When children grow up to be people who do not reflect these desired outcomes, their development is deemed "unsuccessful."

To explore how a "regime of truth" is brought to life by micropractices, I examine three of the eight micropractices in relation to readiness as it is reflected in the social policy being implemented in British Columbia.

Surveillance is the micropractice in which an individual or group of individuals expects to be, or is, observed in reference to particular truths (Gore 1998). The act of observing or monitoring the development of children to assess readiness as defined by child development can be considered surveillance. At present, the Ministry for Children and Families assesses all children in British Columbia in their kindergarten year using the EDI. According to Hertzman and Williams (2009, 68), "monitoring early child development – across a population, over time and with the ability to examine geographic trends – is a key activity in support of the success of a modern developed society." In this way, child development creates both the standard of assessment and the need to monitor children to assure their development conforms to the standards of readiness. Rose (1998, 81) writes that "the stewardship of human conduct has become an intrinsically psychological activity." Thus, if British Columbia's social policy is built on the assumption that child development is a truth, there is a requirement to monitor the development of children to carry out a mandate of ensuring the readiness of individual children.

If readiness is being monitored at the community level, then adults within the community also require surveillance to ensure that they are meeting the developmental needs of the children. The discourses of readiness thus bring forth a particular understanding of the parent – the good parent who readies the child and the bad parent who does not ready the child. Parenting programs are then created to "smarten up the parents" so that they can provide children with optimal and regulated experiences to promote development (Millei and Lee 2007). Parents thus become subject to surveillance by a "fixed and uncontested code of conduct" (Rose, as cited by Millei and Lee 2007, 219), which is measured by the readiness of their child. Although providing support to families and communities is not an inherently bad idea, current literature contends that the idea that maintaining the notion of a universal standard of best practice in parenting further marginalizes populations who receive the intended intervention (Burman 2008a, 2008b; Cannella 1997; Millei and Lee 2007).

Worryingly, the assumptions of child development can create a prescribed support that reflects only one way of understanding children. Li, D'Angiulli, and Kendall (2007) suggest, for example, that, when a community does not identify with the EDI, the support offered is not culturally or linguistically relevant, and this invites resistance by the community. To create a British Columbia where all children reach their potential, as measured by child development, all citizens of the province must agree to the concept of readiness as defined by social policy. Scott (1998, 225) writes that "the most important fact about social engineering is: its efficiency depends on the response and cooperation of real human subjects."

Normalization requires individuals to conform to a standard that reflects a specific truth (Gore 1998). A child is assessed as ready for kindergarten when his or her development is compared with a standard of development that has been constructed by the science of child development. The emotional maturity indicator consists of teachers' observations concerning the child's ability to reflect before acting, deal with feelings, and respond to others' feelings at an age-appropriate level (Janus and Offord 2007). To assess a child, the teacher must compare that child with a standard that defines normalcy. This process illustrates child development's assumption that childhood can be described as a universal and unified sequence of events that over time creates a way for teachers to understand a child as ready or not ready (Rose 1990).

Research that uses the EDI to assess readiness at a community level presents the level of readiness of a community in comparison with other communities. The intent of this practice is to assess communities so that resources and interventions can be allocated to increase the opportunities for children to reach their full potential as defined by child development. When the data are analyzed, however, the results show that communities scoring lower on the readiness scale have higher numbers of children who are not from the dominant culture (e.g., children of Aboriginal descent) than communities scoring higher on the scale (Janus 2002). On the basis of these results, the argument can be made that comparing communities in terms of their level of conformity to an instrument that is culturally and linguistically biased reinscribes social inequities such as racialization (Li, D'Angiulli, and Kendall 2009). In this way, child development creates a norm from which particular communities are rendered inferior, or not normal, based solely on their not conforming to the dominant culture as measured by the EDI. As Lather (1991, 124) asks, though, "to what extent does method privilege findings?" Li, D'Angiulli, and Kendall (2007, 2009) critique the reliability and validity of the EDI, arguing that these criteria have never been formally established in a peer-reviewed journal article. Their critique is important, for the goal of science is in fact the quest for truth and the limitation of error. If the EDI is to be used to measure readiness at a community level across British Columbia's diverse population, then the tool must be able to withstand scrupulous evaluation and meticulous seeking out of evidence that might contradict or modify that claim (Murphy and Dingwall 2003).

Li, D'Angiulli, and Kendall (2007) further assert that the EDI is limited as a universal screening tool since it is not sensitive to linguistic or cultural diversity and does not successfully predict the academic trajectory of children who are members of minority linguistic and cultural groups. Since the EDI relies on a standard of measurement that is culturally and linguistically biased, children who are not of the dominant culture can incorrectly be identified as not being ready. In response to this criticism, Li, D'Angiulli, and Kendall argue that the EDI results pertaining to Aboriginal children might "simply reflect the consequences of endemic generational disadvantages created by an inherently racist and colonialist educational system evolved from the Canadian residential schools in the 1880s" (224).

Classification involves using truth to differentiate between individuals or groups of individuals. A child is identified as being ready for kindergarten by classifying his or her behaviour according to specific developmental standards. The micropractice of classification creates social policy that relies on the existence of a binary: ready/not ready. Derrida argues that the majority of Western languages depend on oppositions, or binaries, to produce meaning (cited in MacNaughton 2005, 81). Readiness, for example, can only be understood in relation to its opposite, unreadiness: "They form a binary opposition in which ... we are offered two mutually exclusive meanings." The significance of binaries is that one of the pair is always more valued than the other. The more valued or privileged term defines the cultural standard of normalcy.

When the notion of binaries is applied to readiness, a ready child is understood in comparison to a child who is not ready. A child identified as ready is considered normal by the standards of child development, whereas the child who is identified as not ready is seen as not normal. When the notion of binaries is applied to the readiness of communities, as assessed by the EDI, there are communities that are normal and communities that are not normal. In this way, differences between communities take on value and meaning that are hierarchical. From a social constructionist view, *ready* is privileged over *not ready* and creates an inequity between children and communities. If we juxtapose ready versus not ready with dominant culture versus minority culture, then the inequities become more pronounced. This is borne out in the previously cited results indicating that communities where the majority of children are not members of the dominant culture are more likely to be identified as not achieving the correct measure of readiness.

Summary of the Implications of Micropractices of Power for Social Policy

Examining the discourse of readiness using three of Gore's (1998) micropractices illustrates how practice brings to life a regime of truth. Practice focused on readiness articulates the language of child development, and, in the implementation of practice, the influence of child development is strengthened. Readiness can be discussed, children can be identified as ready, and programs can support readiness only if child development is accepted as a truth. Rose (1998) writes that the truth is made visible by language and is inscribed by the techniques or devices used to practise truth.

From a social constructionist perspective, one can argue that practices in the name of readiness comprise a technique of governance that operates as a form of surveillance. "What I mean, in fact, is the development of power techniques oriented towards individuals and intended to rule them in a continuous and permanent way" (Foucault, cited in Rabinow and Rose 2003, 182). Readiness creates the need to monitor children's development, and the behaviours of those involved in their care and education, to create the normal citizen.

Seeking Alternative Perspectives

The goal of the government of British Columbia (n.d., 43), as stated in *Strategic Plan 2006/07-2008/09*, is to have "the best educated and most literate jurisdiction on the continent." This vision is not without some merit and speaks to the province's commitment to children and youth; yet, to quote Foucault (cited in MacNaughton 2005, 201), "my point is not [that] everything is bad but that everything is dangerous." The concept of readiness is not inherently a bad thing, but the implications of readiness as a single story void of critical reflection can be dangerous.

I would now like to consider some alternative perspectives that seek to transform social policy on readiness. MacNaughton (2003) writes that a transforming perspective aims to change in order to create something new or different. This view implies that social policy as it relates to readiness needs to challenge existing injustices so as to create a more just and equitable society. I would argue that children need to be viewed as "human beings" rather than "human becomings" (Qvortrup 2008, 4). "Each time we use expressions such as 'children are our future' we colonize their lives and make them instruments of our redemption" (Moss and Petrie 2002, 102). Readiness privileges the child as a future adult or citizen and marginalizes his or her value as a child in the present. I would suggest that social policy has an obligation to address the child as a citizen of today and provide children with opportunities to reach their potential on the basis of that citizenship and not on some future value.

Furthermore, I would argue that, by presenting the future as a known commodity, we fail to recognize that the future is unpredictable and will hold circumstances we cannot anticipate (Moss and Petrie 2002).

In preparing children for a predetermined future, we risk seeing learning as a singular pathway that limits the possibilities of diversity in the future. If we were to value diversity, then we would maximize the possibility that future citizens will have a diverse set of skills and knowledge. Children who learn in an environment that values diversity and multiple perspectives might be more open to alternative ways of seeing and thinking about the issues and problems that confront them in an unknown future (MacNaughton 2003).

"Throughout our everyday interactions we speak and perform discourses into existence" (Robinson and Diaz 2006, 30). By speaking of readiness, we bring into being the ready and unready child and reinscribe the inequities associated with that binary. Transforming social policy to create a more just society asks us to think differently in order to change something. By removing the discourse of readiness from learning, we begin to challenge discrimination and make visible the effects of discrimination on the learner. The elimination of readiness invites those who work with young children to "build their own pictures of children as learners and capture specific children, in specific circumstances, at specific times" (Davis, cited in MacNaughton 2003, 77).

Giving up the discourse of readiness evident in current social policy would also require a move away from employing child development as the sole source of expertise in understanding children. The removal of readiness would make room for the voices of other cultures, other disciplines, and other understandings of children that have been silenced or marginalized in social policy as a result of the hegemony of child development (MacNaughton 2003). If we disrupt the dominant discourses of child development, including the discourse of readiness, then childhood might more easily be recognized as a social construct in which children are not a universal entity but complex, diverse, and at times contradictory human beings (Dahlberg, Moss, and Pence 2007). The BC Early Learning Framework (British Columbia 2008) is an example of a first step toward seeing children differently. The following is the image of the child presented in the ELF document:

> It views young children as capable and full of potential; as persons with complex identities, grounded in their individual strengths and

capacities, and their unique social, linguistic, and cultural heritage. In this image, children are rooted in and take nourishment from a rich, supportive ground, comprised of relationships with their families and communities, their language and culture, and the surrounding environment. (4)

Working with an image of a complex and unknown individual opens up the possibility of multiple ways of providing services for children and families.

This image also constructs the image of an educator who creates spaces that are ready to welcome children and not spaces for readying. Rinaldi (2006, 125) writes that "this requires a 'powerful' teacher, the only kind of teacher suitable for our equally 'powerful' child." This powerful educator, Rinaldi explains, is open to the unexpected and engages in learning with the child as a researcher to be open to possibilities in the project of education. The task of the powerful educator is to "create a context in which children's curiosity, theories and research are legitimated and listened to, a context in which children feel comfortable and confident, motivated and respected in their existential and cognitive paths and processes" (126). The question of readiness seems to be extraneous in a classroom in which powerful individuals come together to co-construct understanding and meaning.

Moss, Dillon, and Statham (2000, 250) refer to this image as that of a "rich" child, as opposed to a child in need, who is "born equipped to lead, neither asking nor needing adult permission to start learning." In responding to the image of the rich child, Moss and Petrie (2002, 111) envision spaces where children and adults come together as a community to construct relationships as co-constructors of knowledge. Such spaces would provide opportunities for

> excitement, wonder and the unexpected; children living childhoods not entirely ordered or predetermined for them by adults and their preoccupations; relationships and experiences that are not defined or legitimated only in terms of work and outcomes; the value of play and playfulness in its own right, and not just as means to an end; a childhood where children's questions and questionings are taken

seriously and respected by adults who themselves are open to learning from children.

Within this vision, communities would be supported through public policy to create spaces for children to be with other children and adults as complete beings, engaged in meaningful and relevant activities that reflect their daily lives and not a predetermined future.

Finally, competent and complex children must be recognized as "experts on their own lives," and adults should be seen as often having "a limited understanding of children's lives and experiences" (Dockett and Perry 2005, 4). A transforming position moves children from the position of "objects of inquiry" to contributors to research (Dockett and Perry 2002). In a study in which children were viewed as experts on the discourses of readiness, Dockett and Perry (2005, 8) asked young children these questions: "What did you need to know when you started school?" "There are some children who are going to start school soon. What is important for them to know about this school?" The significance of this study lies not just in what the children said but also in the fact that their opinions were deemed worthy. The research repositioned children as competent and knowledgeable actors in the readiness process.

Conclusion

In speaking to the issues of race and power in education, Delpit (1988) warns educators and researchers that to hold on to one assumed right answer silences other opinions and represses issues of social justice. It is my hope that this chapter will help to disrupt the discourses of readiness, that it will *open up* new possibilities for developing early years programs and social policies that speak *with* children about learning. I suggest that the discourses of readiness hold a single story that reduces child development to a simple, linear process.

My intent is not to condemn the project of readiness but to invite a conversation that makes visible the possible dangers inherent in a project based on a Western scientific conceptualization of "the child," one that is primarily concerned with the future (Lather 2007). Scott (1998, 95) labels projects with a future focus and whose authority is derived from scientific knowledge as high modernism. The high modernist project is problematic, Scott argues, because it has a "tendency to disallow other competing sources of judgment."

Readiness, I contend, needs to be understood as a complex, diverse, and problematic concept. Readiness should not be heard as a single story in which children are ready or not ready. As a social construct, readiness must be interpreted from multiple perspectives and not just from a measurable set of characteristics within a child. By inviting into the conversation other understandings of readiness, we might be surprised and inspired to discover infinite possibilities for welcoming children into schools.

Note

1   Division 1, section 3(1), states that children in British Columbia must enrol in an educational program the year of their fifth birthday. Note that section 3(2) allows parents to defer enrolment by one school year.

References

Adichie, C. 2009. "The Danger of a Single Story." Interactive transcript. http://www. ted.com/.

Ailwood, J. 2008. "Learning or Earning in the 'Smart State': Changing Tactics for Governing Early Childhood." *Childhood: A Global Journal for Childhood Studies* 15, 4: 535-51.

Arnett, J.J. 2008. "The Neglected 95%: Why American Psychology Needs to Become Less American." *American Psychologist* 63, 7: 602-14. http://web.ebscohost.com.ezproxy.library. uvic.ca.

Barbarin, B., D. Early, R. Clifford, D. Bryant, P. Frome, M. Burchinal, C. Howes, and R. Pianta. 2008. "Parental Conceptions of School Readiness: Relation to Ethnicity, Socioeconomic Status, and Children's Skills." *Early Education and Development* 19, 5: 671-701.

British Columbia. N.d. *Province of British Columbia Strategic Plan: 2006/07-2008/09.* Victoria: Queen's Printer. http://www.bcbudget.gov.bc.ca/.

–. 1996. *School Act,* Revised Statutes of British Columbia, c. 28. http://www.bced.gov.bc. ca/legislation/schoollaw/revisedstatutescontents.pdf.

–. Ministry of Education, Ministry of Health, and Ministry of Children and Family Development. 2008. *British Columbia Early Learning Framework.* Victoria: Queen's Printer.

Burman, E. 2008a. *Deconstructing Developmental Psychology.* 2nd ed. London: Routledge.

–. 2008b. *Developments: Child, Image, Nation.* London: Routledge.

Canadian Council on Learning. 2007. *State of Learning in Canada: Toward a Learning Future.* http://www.ccl-cca.ca/.

Cannella, G. 1997. *Deconstructing Early Childhood Education: Social Justice and Revolution.* New York: Peter Lang.

Carlton, M., and A. Winsler. 1999. "School Readiness: The Need for a Paradigm Shift." *School Psychology Review* 28, 3: 338-51. http://web.ebscohost.com.ezproxy.library. uvic.ca/.

Dahlberg, G., P. Moss, and A. Pence. 1999. *Beyond Quality in Early Childhood Care and Education: Beyond Quality.* London: Routledge.

–. 2007. *Beyond Quality in Early Childhood Care and Education: Postmodern Perspectives*. 2nd ed. London: Routledge.

Delpit, L. 1988. "The Silenced Dialogue: Power and Pedagogy in Educating Other People's Children." *Harvard Educational Review* 58, 3: 280-98. http://web.ebscohost.com.ezproxy.library.uvic.ca/.

Dockett, S., and B. Perry. 2002. "Who's Ready for What? Young Children Starting School." *Contemporary Issues in Early Childhood* 3, 1: 67-89. http://0-ww.wwwords.co.uk.library.capilanou.ca/.

–. 2005. "'You Need to Know How to Play Safe': Children's Experiences of Starting School." *Contemporary Issues in Early Childhood* 6, 1: 4-18. http://0-ww.wwwords.co.uk.library.capilanou.ca/.

–. 2009. "'Readiness for School: A Relational Construct." *Australian Journal of Early Childhood* 34, 1: 20-26. http://web.ebscohost.com.ezproxy.library.uvic.ca/.

Goelman, H., and C. Hertzman. N.d. *What the EDI Is (Not) – and Why It Is Important for British Columbia: Human Early Learning Partnership*. http://www.idpofbc.ca/What_the_EDI_is_(not)_Nov_7.pdf.

Gore, J. 1998. "Disciplinary Bodies: On the Continuity of Power Relations in Pedagogy." In *Foucault's Challenge: Discourse, Knowledge, and Power in Education*, ed. T.S. Popkewitz and M. Brennan, 231-51. New York: Teachers College Press.

Graue, M.E. 1993. *Ready for What? Constructing Meanings of Readiness for Kindergarten*. Albany: State University of New York Press.

–. 2006. "The Answer Is Readiness: Now What Is the Question?" *Early Education and Development* 17, 1: 43-56.

Graue, M.E., and J. DiPerna. 2000. "Redshirting and Early Retention: Who Gets the 'Gift of Time' and What Are Its Outcomes?" *American Educational Research Journal* 37, 2: 509-34.

Graue, M.E., J.K. Kroeger, and C.P. Brown. 2002. "Living the 'Gift of Time.'" *Contemporary Issues in Early Childhood* 2, 2: 338-53. http://0-ww.wwwords.co.uk.library.capilanou.ca/.

Hacking, I. 1999. *The Social Construction of What?* Cambridge, MA: Harvard University Press.

Hertzman, C., and R. Williams. 2009. "Making Early Childhood Count." *Canadian Medical Association Journal* 180, 1: 68-71. http://web.ebscohost.com.ezproxy.library.uvic.ca/.

Holmes, D., S. Murray, A. Perron, and G. Rai. 2006. "Deconstructing the Evidence-Based Discourse in Health Sciences: Truth, Power, and Fascism." *International Journal of Evidence-Based Healthcare* 4, 3: 180-86.

Janus, M. 2002. *School Readiness, Neighbourhood Affluence, and Grade 3 Test Results*. Report prepared at the Canadian Centre for Studies of Children at Risk, McMaster University, Hamilton. http://www.offordcentre.com/.

Janus, M., and D. Offord. 2007. "Development and Psychometric Properties of the Early Development Instrument (EDI): A Measure of Children's School Readiness." *Canadian Journal of Behavioural Science* 39: 1-22.

Lather, P. 1991. *Getting Smart: Feminist Research and Pedagogy with/in the Postmodern*. New York: Routledge.

–. 2007. *Getting Lost: Feminist Efforts toward a Double(d) Science*. Albany: State University of New York Press.

Li, J., A. D'Angiulli, and G. Kendall. 2007. "The Early Development Index and Children from Culturally and Linguistically Diverse Backgrounds." *Early Years* 27, 3: 221-35.

–. 2009. "Response to 'Reply to Li, D'Angiulli, and Kendall: The Early Development Index and Children from Culturally and Linguistically Diverse Backgrounds' by Janus, Hertzman, Guhn, Brinkman, and Goldfeld." *Early Years* 29, 1: 89-92.

MacDonald, M. 2007. "Developmental Theory and Post-Modern Thinking in Early Childhood Education." *Canadian Children* 32, 2: 8-10.

MacNaughton, G. 2003. *Shaping Early Childhood: Learners, Curriculum, and Contexts.* Berkshire: Open University Press.

–. 2005. *Doing Foucault in Early Childhood Studies: Applying Poststructural Ideas.* London: Routledge.

Meisels, S. 1998. *Assessing Readiness.* Report 3-002. Ann Arbor: Center for the Improvement of Early Reading Achievement. http://www.ciera.org/library/reports/inquiry-3/3-002/3-002.pdf.

Millei, Z., and L. Lee. 2007. "'Smarten Up the Parents': Whose Agenda Are We Serving? Governing Parents and Children through the Smart Population Foundation Initiative in Australia." *Contemporary Issues in Early Childhood* 8, 3: 208-21.

Moss, P., J. Dillon, and J. Statham. 2000. "The 'Child in Need' and the 'Rich Child': Discourse, Construction, and Practice." *Critical Social Policy* 20, 2: 233-54.

Moss, P., and P. Petrie. 2002. *From Child's Services to Children's Space: Public Policy, Children, and Childhood.* London: RoutledgeFalmer.

Murphy, E., and R. Dingwall. 2003. *Qualitative Methods and Health Policy Research.* New York: Walter de Gruyter.

Pence, A., and H. Hix-Small. 2007. "Global Children in the Shadow of the Global Child." *International Journal of Educational Policy, Research, and Practice: Reconceptualizing Childhood Studies* 8, 1: 83-100. http://web.ebscohost.com.ezproxy.library.uvic.ca/.

Qvortrup, J. 2008. *Childhood Matters: Social Theory, Practice, and Politics.* London: Avebury Publishing.

Rabinow, P., and N. Rose. 2003. "Omnes et Singulatim: Toward a Critique of Political Reason." In *The Essential Foucault,* ed. P. Rabinow and N. Rose, 180-91. London: New Press.

Rinaldi, C. 2006. *In Dialogue with Reggio Emilia.* London: Routledge.

Robinson, K., and C. Diaz. 2006. *Diversity and Difference in Early Childhood Education.* London: Open University Press.

Rose, N. 1990. *Governing the Soul: The Shaping of the Private Self.* London: Routledge.

–. 1998. *Inventing Ourselves: Psychology, Power, and Personhood.* New York: Cambridge University Press.

Scott, J.C. 1998. *Seeing Like a State: How Certain Schemes to Improve the Human Condition Have Failed.* New Haven: Yale University Press.

Scott-Little, C., S. Kagan, and V. Frelow. 2006. "Conceptualization of Readiness and the Content of Early Learning Standards: The Intersection of Policy and Research?" *Early Childhood Research Quarterly* 21: 152-73.

Walkerdine, V. 1988. *The Mastery of Reason: Cognitive Development and the Production of Rationality.* London: Routledge.

Weiss, J. 2002. *Take the Ride of Your Life: Shift Gears for More Balance, Growth, and Joy.* Scottsdale: Bloomfield Press.

Wesley, P., and V. Buysse. 2003. "Making Meaning of School Readiness in Schools and Communities." *Early Childhood Research Quarterly* 18: 351-75.

Winter, S., and M. Kelley. 2008. "Forty Years of School Readiness Research: What Have We Learned?" *Childhood Education* 84, 5: 260-67. http://web.ebscohost.com.ezproxy. library.uvic.ca/.

Wright, C., M. Diener, and S. Kay. 2000. "School Readiness of Low-Income Children at Risk for School Failure." *Journal of Children and Poverty* 6, 2: 99-117. http://web.ebscohost. com.ezproxy.library.uvic.ca/.

Afterword

JENNIFER WHITE AND ALAN PENCE

As these diverse chapters attest, child and youth care is a dynamic and evolving field. Long defined by its focus on children, youth, and families across a broad range of institutions and contexts, the field embraces an array of professional practice interventions, pedagogical efforts, scholarly investigations, and policy activities at local, national, and international levels.

With this book, we have attempted to demonstrate that critically oriented perspectives and postfoundational theories, in all their varied, multiple, and complex forms, are useful intellectual resources for theorizing and reimagining CYC. For example, embodying a critical reflexivity toward what and how they know, as well as showing a deep and abiding concern for history, context, knowledge, language, and power, each of the contributors has shown some of the fresh possibilities opened up by critically working the borders of CYC pedagogy, practice, and policy.

Although such postfoundational, critical perspectives are hardly new, they remain relatively underexplored in CYC. Importantly, then, we see this volume as capturing the field's development at a particular moment in time. Although much of the field's early history was dedicated to carving out a unique professional identity, which often included defining CYC relative to other existing professions, over the past several decades the field has expanded in multiple, sometimes contradictory, directions, leaving any idea of linear progress or a single, stable core far behind.

The chapters assembled here reveal CYC as a highly pluralistic set of social practices and commitments. In other words, earlier efforts to define CYC in sharp, singular, and static terms have recently given way to recognizing the multiplicities, diversities, and contingencies of CYC as an emerging and dynamic field. Although this might cause consternation for some, we welcome the creativity and freedom that these messy borders and indeterminate edges invite. We are intrigued about where these ideas might take us next.

Working against any universalizing tendencies to capture CYC once and for all, and resisting the temptation to prescribe a singular set of practices that will transcend time and place, it is our sincere hope that the material gathered here will challenge readers, enable new questions, and provoke stimulating debates. By supporting greater epistemological diversity, adopting an ongoing critical posture toward our taken-for-granted assumptions, and accommodating a wide range of divergent points of view, we believe that this book signals an exciting new era for CYC, one in which critique, deconstruction, reflexivity, multiplicities, and blurred borders are embraced as useful and welcome tools for creative thought and action.

Contributors

B R O O K E A L S B U R Y holds a master's degree in child and youth care from the University of Victoria. She has been a CYC professional for over fifteen years working in wilderness, recreation, education, residential treatment, outreach, and office-based settings. She lives in the Yukon, where she is an instructor for various post-secondary institutions, including Yukon College and Aurora College in the Northwest Territories. In her teaching and research, she seeks to understand how the northern Canadian context creates a unique environment for training individuals to work with children, youth, and families and how that context can offer promising practice approaches for helping professionals trained in the North.

M A C K E N Z I E D E A N is a graduate student in the School of Child and Youth Care at the University of Victoria. She has been working in the field of CYC for the past eleven years, and her focus has been primarily on working with adolescents in residential care settings. Currently, she coordinates after-school programs in south Burnaby for children who are, for various reasons, excluded from being involved in mainstream programming. Her current research examines the complexities of diversity in practice and seeks to explore how CYC practitioners understand and work with discourses of difference in their professional roles.

SANDRINA DE FINNEY is an associate professor in the School of Child and Youth Care at the University of Victoria. Rooted in her experience as a youth worker, community researcher, and activist, her practice and research are informed by participatory, arts-based, change-centred frameworks. Her work interrogates minoritized subject formation, engagement, and resistance in neocolonial contexts. She is the co-founder and past president of the award-winning antidote network for racialized girls and women and is the research adviser for the Indigenous Child Welfare Research Network (ICWRN).

B. DENISE HODGINS is a doctoral student and sessional instructor in the School of Child and Youth Care at the University of Victoria. She has worked with children, youth, and families in a variety of capacities in the human service sector since 1989, including as a school-age child-care provider, an early childhood educator, and a program director. Her research interests include the role that gender plays in the (re)construction of parenting practices and the implications of postfoundational theories and methodologies for research and practice.

MARK L. KELLY has provided counselling, program development, and group facilitation to youth, families, and marginalized populations for twenty years. He provides specialized instruction to students and professionals working with children, youth, and families. He has a proven track record of advocacy for those facing poverty in the Yukon and across northern Canada. He holds a BA degree in child and youth care from the University of Victoria and an MEd degree in counselling from Acadia University. He has researched and written in the areas of addiction, marginalization, recreation, and therapeutic approaches for youth. He is currently in private counselling practice and lives in Whitehorse, Yukon.

KATHLEEN KUMMEN is a lecturer in the Department of Early Childhood Education at Capilano University and a PhD candidate at the School of Child and Youth Care at the University of Victoria. She is part of Research in Early Childhood Care, Education, and Health (REACH), a consortium of early childhood researchers at the University of Victoria. Her research interests focus on exploring theory and practice in pre-service training and ongoing professional development of early childhood educators.

J.N. LITTLE is a theoro-practivist who teaches in the School of Child and Youth Care at the University of Victoria and counsels in eating disorders. Her most recent research was an arts-based inquiry with youth activists from Youth Combating Intolerance. When not waxing peda-gogical, she can be found in her studio collaging or spending time in her garden with her family.

ELICIA LOISELLE is completing her MA degree in the School of Child and Youth Care at the University of Victoria. Her academic career is heavily informed by more than a decade of community work in fem-inist organizing, sexual health education, sexualized violence prevention, queer community development, and youth work. Her current research interests include critical feminist Youth Participatory Action Research with minoritized girls and youth, youth work as social justice praxis, and queer(ing) family formation.

JONATHAN MORRIS has practised across several contexts in CYC over the past ten years, including programs for children responding to violence at home, hospital-based psychiatric treatment, school-based youth suicide prevention education, and campus mental health promo-tion. He has recently completed his master's degree in child and youth care, exploring how the ideas of Michel Foucault can be used to critically examine youth suicide prevention curricula. Other scholarly interests include the role of communities of practice in campus mental health promotion and narrative-informed approaches to CYC work. He is a sessional instructor in the undergraduate program at the University of Victoria.

JANET NEWBURY is a PhD candidate in the School of Child and Youth Care at the University of Victoria. She is currently exploring alternatives to what she sees as the widespread individualization of social problems. She has also published academic articles on the topics of addiction support, social justice, and research methodology and non-academic articles about current global and social events.

VERONICA PACINI-KETCHABAW is an associate professor and coordinator of early years specialization at the School of Child and Youth Care at the University of Victoria. Her research interests revolve around the history of childcare in Canada; racialized immigrant and refugee communities; the problematization of prescriptive practice in early childhood; and post-humanist, post-structural, post-colonial, and anti-racist feminist practices in early childhood education.

ALAN PENCE is the UNESCO chair for Early Childhood Education, Care, and Development and a professor in the School of Child and Youth Care at the University of Victoria. He is the former director of the school, and he founded the Unit for Early Years Research and Development (EYRD), the First Nations Partnerships Program (FNPP), and the Early Childhood Development Virtual University (ECDVU) within the school. His major areas of research and development work focus on leadership promotion for early childhood care and development in the majority (developing) world, with particular emphases on Africa and Indigenous communities internationally.

LORINDA STONEMAN is a doctoral student in the University of Victoria's School of Child and Youth Care and is engaged in research and writing on youth justice policy. She received her master's degree in criminology from Simon Fraser University in 2008, and the intersections between criminology and child and youth care form a key area of interest. Other interests range from qualitative and community-based research methods to criminological and post-structural theory.

JENNIFER WHITE is an associate professor in the School of Child and Youth Care at the University of Victoria. She has practised as a clinical counsellor, educator, policy consultant, researcher, and community developer. She has a long-standing interest in studying everyday practice in CYC, which includes consideration of the diverse ways of knowing, doing, and being that inform this work. She is particularly interested in better understanding CYC practice as a unique site of multiple ethical, socio-political, and relational engagements.

Index

Aboriginal children: and readiness, 209; residential schools/foster homes and, 105

Aboriginal peoples: fathers, 105-6, 107; girls, 73; human services professions and, 167-68, 171-72; as more "at risk" than non-Aboriginals, 171-72

activism: in CYC practice, 14-15, 38; ethical, 44; in feminism, 7; teaching as, 14-15

actuarial justice, 192-93, 194

adolescence: and future risk, 193; mapping of, 25-26. *See also* youth

advocacy: critical, 90; in CYC, 14; girls and, 85-86; and minoritized girls, 89; and political action, 14; for street-involved youth, 142

Ailwood, J., 206

Alsbury, Brooke, xx

Alvi, S., 184, 187, 188, 189

Anderson, J., 143-44

Armitage, A., 169

assimilation, 40, 105, 107, 108

Association of Child and Youth Care Practice, Ethics of Child and Youth Care Professionals, 36

Austin, B.D., 134

Ball, J., 106, 107

Barbarin, B., 202

Barbershop Fatherhood Organization, 103

Barclay, L., 97-98, 100-1, 103, 108-9

Barrett, F.J., 141

Barron, C.L., 194

Bauman, Z., 39

Beccaria, Cesare, 184

Beker, Jerome, 124, 130

Bellefeuille, G., 41

Benhabib, S., 194

Bentham, Jeremy, 184

bereavement, 161, 174n2. *See also* grief

Berland, Jeremy, 159

Bill C-25 (Act to Amend the Youth Criminal Justice Act), 179

Bill of Rights, 188

Birthing Project, 103

Blaise, M., 61-62, 67

Bloustien, G., 11

Bradford, S., 126, 128, 131

British Columbia: Early Learning Framework (ELF), 212-13; Ministry for Children and Families, 207; *Strategic Plan 2006/07-2008/09*, 211

Bronfenbrenner, Urie, 202

Broughton, T.L., 98
Brown Commission (1849), 184
Burbules, N., 58-59
bureaucracy: in northern communities,
127; and professions, 127, 128; and social problems, 128; and street-involved
youth, 142
Burman, Erica, 23, 56, 204
Butler, J.: and compulsory heterosexuality,
60; and gender trouble, 111; on grief,
172-73; on grieving of losses, 163-64;
and implication of individual and other
lives, 159; on isolation of involved individuals, 158; on self-generated acts, 38;
and September 11 losses, 166, 170; and
transformative effect of loss, 167

calculability: of persons, 192-93
Callahan, M., 171, 192
Canadian Charter of Rights and
Freedoms, 189
Canadian Council on Learning, 204-5
Canadian Women's Foundation, 86
Canales, M.K., 145
Cannella, G.S., 25
Caputo, J.D., 136, 154, 158
Caputo, T., 143-44
Caragata, L., 96-97
Carlton, M., 199
Carr, D., 37, 41
Carrigan, D.O., 181, 183, 186
Casey, R., 133-34
Catlett, B.S., 96
Cerulo, K.A., 125
Chambers, C.M., 126
change, CYC and, 136; individual(s) and,
158-59, 164, 168. *See also* social change
Chantler, K., 84
Charles, G., 136
Chesney, Lind, M., 80
child development, dominant discourses
of, 205, 212; ecological perspective and,
202; father involvement and, 102; and
learning, 201; maturationist view of,
201; and "natural" knowledge, xix;
population health and, 202-3; and readiness, 201, 205, 208, 212, 214; stages of,

22; as truth, 210; universality in, xviii,
22, 204-5; and Western children, 205.
See also developmental psychology
child offender(s). *See* young offender(s)
child welfare: approach to youth criminal
justice system, 191; and decision making
in children's best interests, 128-29; and
individual, 168; and loss, 169; policy
makers and, 159; poverty and, 168
child and youth care (CYC): about, xv;
academic/practitioner dichotomy in, 3,
16; certification, 10; Code of Ethics,
36-37, 46; competencies, 29, 131; as
contested field, xvii; contexts of practice,
6; critical engagement in, 45; developmental psychology and, 19-20, 29; developmental theories and, 20, 30-31;
distinctiveness of, 33-34; essentialism in,
13; ethical decision-making models in,
41; evolutionary vs. revolutionary changes in, 29-30; gender and, 66-68; liberal
humanism and, 43; modernist discourses of professionalism in, xv-xvi;
multi/interdisciplinarity in, 9-10, 46;
multiple philosophies, 15-16; and normative, xviii, 10; other caring professions
and, 34; participatory action research
(PAR) methodologies, 15; patterning
after other professions, 39-40; philosophy, 6, 10-11; philosophy vs. practice,
7-8; postmodernism and, 45-46; power
relations and, 89, 168; practice, 13-14;
professional codes of behaviour, 42;
professional ethics in, 35-37; professionalism discourses in, 40-44; professionalization and, 121, 130-31;
reconceptualization of, xvi; relational
vs. individual in, 168; relational vs.
political in, 10; roles in, 5-6; schools of,
9-10; student grooming in, 13; theoro-
practivist model, 4-5, 11-15, 16; theory,
12-13; worker identity in, 125
Child and Youth Care Forum, 35
childhood, child development and, 208;
gender and, 55, 61; history of attitudes
toward, 184-85; sexuality and, 55; as
social construct, 212

children: Aboriginal, 105, 209; child savers movement and, 186-87; constructions of, 20; as consumers, 188; as contributors to research, 213, 214; criminal justice system and, 180; developmental testing of, 27; Doyle report and, 183; early Canadian attitudes toward, 182-83; education of, 185; employment of, 183, 185, 187; as experts on own lives, 214; fathers and, 96, 99-100; and future, 187, 211-12; gender and, 66, 67; heterosexualization and, 56, 61, 65-66; immigration to Canada, 181; as independent, 188; normal/typical, 204-6; *parens patriae* and, 186, 189; punishment of, 183; self-determination of, 188, 189; sexuality and, 64, 66; state and, 186. *See also* girls; youth
Clark, D., 106
clients: as co-experts, 135-36; professions and best interest of, 129
codes of ethics: CYC, 36-37, 42, 46; de-politicized concepts in, 42; loneliness/doubt/uncertainty and, 39; and professionalism, 40; and respectability, 42; and restrictive approach, 41; and small communities, 129
collective biography, xx, 56-58, 61, 68
colonialism: and Aboriginal fathers, 105-6; and advocacy for best practices, 129; and developmental theories, 25; and Indigenous peoples, 40; in northern communities, 123
Colton, M.J., 128-29
Coltrane, Scott, 103
Columbine school shooting, 163
Comacchio, C., 98, 99
competencies: CYC, 131; and suicide, 38
Competencies for Professional Child and Youth Work Practitioners (CPCYWP), 36-37, 41, 42, 46
connectedness, 159, 165-66
Connell, R.W., 60, 110
context: of gender, 60; and meaning, 58-59
Corson, D., 26-27

crime: deterrence, 184; hedonism and, 184; individual responsibility for, 183-84; minoritized girls and, 80; prevention, 179, 180
criminal justice, actuarial methods used in, 192; child welfare approach to, 191; disappearance of children as category, 180; probability in, 194; relational theory in, 195; retributive approach, 191; schooling and, 185. *See also* youth justice
critical spaces, girls and, 86-88; and power relations, 87
culture: and child welfare, 129; and fatherhood, 100-1, 104-5; and reflexivity, 124; of street-involved youth, 153-54

D'Angiulli, A., 205-6, 208, 209
Damousi, J., 162, 163
Davies, Bronwyn, 56, 59-60, 63, 85, 111
Day, C.A., 134
de Finney, Sandrina, xx
Dean, Mackenzie, xx
Deleuze, G., 26, 27, 28, 43-44
Delpit, L., 214
Denov, M., 189
Derrida, J., 164, 166, 167, 169, 210
developmental psychology, contextualization of, 20; critical stance on, 20, 21; and CYC practice/training, 19-20, 29; dominance of, 59; and evolutionary tree, 25-26; feminist post-structuralism and, 68; as framework, 26; and gender, 66-67; and lifespan development, 28; modernity and, 22-26; predefined outcomes in, 23; as science, 19; social technologies of, 27; in societies of control, 26-28; testing of children, 27. *See also* child development
developmental theories, 19; contextualization of, 30-31; CYC and, 20, 30-31; and disciplinary societies, 26; Enlightenment and, 25; as frameworks, 20; political positioning of, 21; power relations and, 28-29; and progress, 25; and social movements, 21; of stages, 25; and subjectivities, 30

deviancy, homelessness and, 145; street-involved youth and, 145, 146
Diagnostic and Statistical Manual of Mental Disorders (DSM-IV), 5, 6
Dillon, J., 213
DiPerna, J., 201
disadvantage. *See* marginalization
discourses: and inscription, 59; and subjectification, 59-60. *See also* dominant discourses
diversity, xx; in fatherhood, 96, 107, 108; and girls, 84; learning and, 212; in practice, 84; within professional identities, 134; readiness and, 212; of standards in control society, 28; of street-involved youth, 143-44
Dockett, S., 199-200, 204, 214
Dollahite, D.C., 101
dominant discourses: and alternative knowledges, 65; of child development, 205, 212; defined, 40; and inscription, 111; liberal humanism as, 45-46; neo-liberalism and, 72; resistance to, 65
Doucet, A., 103, 111
Duncombe, Charles, 184

Early Development Instrument (EDI), 27, 202-3, 205-6, 207, 208-10
Eberle, S.G., 161
Emerson, Ralph Waldo, 203
Enlightenment: and childhood, 185; and developmental theories, 25
environment: and child development, 202; and readiness, 202
Erikson, Erik, 25
Ermine, W., 3-4, 44-45
Esté, D., 106-7
ethics, activism and, 44; big questions vs. micro-ethics, 46-47; critical engagement in, 45; as depoliticized, 48; dilemmas in, 39, 48; enlarged perspective on, 44-45, 47; ethical space, 3-4, 45; and families, 41; human caring practices and, 37-40; Indigenous knowledge/philosophy and, 44-45; instrumentalist view of, 42, 48; postmodern, 39; as product, 41-42; re-storying in, 48; of resistance, 38; and

responsibility for others, 39; restrictive frameworks, 40-41; self-awareness and, 43; and social justice, 44; and suicide, 38; teaching of, xix-xx, 44-48; traditional/rule-based vs. postmodern, 39
Ethics of Child and Youth Care Professionals (Association of Child and Youth Care Practice), 36
evidence-based practice (EBP), 170, 171
experts, children as, 214; clients as co-, 135-36; northern, 126-27; youth as co-, 135

Factory Act, 185
family/families, constructions of, 20; criminal justice system and, 191; fatherhood and model of, 103; and juvenile delinquency, 184; maternal focus in, 95; privileging of, 112; professional ethics and, 41; Western, 95-96
Father Initiative, 101
father involvement, xx; and children's development, 102; as concept, 100-1; heterogeneity of, 104; initiatives, 112; maternal overprotection and, 99
Father Involvement Research Alliance (FIRA), 101, 104
Father Responsibility Movement, 103
fatherhood: in Canada, 99, 101; changes in, 96, 112; culture and, 100-1, 104-5; diversity in, 96, 107, 108; and egalitarian parenting, 100; ethnicities and, 104-5; family model and, 103; gendering of, 108-12; government initiatives in, 101, 103, 109; heterogeneity of, 107; heterosexuality and, 104; history of, 97-100; ideal of, 98, 104; normative, 103; research on, 100, 102; social classes and, 97-98; social construction of, 110-11; societal expectations of, 102-3; in US, 99, 101; Western image of, 95-96
fathers: Aboriginal, 105-6, 107; as breadwinners, 96-97, 99; changes in conduct vs. image, 96; as citizens, 97; essentiality of, 109, 110; immigrant, 106-7; refugee, 106-7; as sex role models, 99-100; social inclusion for, 107-8, 109, 112; societal

expectations of, 107; as support persons/
helpers, 103; and work-parenthood
relationship, 111-12
feminism(s): activism, 7; and egalitarian
parenting, 100; essentialist, 13; expert
vs. non-expert, 16; and girls, 76, 86;
theory vs. practice in, 7; transnational, 4
feminist post-structuralism, 59-60, 61;
and collective biography, 56; and
developmental psychology, 68
feminity, 60
Fendler, L., 21-22, 27
Fewster, G., 8, 13
Fine, M., 78, 79, 83
Foucault, Michel, 23, 26, 58, 171, 193, 200,
205, 206, 211
Freidson, E., 125, 128, 131, 133, 134
Frelow, V., 199, 201
Funiciello, T., 152

Gabor, P., 148
Gale, A.G., 134
Gannon, S., 59-60
Garfat, T., 41, 136
Gastaldo, D., 45
Gavanas, A., 103
gender, xx; and childhood, 55, 61; children
and, 66, 67; clothing and, 62-65; collective biography and, 57, 58, 61; construction of, 55, 60, 108; context of, 60; CYC
pedagogy/practice and, 66-68; developmental psychology and, 66-67; dichotomized structure of, 88-89; and
fatherhood, 108-12; fathers as role
models, 99-100; girls and structures of,
73, 74; heterosexualization and, 55-56,
109; loss and, 163; and male/female
dualism, 55, 67; and parenthood, 111-12;
power relations and, 55, 60, 61, 67, 68;
and social order, 60, 61, 63-64, 66-67;
and subjectification, 59-60; "trouble,"
111
George, R., 107
Gergen, K.J., 4, 5, 110, 141, 148
Giles, C., 190
Girl Power, 77-79, 81, 84
girl studies, 71, 75-76

girlhood(s), concepts of, 76-80; as contested space, 70; definition of, 71; essentialism and, 70; neoliberalism and, 70
girls: Aboriginal, 73; and advocacy, 85-86;
agency, 84-86; of colour, 82-83; and
critical spaces, 86-88; with disabilities,
74, 82-83; diversity and, 84; empowerment of, 65, 77, 85; feminism and, 76,
86; gender structures and, 73, 74; gendered clothing and, 62-65; girl/boy
dichotomy and, 88-89; heterosexualization of, 64; immigrant, 82-83; interventions and, 72-73, 79, 82; lesbian/bisexual,
74; mean, 79, 80; minoritization of, xx,
71-74, 78-79, 85-86; neoliberalism and,
77-78, 81, 84-85; party, 79-80; pregnant,
83; racialization and, 74, 80; at risk, 82,
85; sexuality and, 82-83, 88; UN decade
of the girl child, 71; violence and, 82;
voiceless, 79; vulnerable, 79-81; youth
development theories and, 76
Girls Action Foundation, 84
Goffman, Erving, 145-46
Gordon, Colin, 192-93
Gore, J., 206, 210
Gove, Thomas J., 169
Grant, M., 12
Graue, M.E., 200, 201, 203
Greenwood, E., 125-26, 131, 133
grief: and community, 159; cross-cultural
comparisons, 161; defined, 174n1; pur-
pose of, 161; and solidarity, 163, 164. *See
also* loss
Griffin, C., 70, 76, 81
Griswold, R.L., 96, 98, 99
Guattari, Félix, 43-44
Gulcur, L., 147-48

Hacking, I., 144-45, 203
Hagarty, Judge, 185
Hall, G. Stanley, 25
Hannah-Moffat, K., 193, 194
Hansen, J., 43
Harris, A., 80-81
Hawkins, A.J., 101
herising, F., 15-16
Hertzman, C., 202, 207

heterosexuality/heterosexualization: and children, 56, 61, 65-66; compulsory, 56, 60, 63, 66; conceptualization of, 60; and fatherhood, 104; and gender, 55-56, 61, 67, 109; and sexuality, 67
Hewlett, Barry, 96, 100
Higgett, N., 144
Hix-Small, H., 129
Hodge, M.N., 125
Hodgins, B. Denise, xx
Holmes, D., 45
homelessness: absolute vs. relative, 144; and deviancy, 145; outreach professionals and, 147-48; street involvement and, 145
Hondagneu-Sotelo, Pierrette, 96
hooks, bell, 7
hope, 166-67
Houston, S.E., 182
human services: and Aboriginal peoples, 167-68, 171-72; alternatives within, 158; EBP and, 170; economic rationalism and, 171-72; evidence-based practice in professions, 128; and individual, 168; loss and, 169; minoritized girls and, 81-82, 85-86; and relational/contextualized nature of hardships, 168; street-involved youth and, 150
Hunter, K., 161-62

identity/identities: as borderless, 9; construction of, 59; creation of, 9; CYC youth worker, 125; diversity of, 134; and fatherhood, 112; formation of binaries, 59; outreach professionals and, 147; personal vs. professional, 4; politics, 8; professional, xv-xvi, 43, 121, 125, 134; of street-involved youth, 146
Indigenous peoples, assimilation/ colonization and, 40; and ethics, 44-45; Western worldviews and, 45. *See also* Aboriginal peoples
individual(s): agency, 164-65; and change, 158-59, 164, 168; child welfare and, 168; children as, 183; CYC practice and, 168; disenchantment and, 164; generic vs. unique, 169-70; human services and,

168; juvenile delinquency and, 187; liberal humanism and, 42; psychology and, 24-25; responsibility, 150, 183-84, 191, 194; restrictive ethical frameworks and, 40; social conditions and, 173; and society, 164-65; socio-political influences vs., xvii; unique vs. generic, 173
inequities: social, 209, 212; structural, 82, 84, 85, 89, 90. *See also* marginalization
intersectionality theory, 4, 60
interventions, economic rationalism and, 171-72; and girls, 72-73, 79, 82; loss and, 172; power relations and, 172; reduction to essential, 158; risk assessment and, 194-95; and structural inequities, 84
Irwin, K., 80

Jackson, M., 190
Jal, Emmanuel, 166-67
juvenile delinquency: Act for the More Speedy Trial and Publishment of Juvenile Offenders, 185-86; Act Respecting Arrest, Trial, and Imprisonment of Youthful Offenders, 186; anti-social behaviour and, 183-84; class and, 182, 186, 187; and individual, 187; legislation concerning, 185-91
juvenile delinquents: in colonial Canada, 181-82; construction of, 192; as criminals, 189; punishment of, 184; treatment of, 184
Juvenile Delinquents Act (JDA), 186-87, 188-89

Kagan, S., 199, 201
Karabanow, J., 143
Kelly, Mark, xx-xxi
Kempf-Leonard, K., 192
Kendall, G., 205-6, 208, 209
Kermode, S., 132
Klein, N., 163
Knorth, E.J., *Professionalization and Participation in Child and Youth Care*, 130, 135
knowledge, construction of, 47, 203, 213; and thinking, 47-48
Kohlberg, Laurence, 25

Kuehne, V., 149
Kummen, Kathleen, xxi

Lafferty, R., 187
Lamb, M.E., 100, 104
Lather, P., 112, 154, 209
learning, child development and, 201; and diversity, 212. *See also* readiness
Lesko, Nancy, 25-26
Li, J., 205-6, 208, 209
Libel, M., 188
liberal humanism, 42-44, 45-46
Little, Jennifer N., xix, 20-21
Loiselle, Elicia, xx
Long, D., 104-5, 108, 112
Lorde, A.G., 6
Loseke, D.R., 145
loss, child welfare and, 169; collective, 163; and connectedness, 159-60, 165-66; and control, 170; cross-cultural comparisons, 161; functioning of, 160-67; gender and, 163; generic vs. unique individual and, 169-70; hope and, 166-67; and human services, 169; as individual, 165; individual vs. relational aspects, 172-73; and interventions, 172; learning from, 161; nationalism and, 162; political aspects, 162, 163, 164, 165, 167, 172-73; public vs. private grieving of, 163-64; relational aspects, 165, 172-73; and reverence for life, 173; September 11, 2001, attacks and, 165; and social change, 162, 166-67; and social justice, 164, 173; and social responsibility, 167, 173; and unpredictability, 170; war and, 161-62. *See also* grief
Lupton, D., 97-98, 100-1, 103, 108-9
Lutz, M.M., 102

MacDonald, L., 143, 146
MacNaughton, G., 211, 212
Magnuson, D., 41
Maier, H., 124
marginalization, loss and, 162; outreach professionals and, 139, 141, 147, 148; professional, 147, 148; and readiness of disadvantaged children, 205-6; and

stigmatization, 145-46; street involvement and, 143, 144, 145. *See also* inequities
masculinity/masculinities: and fathers' essentiality, 109, 110; hegemonic, 60, 62, 63-64, 98, 110; multiple forms of, 110; and power, 110-11; of sons, 99; transformation of, 111-12
Maurutto, P., 193, 194
McBride, B.A., 102
McClelland, S.I., 83
McKenry, P.C., 96
McKnight, J., 127
McNamee, S., 141
meaning, context and, 58-59
Messer-Davidow, E., 10
Messner, Michael A., 96
Mikel-Brown, L., 77-78
Miller, C.T., 145
Miller, N., 103
Miller, P., 24
Miller, W., 96-97
Minnich, E., 47-48
minoritization, advocacy and, 89; critical practice and, 90; of girls, xx, 71-74, 78-79, 85-86; silence and, 85-86; social services and, 81-82, 85-86; structural inequities and, 90
modernity: and developmental psychology, 22-26; and objectivity, xviii-xix
Moloney, M.M., 126
monitoring. *See* surveillance
Montreal Massacre, 163
Morgan, D., 109, 110
Morris, Jonathan, xx
Moss, P., 203, 213-14
mothers, father involvement and, 112; fathers as support persons/helpers to, 103; and juvenile delinquency, 184; as natural caregivers of children, xviii, 103; social classes and, 97-98
Murray, E., 169
My Daddy Matters Because, 101, 102

Nakae, M., 147-48
National Longitudinal Survey of Children, 204-5
National Project on Fathering, 101

National Youth Agency, 45
Nentwich, J.C., 111-12
neoliberalism, dominant discourses and, 72; and girls, 70, 77-78, 81, 84-85; and individual responsibility, 150; and street outreach work, 141; and structural inequities, 90n3; and youth delinquency, 192
Ngai, S.S., 146
Nicholson, Robert, 179
normativity: about, xviii; and children, xviii, 22, 204-6; fatherhood and, 103; and readiness, 208-9
Norrie, A.W., 194
North American Certification Project Competencies for Professional Child and Youth Care Workers, 67, 131
northern communities, bureaucracy in, 127; experts in, 126-27; professionalization in, 129; segregation in, 123
Nunavik Educational Task Force, 127

objectivity, modernity and, xviii-xix, 22
Oleman, Gerry, 167-68, 172
Ormond, A., 82
outreach professionals: and guerrilla-based strategies, 148; and homelessness, 147-48; mainstream health-care system and, 148; and marginalization, 139, 141; mental health realm and, 148; multidisciplinary approach, 148; as paraprofessionals, 147; and poverty, 153; professional marginalization of, 147, 148; qualities of, 148; and street involvement, 139, 146, 149; as workers vs. practitioners, 146-47; and youth on vs. off the street, 153

Pacini-Ketchabaw, Veronica, xix, 56, 59
Palkovitz, R., 108
parents/parenthood, gender and, 111-12; and readiness, 202, 207-8; surveillance of, 207-8. *See also* family/families; mothers; *and headings beginning* father
Parke, R.D., 104
Pate, K., 193
Pence, A., 29, 129, 152
Pereira, A., 73

Peressini, T., 143, 146
performativity, 60, 61
Perry, B., 199-200, 204, 214
Peters, M., 58-59
Peterson, E., 192
Petrie, P., 203
Phelan, J., 11
Piaget, Jean, 19, 20, 25, 27
Pipher, Mary, *Reviving Ophelia*, 79
Platt, A., 186-87
Pleck, E.H., 97, 98, 99, 100
Pleck, J.H., 98, 99
Polkinghorne, D.E., 170
postmodernism, 26-27; critical perspectives and, xxiiin1; in CYC teaching, 45-46; essentialist politics and, 8; and normativity, xviii; and professionalization, xvi-xvii; and shifts in truth, 8
post-structuralism, 58-59; feminist, 59-60, 61
poverty: and child welfare, 168; of immigrant children, 181; industry, 139, 152-53; minoritized girls and, 78-79; outreach professionals and, 153
power/power relations: and client/professional separation, 40; collective biography and, 56; critical perspectives and, xxiiin1; critical spaces and, 87; CYC practice and, 89, 168; and developmental theories, 28-29; and gender, 55, 60, 61, 67, 68; gendering fatherhood and, 110; governmentality and, 23; intersectionality theory and, 60; interventions and, 172; masculinities and, 110-11; micro
practices of, 206-11; and minoritization, 73; professionalism and, xvi; professions and, 126; and research participants, 124; restrictive ethical frameworks and, 40; and street-involved youth, 141-42; and subjectivities, 59; and unequal girlhoods, 72
practice-based evidence, 129-30, 136
practitioner self-awareness, 33, 35
Prilleltensky, I., 40, 44, 45
Prochner, L., 188
professional ethics. *See* ethics
professionalism, checklist approach to, 42; and client/professional separation,

40; codes of ethics and, 40; competency-based approaches to, 41; as contested, xvi-xvii; decision making in children's best interests, 128-29; modernist discourses of, xv-xvi; postmodernism and, xvi; and power, xvi; re-storying in, 48; and restrictive ethical frameworks, 40; uncertain theory of, 48

professionalization, 124; boundaries of, 131-32; client-based evidence and, 136; as co-construction, 132-36; competencies and, 131; critical/postmodern views and, xvi-xvii; of CYC, 121, 130-31; functionalist, 132, 135-36; medical profession and, xvi; in northern communities, 129; philosophy of, 131-32; process vs. outcome and, 131-32, 133; rise of, 125; values and, 132

Professionalization and Participation in Child and Youth Care (Knorth;Van Den Bergh;Verheij), 130, 135

professions/professionals: and best interests of clients, 129; bureaucracy and, 125; clients as co-experts and, 135-36; criteria for, 125-26; definition of, 125; and definition of client problems, 128; Enlightenment and, 125; expertise of, 126; as generic vs. changing historic concept, 133; identity, xv-xvi, 43, 121, 125; individual vs. collective identity, 125, 133-34; power and, 126; purpose of, 126; rise of, 125; scientific method and, 128; self-awareness, 43; social construction of, 121, 126, 133, 135; and social order, 40, 128; social policy and, 128; and social problems, 127-28; universal understanding of, 135

Proweller, A., 83

psychology, emergence of, 23-24; and governmentality, 24; and individualization, 24-25; and readiness, 204

racialization/racism: and Aboriginal fathers, 105-6; and girls, 74, 80; girls of colour and, 82

readiness: and Aboriginal children, 209; child development and, 201, 205, 208,

212, 214; children as actors in, 214; classification and, 209-10; and communities, 208-9, 210; definitions of, 199, 200-3; and disadvantaged children, 205-6; and diversity, 212; environment/ecological perspective on, 202; future and, 211-12; and marginalization of value of child, 211; micropractices of power and, 206-11; nature vs. nurture and, 201; normalization and, 208-9; parents and, 202, 207-8; population health and, 202-3; psychology and, 204; skills acquisition and, 201; social constructionism and, 203-4, 210, 211; and social inequities, 209, 212; social policy and, 210-11, 212, 214; surveillance and, 207-8, 211; unreadiness vs., 210, 212; views vs. concept of, 199

Reed, P.G., 148

refugee fathers, 106-7

relationality: of CYC practice, 168; and loss, 165, 172-73; politics, 4

responsibility: collective, 159; ethics and, 39; individual, 150, 183-84, 191, 194; social, 167, 173

Reviving Ophelia (Pipher), 79

Reynolds, V., 38

Ricks, F., 41

Rinaldi, C., 213

risk, Aboriginal peoples and, 171-72; assessment, 193-94, 194-95; future, 193; girls and, 82, 85; structural inequities and, 82; youth and, 193-94

Robinson, K., 65-66

Rogers, H., 98

Ropers-Huilman, B., 9

Rose, L., 185

Rose, N., 23, 24, 164, 193, 204, 210

Rose-Sladde, L., 130-31, 132

Rossides, D.W., 129

Rossiter, R., 40, 44, 45

Rowe, M., 147, 148

Schissel, B., 192

School Act, 200

science, evidence of, xviii-xix; modernity and, 22; post-structuralism and, 59

Scott, J.C., 208, 214-15
Scott-Little, C., 199, 201
self-awareness: and ethics, 43; practitioner, 33, 35; professional, 43; self-storying and, 43
services. *See* human services
sexuality: and children, 64, 66; construction of, 55; girls and, 82-83, 88
Shimoni, R., 106
Shope, J.H., 124
Skott-Myhre, Hans, 20-21, 28, 29-30
social change, loss and, 162, 166-67. *See also* change
social classes: and delinquency, 182, 192; and fatherhood, 97-98; involved fatherhood and, 96-97; and juvenile delinquency, 186, 187; and motherhood, 97-98; and treatment of delinquency, 181
social conditions: and individuals, 168, 173; and suicide, 38; youth violence and, 195
social constructionism, 160-61; and readiness, 203-4, 210, 211
social justice, 173; CYC and, xvii; ethics and, 44; loss and, 164
social order, construction and co-option of, 127; gendered, 60, 61, 63-64, 66-67; professions and, 40, 128
social policy, classification and, 209-10; of microsystem explanations vs. complex multilevel understandings, 179; power micropractices and, 210-11; and readiness, 201, 210-11, 212, 214
social problems, professions and, 127-28; and social success, 194; street-involved youth and, 145, 149
social services. *See* human services
Staller, K., 128, 129-30
Standing on the Precipice, 36
Statham, J., 213
Statistical Inventory on Recidivism (SIR), 193
stigmatization, 145-46
Stoneman, Lorinda, xxi
street-involved youth, xx-xxi; bureaucracy and, 142; contributions to society, 153;

culture of, 153-54; definition of, 143, 144-45; and deviancy, 145, 146; diversity of, 143-44; images of, 142-43; mainstreaming and, 145, 150; marginalization of, 144, 145; othering of, 141-42, 145; power and, 141-42; problematizing of, 150-51; and social problems, 145, 149; stereotypes of, 143; "systems" and, 149; as totalized identity, 146
street involvement: and absolute vs. relative homelessness, 144; as choice, 139, 145; continuum of, 144; description of, 143; and homelessness, 145; and marginalization, 143; outreach professionals and, 139, 146
Stronach, I., 48
structural inequities, CYC practice and, 85, 89, 90; and girls' agency, 85; interventions and, 84; and minoritization, 90; neoliberalism and, 90n3; and risk factors, 82
Stuart, C., 42, 131-32
subjectification: about, 63; discourses and, 59-60; gendered, 59-60; poststructuralism and, 59
subjectivity, developmental theories and, 30; feminist post-structural analysis and, 68
suicide, individualism and, 38; privacy and, 38; professional ethics and, 38
surveillance: and objectification, 63; and readiness, 207-8, 211; in societies of control, 27
Sutherland, N., 182-83
Swift, K., 171, 192

Tachble, A., 106-7
Taguchi, H., 34
Tait, C., 44-45
Tamis-LeMonda, C.S., 104
Taylor, C., 164
Thomas, S., 8
Thyer, B., 170
truth: claims as fixed/static, 160; universality of, 58-59
Tsemberis, S., 147-48
Turner, C., 125

UN Commission on the Status of Women, 71
UN Convention on the Rights of the Child, 188
United Nations Convention on the Rights of the Child, 196n2
United States: and September 11, 2001, attacks, 165-66; welfare reforms in, 152
universalism/universality: in child development, xviii, 22, 204-5; of professionalization, 131, 132, 135; of readiness, 204-6; of truth claims, 58-59

Valentine, J., 150
Van Den Bergh, P.M., *Professionalization and Participation in Child and Youth Care*, 130, 135
Varcoe, C., 82
Vaudreuil, Matthew, 168
Verheij, F., *Professionalization and Participation in Child and Youth Care*, 130, 135
violence: and girls, 82; youth, 190, 195
Viruru, R., 25

Walker, K., 171
Walkerdine, V., 21, 83-84, 204
Walsh-Bowers, A., 40, 44, 45
Weedon, C., 59, 65
Weiler, R., 143-44
Weiser, J., 145
White, Jennifer, xix-xx, 4

Williams, R., 202, 207
Winsler, A., 199
Wittgenstein, Ludwig, 4
Wright-DeAgüero, L., 150

Yeatman, A., 16
young offender(s), 179; history of, 181-91; panic discourse surrounding, 191-92; serious, 190; as social construct, 180-81; World War II and, 187-88
Young Offenders Act (YOA), 189-90
youth, alienation of, 145; as co-experts, 135; constructions of, 20, 179-80; disciplinary societies/societies of control and work with, 28; diversion-eligible vs. punishable, 190-91; explanations of criminality among, 184; girls and development theories of, 76; incarceration of, 180, 186, 190; incidence of crime, 191; punishment of, 186; restorative justice and, 191; risk/need assessments with, 193-94; screening of, 193-94; trials of, 186; and violent crimes, 190
Youth Criminal Justice Act, 179, 180, 189-91
youth justice, deterrence in, 179; history of, 181-91; punitiveness in, 179, 180, 191; rehabilitative approaches, 192; remand in, 179; rights-based climate and, 188-89; sentencing in, 179. *See also* criminal justice